全国高职高专专业英语"十二五"规划教材

轨道交通运输与信号专业英语

English for Rail Transportation and the Signal System

主 编 叶清贫 曾 毅
副主编 余红梅 朱 蓓 赵亚军
主 审 夏 栋

华中科技大学出版社
中国·武汉

内 容 简 介

本书是一本实用的轨道交通运输与信号专业英语教材,内容新颖、丰富,以轨道运输与信号为背景,力求切合实用型轨道运输与信号类专业学生的培养目标。本书充分考虑了轨道运输与信号方向的专业性和发展性,教材所选用的大部分资料节选自国外最新的文献,保证了本书文献的纯正性。同时,本书紧跟现代轨道运输与信号的不断发展,尽可能兼顾系统性、实用性和可操作性。

全书分为三大部分。第一部分主要介绍轨道交通客(货)运服务实用英语口语,主要是招待外宾时经常使用的一系列实用情景对话,涉及13课内容,分别为电话订票、购票、退票、检票、列车通告、货运服务、餐车服务、紧急服务、旅游观光景点等。第二部分是轨道运输部分,主要介绍了运输组织方式、轨道车辆等,涉及地铁、轻轨、磁悬浮、高速铁路、动车组等。第三部分是轨道信号部分,主要介绍了铁路道岔、直流轨道电路、交流轨道电路、电码化轨道电路、自动闭塞信号、车站连锁设备、道口预警信号、驼峰信号、工业化铁路系统、调度集中系统等内容。同时,为方便学生学习,文后附有专业英语常用语法知识、轨道运输与信号专业术语、科技英语写作、单词表等。

另外,为方便教学,本书配有电子备课包和教师免费参考电子文档(免费索取请联系QQ:407168192),内容包括所有课后习题参考答案、课文及阅读材料参考译文,可供教师参考。

图书在版编目(CIP)数据

轨道交通运输与信号专业英语/叶清贫,曾毅主编. —武汉:华中科技大学出版社,2013.9(2022.8重印)
ISBN 978-7-5609-9126-9

Ⅰ.①轨… Ⅱ.①叶… ②曾… Ⅲ.①轨道交通-英语-高等职业教育-教材 ②轨道交通-交通信号-英语-高等职业教育-教材 Ⅳ.①H31

中国版本图书馆 CIP 数据核字(2013)第 123707 号

轨道交通运输与信号专业英语	叶清贫 曾 毅 主编

策划编辑:刘 平
责任编辑:刘 平
封面设计:李 嫚
责任校对:朱 霞
责任监印:张正林
出版发行:华中科技大学出版社(中国•武汉) 电话:(027)81321913
　　　　　武汉市东湖新技术开发区华工科技园　邮编:430223
录　排:华中科技大学惠友文印中心
印　刷:武汉市首壹印务有限公司
开　本:787mm×1092mm　1/16
印　张:11
字　数:300千字
版　次:2022年8月第1版第8次印刷
定　价:29.80元

本书若有印装质量问题,请向出版社营销中心调换
全国免费服务热线:400-6679-118　竭诚为您服务
版权所有　侵权必究

前　言

近年来中国城市轨道交通不断发展，新的闭塞设备、新的机车车辆、新的运输组织方式不断更新，中国轨道运输持续迅速发展并逐步完善。

为了实现轨道运输与信号现代化的发展，特编写了本书。教材所选用的大部分资料节选自国外最新的文献，保证了本书文献的纯正性。同时，本书紧跟现代轨道运输与信号的不断发展，尽可能兼顾系统性、实用性和可操作性。

本书主要介绍了有关轨道交通方面的运输部分和通信信号方面的内容，全书分为三大部分。第一部分主要介绍轨道交通客（货）运服务实用英语口语，主要是招待外宾时经常使用的一系列实用情景对话，涉及13课内容，分别为电话订票、购票、退票、检票、列车通告、货运服务、餐车服务、紧急服务、旅游观光景点等。第二部分是轨道运输部分，主要介绍了运输组织方式、轨道车辆等，涉及地铁、轻轨、磁悬浮、高速铁路、动车组等。第三部分是轨道信号部分，主要介绍了铁路道岔、直流轨道电路、交流轨道电路、电码化轨道电路、自动闭塞信号、车站连锁设备、道口预警信号、驼峰信号、工业化铁路系统、调度集中系统等内容。

本书针对高职学生的特点，编排了课文、单词和词组、专业术语、难点注释等内容，强调了运输与通信信号专业词汇的应用，有利于学习者在获得专业知识的同时，提高专业英语水平。本书内容全面、翔实，第一部分轨道交通客(货)运服务实用口语部分，内容简洁、实用，第二、三部分是轨道交通运输与信号专业知识的详细介绍。这有利于学生在掌握口语的同时提高专业知识阅读能力，拓宽视野。建议单篇课文课堂教学用时2~4学时。教师可结合教学实际，对部分课堂教学内容自主选择使用。

本书由武汉铁路职业技术学院叶清贫、曾毅主编，余红梅、朱蓓、赵亚军任副主编，夏栋任主审，同时，在编写过程中，还得到了郭强、奚进、朱宛平、王珏、王学忠等老师的支持和帮助。同时，在本书的编写过程中，华中科技大学出版社刘平编辑给予了积极的支持和帮助，在此一并表示感谢。

本书旨在提高学生专业英语的能力，了解轨道运输与信号领域国内外的最新发展动态。此教材既可作为轨道运输与信号专业本科（含二级学院）、高职高专院校的专业英语教材，又可供轨道运输及信号相关专业的学生及英语爱好者使用。

由于作者水平有限，书中难免有不当之处，敬请读者批评指正。

编　者

2013 年 6 月

CONTENTS (目录)

Part 1　Practical Oral English for Rail Passenger (Freight) Service (轨道交通客 (货) 运服务实用英语口语)

Lesson 1　Booking Tickets on the Telephone(电话订票) ···2
Lesson 2　Buying Tickets(购票) ··2
Lesson 3　Refunding Tickets(退票) ··3
Lesson 4　Checking Tickets(检票) ···4
Lesson 5　Inquiring in the Station(车站问讯) ···4
Lesson 6　The Luggage Storage Service(行李寄存服务) ···5
Lesson 7　Announcements in the Station(站内通报) ··7
Lesson 8　On-Train Service(列车服务) ···7
Lesson 9　Announcements on the Train(列车通告) ···9
Lesson 10　Freight Service(货运服务) ··10
Lesson 11　Dining Car Service(餐车服务) ···10
Lesson 12　Emergency(紧急服务) ··11
Lesson 13　Travelling and Seeing Attractions(旅游观光景点) ··12

Part 2　Rail Transportation (轨道运输)

Lesson 1　High-Speed Rail(高速铁路) ··16
Lesson 2　Monorail(单轨铁路) ···20
Lesson 3　Light Rail(轻轨) ··23
Lesson 4　Maglev Train(磁悬浮列车) ··28
Lesson 5　Subway(地铁) ···33
Lesson 6　Multiple Units(动车组) ··39
Lesson 7　Beijing West Terminal（北京西站） ··43
Lesson 8　Passenger Rail Transport in China(中国铁路客运) ··49
Lesson 9　Railroad Car(铁路车厢) ···54
Lesson 10　Freight Traffic(货运) ··60
Lesson 11　The Railroad Track(铁路轨道) ··65
Lesson 12　Railway Signaling(铁路信号) ··69

Part 3　Rail Signal System (轨道信号)

Lesson 1　Railroad Switch(铁路道岔) ···76
Lesson 2　D-C Track Circuits(直流轨道电路) ··80

Lesson 3   A-C Track Circuits(交流轨道电路) ………………………………………………… 85
Lesson 4   Electronic-Coded Track Circuits (电码化轨道电路) …………………………… 89
Lesson 5   Basic Automatic Block Signals(自动闭塞信号) ………………………………… 95
Lesson 6   Interlocking(车站连锁设备) ……………………………………………………… 99
Lesson 7   Highway Crossing Warning Signals (道口预警信号) ………………………… 105
Lesson 8   Centralized Traffic Control(调度集中) ………………………………………… 110
Lesson 9   Industrial Railroad Systems(工业铁路系统) …………………………………… 115
Lesson 10   Hump Classification Yard(驼峰编组场) ………………………………………… 119

附录 A 专业英语中的常用语法知识 …………………………………………………………… 125
附录 B 轨道交通运输与信号专业英语术语 …………………………………………………… 135
附录 C 科技英语写作 …………………………………………………………………………… 142
附录 D 单词表 …………………………………………………………………………………… 152
参考文献 …………………………………………………………………………………………… 169

Part 1

Practical Oral English for Rail Passenger (Freight) Service (轨道交通客(货) 运服务实用英语口语)

Lesson 1 Booking Tickets on the Telephone (电话订票)

Dialogue   Booking Tickets

A: Ticket office.

B: I'd like to **reserve** berth tickets on T95 for Shenzhen.

A: Sorry, today and tomorrow's tickets are all booked up. How about the day after tomorrow's? There are berths available on that train.

B: OK, I have no choice. Please reserve two tickets.

A: Semi-cushioned berth or **soft berth**?

B: Soft berth, please.

A: All right, give me your ID card number and your name.

B: Liu Ye, 123456789.

A: OK, your tickets have reserved. Please take your tickets before 12 o'clock tomorrow night.

B: OK, I will. Thank you.

Lesson 2 Buying Tickets (购票)

Dialogue 1   Buying Tickets in the Booking Office

A: Good morning, Sir. May I help you?

B: Yes, I'd like to buy a ticket for tomorrow's Train T246.

A: What is your destination, please?

B: Chengdu.

A: Would you like a **one-way ticket** or **round-trip one**?

B: One-way ticket.

A: **Cushioned berth** or **semi-cushioned berth**?

B: Cushioned berth, please!

A: **Lower berth** or **middle berth** or **upper berth**?

B: Lower berth. By the way, we have two children. How much do they have to pay?

A: How tall are they?

B: One is less than one meter and the other is 1.2 m tall.

A: Children under 1.1m in height are **free of charge.** And children between 1.1 m and 1.4 m are required to pay half the price.

B: How much do I have to pay?

A: 514 yuan, please.

B: Here you are. Is the insurance included in the cost?

A: Sure. These are your tickets and your change.

B: Thank you.

Dialogue 2   Buying Tickets in the Subway Station

A: Excuse me, would you please tell me how can I buy a **single journey ticket?**

B: I am glad to offer help first of all. Let me show you how to buy tickets. This way, please.

A: OK, thanks.

B: First, exchange notes into coins at the ticket booth, then go to the TVM(Ticket Vending Machine). Select the stations of departure and destination, press the Fare Selection Button and deposit coins into the Coin Entry Slot, at last, take a **SJT**(single journey ticket) from the Ticket Exit Slot.

A: Oh, I see. How can I use the ticket?

B: Here, this is the **AGM**(Automatic Gate Machine). Put the ticket in the magnetic area, then you will hear a beep sound, go through as soon as the door opens.

A: Sounds a little bit complex.

B: Don't worry. If you need help, call for us at any time. Oh, one more thing, be sure to put away the ticket and we will collect it when you arrive at your destination.

A: Thanks a lot. How long is the validity period of a SJT?

B: The SJT is valid during the intraday traffic hours. If your ticket exceeds the system time, according to our ticket policy, you should pay the additional fare. Also if your ticket is under fare, you should pay the exact fare.

A: Thank you very much.

Dialogue 3   Buying Group Tickets in the Subway Station

A: How many kinds of current tickets in Wuhan Metro Line 2?

B: There are five kinds of current tickets in Wuhan Metro Line 2, Single Journey Ticket, Store Value Ticket, Student Ticket, Elder Ticket and Value Pass.

A: How about the discount of Store Value Ticket?

B: For a 100 yuan SVT (Store Value Ticket), it has 10 percent discount; a 50 yuan SVT has 5 percent discount. All the SVTs have last ride bonus.

A: How can I get a group ticket, and how about the discount?

B: More than 30 persons can get a group ticket. You can contact with the **station supervisor**. The group more than 30 persons, not exceeding 100 persons may have 10 percent discount; more than 100 persons may have 20 percent discount.

A: There are 40 persons in our tour group. Please give me 40 tickets. What should I pay?

B: You should pay 144 yuan.

A: OK, here is 150 yuan.

B: Here you are, 40 tickets and the change.

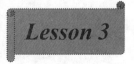 **Refunding Tickets (退票)**

Dialogue   Refunding Tickets

A: Excuse me, but can you help me?

B: Yes, of course.

A: I bought two berth tickets for Shenzhen yesterday, but my friend was ill and I have to take after her. May I get a refund for my tickets?

B: When is your train due to leave?

A: Tomorrow night at 17:00.

B: You have come in time. But you have to pay a **refund service charge**.

A: How much is the refund service charge?

B: According to regulations, the refund service charge is 5 percent of the ticket price.

A: OK, I see. My tickets, please!

B: Here is your refund.

A: Thanks.

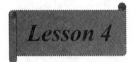

Lesson 4　Checking Tickets (检票)

Dialogue 1　Checking the Tickets at the Entrance

A: Show me your ticket and your ID card, please.

B: Here it is.

A: OK, come into the waiting-room and have a rest.

B: In which waiting-room shall I wait for my train?

C: Your Train is **south-bound**. You should wait in the second waiting-room.

B: Can I buy a **train schedule** there?

C: Yes. You can get one at the entrance of the supermarket in this hall.

B: Thank you. Where do I board the train?

C: At platform 2. You have to go through the platform bridge.

B: Thank you.

C: Not at all.

Dialogue 2　Checking the Tickets at the Exit

A: Your ticket, Please?

B: Here you are.

A: Thanks.

B: How can I get to Huameida Hotel, please?

A: The bus station is over there. There are many buses for you to take. You had better take Bus No.903, and then you can arrive earlier.

B: Thank you very much.

A: You are welcome.

 **Inquiring in the Station (车站问讯)**

Dialogue 1 Inquiring at the Information Office
A: Hello. This is the **inquiry office**.
B: Hi! Could you tell me the times of the trains to Huangshi?
A: There are three **express trains** starting from our station to Huangshi at 8:00, 11:00 and 14:00. There are two **passing trains** at 9:30 and 15:20.
B: Are the passing trains expresses, too?
A: No, they are **local expresses**.
B: What time does the 9:30 train get to Huangshi?
A: It's due to arrive at 12:50.
B: Thank you.

Dialogue 2 Inquiring Station Transference
A: What can I do for you?
B: Could you tell me how to get to Jianghan Road? I just can't figure it out from the subway system at all.
A: You take the downtown Line 1 train and get off at Xunlimen. Xunlimen Station is a **transfer station.** Then you take the Line 2 train and get off at Jianghan Road Station.
B: Thank you. How much is the fare?
A: You can inquire in the AVM(Automatic Vending Machine) over there. The fare is **distance-based.**
B: By the way, should my child buy a ticket?
A: Children below 1.2 meters in height ride for free when accompanied by a paying adult. How tall is your child?
B: 1.1 m.
A: OK, he is free.
B: How do I use this ticket?
A: You swipe it to get through the **AFC**(Automatic Fare Collection) machine. And insert it when you leave the subway.
B: By the way, how can I find the way to get out of the platform after I get off the train?
A: That's very easy. The exits are always open, and there are signs.
B: Thank you very much.
A: I am very happy to help you.

Dialogue 3 Looking for a Toilet in the Station
A: What place are you looking for?
B: I am looking for a toilet.
A: It is over there on that way. The man's room is on the right.
B: Thank you. Can I hear the announcement in the washroom?

A: Sure, but please get a move on. Pay attention to your departure time.

B: OK. By the way, is the toilet free?

A: Yes, it is. Well, it is boarding time for Express T95. Will passengers for Shenzhen please go to the boarding gate?

Dialogue 4   Directing

A: How can I get on the train?

B: Pass through the Entry Gates and go down the escalator to Platform 1.

A: How many minutes is the train headway, now?

B: At peak time, the train headway is 6 minutes, at off-peak time, 8 minutes.

A: How can I go to Huameida Hotel?

B: You can go to Platform 1 via the staircase and board the first available train to Guanggu Station.

A: How long does it take?

B: It takes 10 minutes.

A: What should I do after I get out from the station?

B: You can get out from Entrance A, then you will see the hotel.

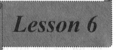

Lesson 6   The Luggage Storage Service (行李寄存服务)

Dialogue   Depositing Luggage

A: Will you please see to my luggage?

B: Sorry, please bring them along with you.

A: My luggage is too heavy. I want to buy something to eat on the train.

B: You can take them to the left-luggage office.

A: Where is the luggage storage service?

B: There are luggage lockers in the waiting hall and luggage storage office outside the waiting hall.

A: OK, thanks.

B: Mind you, don't miss the train. You must be back in an hour.

A: Yes, I will.

C: What can I do for you?

A: May I deposit my luggage here?

C: Of course, you may. I will take care of your luggage. But please be back as soon as possible.

A: I want to withdraw my luggage. Here is the **luggage check**.

C: Here is your luggage, a suitcase and two travelling bags, right?

A: Sorry, it is not my luggage. My luggage is over there.

C: I am sorry. Here you are.

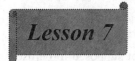 Announcements in the Station (站内通报)

(1) Boarding Announcements

① Attention, please. Train T96 to Wuchang will depart at 17:37. The train is now waiting at Platform 2. Passengers are requested to **check in** and board the train.

② It's time to board the train (It's time to get on board.). It's boarding time for T95. Please get your ticket ready. Passengers for train T95, please go to the **boarding gate.**

③ To ensure punctuality, this barrier may be closed up to 5 minute prior to departure of each train.

(2) If you have something dropped into the track, please contact with the station staffs.

(3) All passengers are requested to leave the station now!

(4) Please follow the instruction of **station staffs** and leave the station in order.

(5) Please avoid the gap between the platform edge and the car body!

(6) Please adjust your footstep when boarding and alighting the train.

(7) Please attention: Crowd Management Plans are now in operation and some of the **entry gates** are temporarily shut down. They will be back in use in about 15 minutes. Please use other transport and accept our apologies for any inconvenience or delay this might cause.

(8) Your attention please! Please buy tickets at the **Customer Service Centers** as the ticket machines are not working.

(9) Please wait in line while passengers exit from the train.

(10) Please take care of your children and belongings.

(11) When traveling on escalators, stand firm and hold the handrail. Please do not run or walk in the wrong direction.

(12) Train service for today has ended. Please leave the station.

(13) The train for Guanggu Station is arriving. Please let passengers exit first.

(14) Please don't squat. It is dangerous.

(15) Hold the handrail and stand firm.

(16) Do not lean against the side of the escalator.

(17) Beware! Rubber shoes may get caught in the escalator mechanism.

(18) Beware! Long skirts may get caught in the escalator mechanism.

(19) Take care of your children.

(20) The elderly are advised to use the elevator or stairs instead.

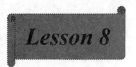 On-Train Service (列车服务)

Dialogue 1   Toilet

A: Is the toilet occupied?

B: No, it is locked.

A: Why?

B: Because the train will arrive at a big station. Toilets on the train are not supposed to be used when it stops at big stations.

A: Oh, I see. But how long will the train stay at this station?

B: Nine minutes. You have to wait a minute. Sorry.

A: I see. Please tell me when it is available.

B: Sure.

Dialogue 2   In a Semi-Cushioned Seat

A: Tickets, please! Could I see your ticket, please?

B: I am sorry. I am afraid I didn't get one.

A: Why?

B: I was a bit late. I have no time to go to the ticket office.

A: Well. You should buy a ticket on the train.

B: Sure.

A: Where did you board the train? And where are you going?

B: Changsha, and I will go to Guangzhou.

A: Single journey ticket?

B: No, I'd like a return.

A: 240 yuan, please.

B: Here is 250 yuan.

A: Here you are , your ticket and change.

Dialogue 3   In a Cushioned Sleeper

A: Good evening, ladies and gentlemen, welcome to our train. I am the **conductor** of this sleeper. My number is 35; I will be with you during this journey. Please let me know whenever you need help.

B: All right.

A: Now please give me your ticket and I will be keeping them for you. I will give you a **ticket check** with your berth number. You will have your ticket back before you arrive.

B: Can you wake me up at mid-night while I arrive at my stop?

A: Yes. It's my duty.

B: When will the lights be turned off?

A: At ten o'clock. But we will have a few necessary bed lights on.

B: Thank you.

Dialogue 4   In a Soft-Cushioned Sleeper

A: Excuse me, would you please show me your ticket?

B: All right.

A: Your berth is in this compartment. Yours is a lower berth.

B: Is the upper berth occupied?

A: I couldn't know if it is reserved yet. What can I do for you?

B: I have something important in that box. It's a master sample of our production. I must keep it in good shape. Can I put it on the upper berth if it is free?

A: Well, we have to keep the berth clean for passengers. And I am afraid that he may get on the train at next station. Why don't you put it on the baggage rack? It's safe there.

B: Isn't the box too big to be there? It's so tall.

A: Let me help you to have a try. See, it's OK.

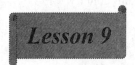

Lesson 9 Announcements on the Train (列车通告)

1. Train Broadcasting Speech

Good morning, everyone. This is the broadcasting studio on the train. Welcome to Train 446 and hope you a happy journey. We will give stop announcement and introduce the scenery spots along the way. We will broadcast some music and songs. At 6:30 am and 20:30 pm. we will relay CCB news. Our studio broadcasts 12 hours a day.

2. Overdue Announcement

Attention, please. Train T95 from Wuchang will be delayed for about 15 minutes. The train is running about 10 minutes late. It will come to Platform 3. We apologize for any inconvenience this may cause.

3. The train is about to leave, those for seeing off leave the train, please.

4. Departing Announcement

This is Express Number T95 from Wuchang to Shenzhen. Please get on the train. In order to avoid any accident, please don't shake hands with those on the platform when the train begins to move. Goodbye. Wish you a good journey.

5. Arriving Announcement

Good morning (afternoon, evening), passengers!

The train has now arrived at Wuchang Station. Warmly welcome to you. For your convenience, there are **luggage barrows** on the platform, and taxis on the station square. After you get off the train, please go to the exit for **ticket-checking.**

6. The next station is Xunlimen; please get ready for your arrival. Xunlimen is an **interchange station** for Line 1. Passengers for Line 1 please get ready to get off.

7. To maintain a healthy clean environment, do not smoke or litter on the train or stairs, and please offer your seats to passengers who needed. Thank you for your cooperation.

8. The train is departing. Please stand back from the **platform screen doors**.

9. Please put your luggage on the rack.

10. Please put the heavy luggage below and the light above.

11. Please hang your coat on the coat-hook.

12. Sorry, don't hang any thing heavy on the coat-hook.

13. Please stand clear of the door!

Lesson 10　Freight Service (货运服务)

Dialogue 1　The Mode of Railway Transportation

A: From what I have heard, **railway freight** service is quite safe.

B: Yes, we promise and arrange the safe delivery of the goods to any part of our country.

A: What is the mode of transportation of everyday use articles?

B: You can choose from transport by **container** or **full container load.**

A: We have some boxes of clothes and food to move.

B: For this kind of big order, we propose to have the goods dispatched by container. Full details regarding packing must be strictly observed.

A: They are packed in **cardboard boxes.** How do you like the goods to be packed?

B: We advocate using smaller container to pack the food. Please make the fruit jar airtight, and the eggs are packed in cartons with beehives lined with shake-proof paper board.

A: How about the clothes? Shirts and cloth are packed in plastic-lined water-proof cartons.

B: Before packed in cases, the cloth should be wrapped in kraft paper, and you should use a polythene wrapper for each shirt.

A: We will pack the goods according to your instruction.

Dialogue 2　The Package of Goods

A: What kind of goods do you want to transport?

B: Medicine. Liquid, capsules and pills.

A: Boxes of injections or glass jars?

B: Plastic bottles of eyedrop. Every bottle is put into a box and 100 boxes into a carton.

A: Do you use cardboard boxes to pack medicine?

B: Yes, each pill is put into a small bag and sealed. We pack them in smaller boxes inside the cardboard, too.

A: The packing must be strong enough to withstand handling and pressure. The crux of packing should lie in protecting the medicine from moisture.

B: We think such boxes packed in cardboard cartons can save freight cost.

A: It would cost more for you to pack the good in wooden cases. But I am afraid the cardboard boxes are not strong enough for long distance medicine transportation.

B: If we can afford time to change the packing, we agree to use wooden cases for outer packing.

Lesson 11　Dining Car Service (餐车服务)

Dialogue 1　Order Dishes

A: Excuse me, Miss. Could we order dishes to the compartment?

B: Sorry, I am afraid you can't.

A: Must we go to the dining car? And do we need a reservation for that?

B: You may go to the dining car of lunch without reservation. Or you could take a box of snack here.

A: What does a box of snack mean?

B: That is a kind of snack we prepare for passengers. It usually includes a box of rice and a box of dishes.

A: Can we choose from the different kind of dishes?

B: Yes, you can.

A: How can we get the snack?

B: Just wait for the salesgirls. They will soon take food to every coach.

Dialogue 2   Dinning Car Service

A: Good morning, welcome to our dinning car.

B: Good morning.

A: Please choose whichever table you like.

B: OK. Thank you.

A: What would you like to order?

B: We'd like to try some Chinese snacks.

A: Here is the menu.

B: We will have four little buns. We had some dumplings yesterday. OK, sweet dumplings today. We want two bowls of sweet dumplings and two bowls of beef with rice noodles as well.

A: Which would you prefer, milk or soybean milk?

B: Two glasses of soybean milk. That is all.

A: I will repeat the order: four little buns, two bowls of sweet dumplings, two bowls of beef with rice noodle, and two glasses of soybean milk as well. Is that right?

B: Right.

A: Please wait a moment. Your order will be here soon.

B: Here is your order: little buns, sweet dumplings, beef with rice noodles and soybean milk. Please enjoy them.

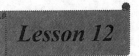

Lesson 12   Emergency (紧急服务)

Dialogue 1   Station Emergency

A: A man on Platform 1 has fallen in a bad faint.

B: Please be calm. I will phone the hospital at once. Wait for the ambulance services, please.

Dialogue 2   Lost Goods

A: Would you please do me a favor to find my lost bag this morning?

B: Okay, I will help you at **The Lost Property Office**.

Dialogue 3 Lost Child

A: I have lost my child somewhere around Platform 1.Please look for my child. She is about six.

B: Please write down you child/son/daughter's personal particulars and we will try our best to locate your child over our system.

Dialogue 4 Emergency on the Train

A: Excuse me , do you have a doctor on the train?

B: Sorry, we haven't. What's the matter?

A: I am suffering a heart trouble and my blood pressure is a little high. Now I feel feverish and nausea. I feel like vomiting.

B: Really? Sit down and have some water, please. Let me get touch with the broadcasting studio and ask for help. There might be a doctor among the passengers.

A: Thank you.

B: You should get plenty of rest. We'd better find a place in the sleep-car. Do you take medicine with you for the journey?

A: Of course. I have four sorts of medicines for my different diseases, I don't know which I should take.

B: That's a problem. Let's wait for the doctor.

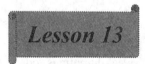

Travelling and Seeing Attractions
(旅游观光景点)

1. The Great wall (长城)

The Great Wall, located in northern China, is 6 700 kilometers long and thus known as the "10 000-li Great Wall". Construction of the wall went on for more than 2 000 years, from 7 th century to 14th century AD. The wall has become a symbol of both China's proud history and its present strength.

2. The Palace Museum (故宫博物院)

The Palace Museum, also called the Forbidden City, is located in the center of Beijing. The imperial palace used by emperors of the Ming and Qing dynasties is the largest and most complete ancient wooden-structure building complex in the world. Construction of the Forbidden City started in 1406 and lasted 14 years. Twenty-four emperors were enthroned there.

3. Zhoukoudian: Home of the Peking Man (周口店：北京人的家)

Remains of the Peking Man (homoerectus) are located on the Dragon Bone Hill at Zhoukoudian Village, Fangshan District, Beijing. In the 1920s, archaeologists discovered the complete skull of Peking Man. Later, more skull bones as well as stone and bone instruments were unearthed. Peking Man lived 690 000 years ago, during Paleolithic times. Findings indicate that Peking Man knew how to make fires.

4. Qinshihuang's Mausoleum and Terra-Cotta Army (秦始皇陵和兵马俑)

Qinshihuang's Mausoleum is located in Lintong District, 35 kilometers east of Xi'an, capital of

Shaanxi Province. Construction of the mausoleum lasted 38 years and involved over 700 000 workers. Over the years, a total of 50 000 important cultural relics have been unearthed. In 1980, two bronze painted horse-drawn chariots were unearthed. They are the largest and most complete bronze chariots and horses discovered so far. In 1974, farmers who were digging a well about 1.5 kilometers east of Qinshihuang's Mausoleum discovered three vaults containing Qinshihuang's Buried Legion. The largest of the three vaults contains 6 000 life-size terra-cotta warriors and horses. The collection of warriors is often dubbed the "eighth wonder of the world".

5. The Mogao Grottoes at Dunhuang (敦煌莫高窟)

The Dunhuang Grottoes comprise of the Mogao Grottoes, West 1 000-Buddha Cave, and Yulin Cave. The Mogao Grottoes, representative of the three sites, are located 25 kilometers southwest of Dunhuang City, Gansu Province. Construction of the grottoes began in 366 AD. The well-designed grottoes are a treasure house containing paintings, sculptures, documents, and cultural relics.

6. The Huangshan Mountain (黄山)

Located in Huangshan City in southern Anhui Province, the scenic area of the Huangshan Mountain covers 154 square kilometers and is famous for its four wonders: strangely-shaped pines, grotesque rock formations, seas of clouds and hot springs. It also features a natural zoo and botanical garden.

7. Huanglong (黄龙)

The Huanglong Scenic Area is located in Songpan County, Sichuan Province. Calcified ponds, beaches, waterfalls and embankments characterize Huanglong scenery.

8. Chengde Summer Resorts and Surrounding Temples (承德避暑胜地和周围寺庙)

Chengde Summer Resort, known as "The Mountain Hamlet for Escaping the Heat", is located in northern Chengde, Hebei Province. Qing Emperors used to spend their summer days handling state affairs at the resort. Construction of the resort lasted from 1703 to 1792. It is the largest and best-preserved imperial palace outside the capital. Many of the scenic spots around the resort's lake area mimic famous landscaped gardens in southern China, and the buildings of the Outer Eight Temples feature architectural style of minority ethnic groups such as Mongolian, Tibetan and Uygur.

9. Ancient Buildings on the Wudang Mountain (武当山古建筑)

The Wudang Mountain, located in northwestern Hubei Province, is a sacred Taoist mountain that is best known as the birthplace of Wudang martial arts. The Gold Hall built on the mountain in 1416 represents advanced architectural style and building techniques of that period.

10. Potala Palace (布达拉宫)

Potala Palace in Lhasa is situated on the Red Hill 3 700 meters above the sea level. The palace was built by Tibetan King Songtsan Gambo in the 7th century for Tang Princess Wencheng. Potala features the essence of ancient Tibetan architectural art and houses many artifacts of the Tubo Kingdom.

11. The Lushan Mountain (庐山)

The Lushan Mountain, located south of Jiujiang City, Jiangxi Province, is one of the most famous mountains in China. The mountain features beautiful peaks, seas of clouds, waterfalls and historical sites. Bailu Academy is one of Chinese first schools of higher learning.

12. The Emei Mountain and Leshan Giant Buddha (峨嵋山和乐山大佛)

The Emei Mountain is one of China's four famous Buddhist Mountains. It is located 7 kilometers southwest of Emeishan City, Sichuan Province. There are 150 temples on the mountain. The mountain features more than 3 000 plant species and 2 000 varieties of animals. Leshan Giant Buddha is located on the east bank of the Minjiang River in Leshan city, Sichuan Province. The Buddha is carved out of a cliff and, being 70.7 meters tall, is the largest sitting Buddha in China. Carving of the Buddha started in 713 and was completed in 803. The body of Buddha has a water drainage system to prevent erosion.

13. Lijiang Ancient City (丽江古城)

Lijiang ancient city, located in Lijiang, Yunnan Province, is an ancient town inhabited mainly by the Naxi minority people. The town was founded in 1127. The roads in the town are paved with colored pebbles produced in Lijiang, and there are many stone bridges and memorial archways built during the Ming and Qing dynasties. Most of the residences are made of earth and wood. Palace murals depicting religious themes were painted during the Ming dynasty. The traditional Dongba Culture of the Naxi ethnic group has been preserved in Lijiang.

14. Pingyao Ancient City (平遥古城)

Pingyao of Shanxi Province was built 2 000 years ago during the Zhou dynasty. The city wall was renovated in 1370. It is one of China's earliest and largest county-level city walls. Ancient streets, government offices, markets, stores and residences have been preserved, providing invaluable resources for research on China's ancient Ming dynasty county seat.

15. Suzhou Gardens (苏州园林)

Suzhou in Jiangsu Province is a famous historic and cultural city that is more than 2 500 years old. Suzhou features more than 200 ancient gardens. The small private gardens are especially famous nationwide and reflect architectural styles of the Song, Yuan, Ming and Qing dynasties.

16. The Summer Palace of Beijing (北京颐和园)

The Summer Palace, featuring the best of China's ancient gardens, is located in the western suburbs of Beijing. The palace was built in 1153 as a temporary imperial palace. It was rebuilt in 1888. The Summer Palace consists of the Longevity Hill and the Kunming Lake. The Long Corridor, painted with exquisite paintings, was included in the Guinness Book of World Records in 1992 as the longest corridor in the world. The corridor links the area where Empress Dowager Cixi handled state affairs with the residential and sightseeing areas.

17. The Temple of Heaven of Beijing (北京天坛)

The Temple of Heaven, built in 1420, is located in southern Beijing. During the Ming and Qing dynasties, emperors came to the temple to worship the God of Heaven and pray for a good harvest.

Part 2

 Rail Transportation (轨道运输)

High-Speed Rail (高速铁路)

High-speed rail is public transport by rail at speeds in excess of 200 km/h. Typically, high-speed trains travel at top service speeds of between 250 km/h and 300 km/h. The world speed record for a conventional wheeled train was set in 1990, by a French TGV[1] (Train à Grande Vitesse) that reached a speed of 515.3 km/h, and an experimental Japanese magnetic levitation train has reached 581 km/h.

The International Union of Railway's high-speed task force provides definitions of high-speed rail travel. There is no single definition of the term, but rather a combination of elements—new or upgraded track, rolling stock, operating practices—that lead to high-speed rail operations.[2] The speeds at which a train must travel to qualify as "high-speed" vary from country to country, ranging from 160 km/h to over 300 km/h.

There are constraints on the growth of the highway and air travel systems, widely cited as traffic congestion, or capacity limits. Airports have limited capacity to serve passengers during peak travel times, as do highways. High-speed rail, which has potentially very high capacity on its fixed corridors, offers the promise of relieving congestion on the other systems. Prior to World War II, conventional passenger rail was the principal means of intercity transport. Passenger rail services have lost their primary role in transport, due to the small proportion of journeys made by rail.

High-speed rail has the advantage over automobiles in that it can move passengers at speeds far faster than those possible by car, while also avoiding congestion.[3] For journeys that do not connect city centre to city centre, the door to door travel time and the total cost of high-speed rail can be comparable to that of driving. A fact often mentioned by critics of high-speed trains. However, supporters argue that journeys by train are less strenuous and more productive than car journeys.

While high-speed trains generally do not travel as fast as jet aircraft, they have advantages over air travel for relatively short distances. When traveling less than about 650 km, the process of checking in and going through security screening at airports, as well as the journey to the airport itself, makes the total journey time comparable to high-speed rail. Trains can be boarded more quickly in a central location, eliminating the speed advantage of air travel. Rail lines also permit far greater capacity and frequency of service than what is possible with aircraft.

High-speed trains also have the advantage of being much more environmentally friendly, especially if the routes they serve are competing against clogged highways.[4]

The early target areas, identified by France, Japan, and the U.S., were connections between pairs of large cities. In France this was Paris-Lyon, in Japan Tokyo-Osaka, and in the U.S. the proposals are in high-density areas. The only high-speed rail service at present in the U.S.A. is in the Northeast Corridor between Boston, New York and Washington, D.C.; it uses tilting trains to achieve high speeds on existing tracks, since building new, straighter lines was not practical, given the amount of development on either side of the right of way.[5]

　　Five years after construction began on the line, the first Japanese high-speed rail line opened on the eve of the 1964 Olympics in Tokyo, connecting the capital with Osaka. The first French high-speed rail line was opened in 1981, the French rail agency, planning starting in 1966 and construction in 1976. The opening ceremonies were significant events, being reported internationally, but not associated with a major showpiece such as a World's Fair or Olympic Games.[6]

　　Market segmentation has principally focused on the business travel market. The French focus on business travelers is reflected in the nature of their rail cars. Pleasure travel is a secondary market, though many of the French extensions connect with vacation beaches on the Atlantic and Mediterranean, as well as major amusement parks. Friday evenings are the peak time for TGVs. The system has lowered prices on long distance travel to compete more effectively with air services, and as a result some cities within an hour of Paris by TGV have become commuter communities, thus increasing the market, while restructuring land use. A side effect of the first high-speed rail lines in France was the opening up of previously isolated regions to fast economic development. Some newer high-speed lines have been planned primarily for this purpose.

New Words and Expressions

typically ['tipikəli] *adv.* 代表性地，作为特色地
record ['rekɔːd] *n.* 最高纪录
experimental [ikˌsperi'mentl] *adj.* 实验的
single ['siŋgl] *adj.* 单一的，专一的，个别的
combination [ˌkɔmbi'neiʃ(ə)n] *n.* 结合，联合，合并
element ['elimənt] *n.* 元素，成分
definition [ˌdefi'niʃən] *n.* 定义，规定
vary ['vɛəri] *vt.* 改变，变更，修改
upgrade [ʌp'greid] *vt.* 使升级，提升
qualify as 取得……资格
constraint [kən'streint] *n.* 约束，强制，局促
capacity [kə'pæsiti] *n.* 容量，才能，能力
potentially [pə'tenʃəli] *adv.* 潜在地
peak [piːk] *n.* 顶点，最高峰
cite [sait] *vt.* 引用，引证，举(例)
offer ['ɔfə] *vt.* 提供，使出现
fixed [fikst] *adj.* 固定的，确定的
corridor ['kɔridɔː] *n.* 走廊，通道
corridor train 从头到尾有走廊的列车
promise ['prɔmis] *n.* 允诺，答应
primary ['praiməri] *adj.* 主要的，初步的，初级的，原来的
relieve [ri'liːv] *vt.* 减少，解除
strenuous ['strenjuəs] *adj.* 奋发的，使劲的，紧张的
principal ['prinsip(ə)l] *adj.* 主要的，首要的

intercity [ˌintə'siti] *adj.* 城市间的
advantage [əd'vɑ:ntidʒ] *n.* 优势，有利条件，利益
automobile ['ɔ:təməubi:l] *n.* 汽车
avoid [ə'vɔid] *vt.* 避免，消除
be comparable to 可比较的，比得上的
mention ['menʃən] *vt.* 提起，说及
critic ['kritik] *n.* 批评家，评论家
argue ['ɑ:gju:] *vi.* 争论，辩论
productive [prə'dʌktiv] *adj.* 生产的，多产的
eliminate [i'limineit] *vt.* 排除，消除
frequency ['fri:kwənsi] *n.* 频率，周率，发生次数
construction [kən'strʌkʃən] *n.* 建筑，施工，建筑物
showpiece ['ʃəupi:s] *n.* 展览品，供展览的样品
clog [klɔg] *v.* 障碍，妨碍，填满
secondary ['sekəndəri] *adj.* 次要的，二级的，中级的，第二的
vacation [və'keiʃən] *n.* 假期，休假
amusement [ə'mju:zmənt] *n.* 娱乐，消遣
compete [kəm'pi:t] *vi.* 比赛，竞争
isolate ['aisəleit] *vt.* 使隔离，使孤立
segmentation [ˌsegmən'teiʃən] *n.* 分割，分节现象
target ['tɑ:git] *n.* 目标，对象；靶
strive to 努力
in excess of 超过
check in 签到
due to 由于，应归于
high-density 高密度
focus on 集中

Notes to the Text

1. TGV：Train à Grande Vitesse (法文) 超高速列车。
2. There is no single definition of the term, but rather a combination of elements—new or upgraded track, rolling stock, operating practices—that lead to high-speed rail operations.
   译文 该定义并不唯一，而是众多因素的集合，如全新的或升级了的铁轨、车辆、实际运营，这些都与高速铁路营运有关。
3. High-speed rail has the advantage over automobiles in that it can move passengers at speeds far faster than those possible by car, while also avoiding congestion.
   译文 高速铁路比汽车运输更有优势，因为它不仅比汽车快得多，而且也避免了交通拥挤。
4. High-speed trains also have the advantage of being much more environmentally friendly, especially if the routes they serve are competing against clogged highways.
   译文 如果高速铁路与拥挤的高速公路相比，高速铁路还具有更环保的优势。
   being much more environmentally friendly 现在分词作宾语。they serve 前面省略了 that，修饰 the

routes.

5. ...it uses tilting trains to achieve high speeds on existing tracks, since building new, straighter lines was not practical, given the amount of development on either side of the right of way.

译文　考虑到原有铁路沿线两边已发展成熟，再修建新的、较直的铁路线并不实际，所以采用摆式列车在原有轨道上获取高速度。

the right of way，建有铁路、公路、管道设施等的公用事业用地

6. The opening ceremonies were significant events, being reported internationally, but not associated with a major showpiece such as a World's Fair or Olympic Games.

译文　通车典礼当时在世界上广为报道，是盛况空前的大事，却没有被认为像世界博览会或奥林匹克运动会那样具有影响力。

Exercises to the Text

Ⅰ. **Translate the following terms into Chinese.**

(1) public transport　　　　(2) high-speed rail　　　　(3) rolling stock
(4) urban mass transport system　　(5) security screen　　(6) traffic congestion
(7) side effect　　　　(8) tilting train　　　　(9) conventional wheeled train
(10) market segmentation　　(11) peak travel times
(12) intercity transport　　(13) commuter communities

Ⅱ. **Fill in the blanks with appropriate words.**

(1) High-speed rail is public transport by rail at speeds in excess of _____ km/h.
(2) It uses _____ to achieve high speeds on existing tracks.
(3) Friday evenings are the _____ time for TGVs.
(4) The speeds at which a train must travel to quality as "high-speed" vary from country to country, ranging from _____ km/h to over _____ km/h.

Ⅲ. **Answer the following questions according to the text.**

(1) When was the world speed record for a conventional wheeled train set by a French TGV that reached a speed of 515.3 km/h?
(2) How to definite the term "high-speed railway"?
(3) What advantages do high-speed rail have?
(4) What is the side effect of the first high-speed rail lines in France?

Reading Material

German High-Speed Lines

　　Construction on first German high-speed lines began shortly after that of the French TGVs. Legal battles caused significant delays, so that the InterCity Express (ICE) trains were deployed ten years, after the TGV network was established. The ICE network is more tightly integrated with pre-existing lines and trains as a result of the different settlement structure in Germany, which has almost twice the population density of France. ICE trains reached destinations in Austria and Switzerland, soon after they entered service, taking advantage of the same voltage used in these countries. Starting in 2000, multi-system third-generation ICE trains entered the Netherlands and Belgium. The third generation of the ICE reaches a speed up to 363 km/h. Admission of ICE trains onto French TGVs was applied for in 2001, but trial runs had only just been completed in 2005. Unlike the TGV or Shinkansen, the first generation ICE had a fatal high-speed crash, following numerous complaints of excessive shaking. Since the crash, the ICE wheels have been redesigned.

Germany is also developing Transrapid, a magnetic levitation train system. The Transrapid reaches speeds up to 550 km/h. A test track with a total length of 31.5 km is operating in Emsland. In China, Shanghai Maglev Train, a Transrapid technology based maglev built in collaboration with Germany, has been operational since March 2004.

New Words and Expressions

Shinkansen [ˈʃiːnˈkɑːnsen]　新干线(日本的高速客运列车)
InterCity Express　城市特快
Transrapid　一种德国的磁悬浮列车
crash [ˈkræʃ] n.　撞车事故, 失事

Exercises to the Material

Decide whether each of the following statements is true or false according to the material.
(1) The first German high-speed railway lines began construction before that of the French TGVs. (　　)
(2) The ICE network hasn't used the existing lines. (　　)
(3) The third generation of the ICE has reached a speed up to 363 km/h. (　　)
(4) Germany isn't developing Transrapid. (　　)
(5) The first generation ICE had a fatal flaw. (　　)

Monorail (单轨铁路)

A monorail is a single rail serving as a track for a wheeled or magnetically levitating vehicle; also, a vehicle traveling on such a track.

Types and technical aspects

Modern monorails depend on a large solid beam as the vehicles' running surface. There are a number of competing designs divided into two broad classes, straddle-beam and suspended monorails.

The most common type of monorail in use today is the straddle-beam monorail, in which the train straddles a reinforced concrete beam in the range of two to three feet(about 0.6-0.9 m)wide.[1] A rubber-tired carriage contacts the beam on the top and both sides for traction and to stabilize the vehicle. The straddle-beam style was popularized by the German company ALWEG.

There is also a form of suspended monorail developed by the French company SAFEGE, in which the train cars are suspended beneath the wheel carriage.[2] In this design the carriage wheels ride inside the single beam. The Chiba Urban Monorail is presently the world's largest suspended monorail network.

Power

Almost all modern monorails are powered by electric motors fed by dual third rails, contact wires or electrified channels attached to or enclosed in their guidance beams.

Advantages

- The primary advantage of monorails over conventional rail systems is that they require minimal space, both horizontally and vertically. Monorail vehicles are wider than the beam, and monorail systems are commonly elevated, requiring only a minimal footprint for support pillars.
- Due to a smaller footprint they are seen as more attractive than conventional elevated rail lines and block only a minimal amount of sky.
- They are quieter, as modern monorails use rubber wheels on a concrete track(though some non-monorail subway systems, like certain lines of the Paris Metro and all of the Montreal Metro, use the same technique and are equally quiet).
- Monorails are capable of climbing and descending steeper grades than heavy or light rail systems.
- Unlike conventional rail systems, straddle monorails wrap around their track and are thus not physically capable of derailing, unless the track itself suffers a catastrophic failure, which is why monorails have an excellent safety record.[3]

Disadvantages

- Monorail vehicles are not compatible with any other type of rail infrastructure, which makes(for example)through services onto mainline tracks impossible.
- Althongh a monorail's footprint is less than an elevated conventional rail system, it is larger than an underground system's.
- In an emergency, passengers may not be able to immediately exit because the monorail vehicle is high above ground and not all systems have emergency walkways. The passengers must sometimes wait until a rescue train, fire engine or a cherry picker comes to the rescue. Newer monorail systems resolve this by building emergency walkways alongside the entire track, at the expense of visual intrusion. Suspended railways resolve this by building aircraft style evacuation slides into the vehicles.[4] Japanese systems use the next train to tow broken down trains to the next station, but this has yet to occur.

New Words and Expressions

monorail ['mɔnəureil] *n.* 单轨铁路
straddle ['strædl] *v.* 跨骑
reinforce [,ri:in'fɔ:s] *vt.* 加强，增援，补充

     vi. 求援，得到增援
rubber-tired 轮胎式的，胶轮式的
traction ['trækʃən] *n.* 牵引
stabilize ['steibilaiz] *v.* 稳定
suspend [səs'pend] *vt.* 吊，悬挂
footprint ['futprint] *n.* 足迹，脚印
block [blɔk] *vt.* 妨碍，阻塞
descend [di'send] *v.* 下去，下来
wrap [ræp] *vt.* 包装，卷，缠绕
catastrophic [ˌkætə'strɔfik] *adj.* 悲惨的，灾难的
rescue ['reskju:] *n.* 援救，营救

Notes to the Text

1. The most common type of monorail in use today is the straddle-beam monorail, in which the train straddles a reinforced concrete beam in the range of two to three feet(about 0.6-0.9 m)wide.
   译文　目前采用的最普通的单轨铁路类型就是跨座式单轨铁路，列车跨座在两到三尺宽的钢筋混凝土梁上。

2. There is also a form of suspended monorail developed by the French company SAFEGE, in which the train cars are suspended beneath the wheel carriage.
   译文　法国 SAFEGE 提出了另外一种悬挂式单轨铁路。该种类型的列车车厢悬挂在车轮下。

3. Unlike conventional rail systems, straddle monorails wrap around their track and are thus not physically capable of derailing, unless the track itself suffers a catastrophic failure, which is why monorails have an excellent safety record.
   译文　不像常规轨道系统，跨座式单轨铁路环抱住轨道梁，因而不会发生脱轨事故，除非轨道自身经历了灾难性故障，这就是单轨铁路系统具有良好安全记录的原因。

4. Suspended railways resolve this by building aircraft style evacuation slides into the vehicles.
   译文　悬挂式单轨铁路通过修建滑行至交通工具的类似飞机的撤退通道来解决该问题。

Exercises to the Text

Ⅰ. **Translate the following words and phrases into English.**
 (1) 单轨铁路   (2) 跨座式单轨铁路   (3) 悬挂式单轨铁路
 (4) 轮胎式客车   (5) 道岔   (6) 营救列车
 (7) 消防车   (8) 轻轨系统

Ⅱ. **Answer the following questions according to the text.**
 (1) How to define a monorail?
 (2) What types are modern monorails divided into?
 (3) What is the most common type of monorail today?
 (4) What is the primary advantage of monorail over conventional rail systems?
 (5) Why is it said that passengers may not be able to immediately exit from monorail?

Reading Material

Overview of Chongqing Monorail No.2 Line

The line opened for business is the 12.5 km of double track between Dongwuyuan and Jiaochangkou(13 stations, comprising 10 elevated stations and 3 underground stations with an average distance of 1 km between stations), which is the first commercial phase of the Jiao-Xin Line(covering 18 km from Jiaochangkou to Xinshancun). The minimum radius of curvature of the track is 100 m, maximum gradient is 50‰, and the minimum radius of curvature of the train depot is 50 m.

Situated on the upper floors of a highrise block in Daping Station, an integrated government office housing an operation room and other management departments runs the monorail system. Moreover, the platforms of the three underground stations are fitted with screen-type safety doors.

At present the second phase of track construction between Dongwuyuan and Xinshancun is under way, and when it is completed, 5.5 km of track with five elevated stations will be added. The assumed passenger volume(one way for the one-hour peak)that can be transported was taken as 12 600 people for four-compartment trains in the initial period, 23 000 for six-compartment trains in the medium term, and 32 000 people for eight-compartment trains in the future. The length of the station platforms—which can accommodate trains with up to eight compartment—is 120 m.

New Words and Expressions

double track 复线，双线
passenger volume 客运量
curvature ['kɜːvətʃə] n. 弯曲，曲率
radius ['reidiəs] n. 半径

Exercises to the Material

Answer the following questions according to the material.
(1) What is the minimum radius of curvature of the track?
(2) Who runs the monorail system?
(3) How long is the Chongqing monorail No.2 line?
(4) What is the maximum gradient?
(5) How many people can be transported by four-compartment trains in the initial period?

Lesson 3 Light Rail (轻轨)

Light rail is a term coined in the 1970s, during the re-emergence of streetcars. In general, it refers to streetcar with rapid transit-style features, it is named to distinguish it from heavy rail.

Most rail technologies, including high-speed rail, freight, commuter, and metro/subway are considered to be "heavy rail" in comparison. A few systems such as people movers and personal rapid transit could be considered as even "lighter", at least in terms of how many passengers are moved per

vehicle and the speed at which they travel. Monorails are also considered to be a separate technology. Light rail systems can handle steeper inclines than heavy rail, and curves sharp enough to fit within street intersections. They are typically built in urban areas, providing frequent service with small, light trains or single cars.

Many light rail systems—even fairly old ones—have a combination with both on road and off-road sections.[1] In some countries, only the latter is described as the light rail. In those places, trams running on mixed right of way are not regarded as light rail, but considered distinctly as streetcars.

Light rail systems are almost universally operated by electricity delivered through overhead lines, although several systems are powered through different means, such as AirTrain JFK,[2] which uses a third rail for its electrical power, and the River Line[3] in New Jersey which uses diesel powered vehicles; such as the Docklands Light Railway, which uses a standard third rail for its electrical power, and trams in Bordeaux, France which use a special third-rail configuration in which the rail is only powered while a tram is on top of it.[4] Several systems in Europe, as well as a few recently-opened systems in North America use diesel-powered trains. Diesel operations are chosen in corridors where lower ridership is expected or which have an "interurban" nature with stations spaced relatively far apart. Operations with diesel-powered trains can be an interim measure until ridership growth and the availability of funding allow the system to be upgraded to electric power operations.

Light rail systems are generally cheaper to build than heavy rail, since the infrastructure does not need to be as substantial, and tunnels are generally not required as is the case with most metro systems. Moreover, the ability to handle sharp curves and steep gradients can reduce the amount of work required.

Traditional streetcar systems as well as newer light rail systems are used in many cities around the world because they typically can carry a larger number of people than any bus-based public transport system. They are also cleaner, quieter, more comfortable, and in many cases faster than buses. In addition, light rail has none of the negative connotations of being a system used by the "transit dependent" that can plague bus-rapid-transit ridership levels.[5]

In an emergency, light rail trains are also easier to evacuate than monorail or elevated rapid rail trains.

Many modern light rail projects re-use parts of old rail networks, such as abandoned industrial rail lines. This fact gives some systems built-in right of way; besides the built-in right of way, the hardware generally operates more quietly than commuter rail or metro systems, and noise mitigation is easier to design.[6]

A good example of both points above is the Docklands Light Railway(DLR)in London, which uses a sharp, steep, curve to enable it to transfer from running alongside an existing railway line to a disused railway line which crosses underneath the first line. A direct connection between these lines would not be practical for conventional rail.

Like all modes of rail transport, light rail tends to be safest when operating in dedicated right of way with complete grade separations. However, grade separations are not always financially or physically feasible.

Monorail advocates like to point out that light rail trolleys are heavier per pound of cargo carried than heavy rail cars or monorail cars, because they must be designed to survive collisions with automobiles.

Furthermore, the opening of new light rail systems has sometimes been accompanied by an epidemic of car accident involving drivers unfamiliar with the physics and geometry of light rail trolleys.

New Words and Expressions

steep [stiːp] *adj.* 陡峭的，险峻的，急剧升降的
incline [inˈklain] *n.* 倾斜，斜坡，斜面，斜坡
monorail [ˈmɔnəureil] *n.* 单轨铁路
curve [kɜːv] *n.* 曲线，弯曲
intersection [ˌintəˈsekʃən] *n.* [数] 交集，十字路口，交叉点，横断，交，交点
section [ˈsekʃən] *n.* 部分，断片，部件，节，项，区，地域，截面
overlap [ˌəuvəˈlæp] *v.* (与……) 交叠，(和……) 重叠
describe [disˈkraib] *vt.* 描写，记述，形容
configuration [kənˌfigjuˈreiʃən] *n.* 构造，结构，配置，外形
ridership [ˈraidəʃip] *n.* [总称] <主美>公共交通工具乘客 (人数)
interim [ˈintərim] *adj.* 中间的，临时的，间歇的
availability [əˌveiləˈbiliti] *n.* 可用性，有效性，实用性
funding [ˈfʌndiŋ] *n.* 资金
upgrade [ˈʌpgreid] *vt.* 使升级，提升，改良品种
substantial [səbˈstænʃəl] *adj.* 坚固的，实质的，真实的，充实的
mitigation [ˌmitiˈgeiʃən] *n.* 缓解，减轻，平静
evacuate [iˈvækjueit] *v.* 疏散，撤出，排泄，撤离，撤退
plague [pleig] *vt.* 折磨，使苦恼，使受灾
connotation [ˌkɔnəuˈteiʃən] *n.* 含蓄，储蓄的东西 (词、语等)，内涵，意义
emergency [iˈmɜːdʒnsi] *n.* 紧急情况，突然事件，非常时刻，紧急事件
abandoned [əˈbændənd] *adj.* 被抛弃的，自甘堕落的，没有约束的，放荡的
hardware [ˈhɑːdwɛə] *n.* 五金器具，(电脑的)硬件，(电子仪器的)部件
transfer [trænsˈfɜː] *vt.* 转移，调转，调任，传递，转让，改变
alongside [əˌlɔŋˈsaid] *prep.* (表示位置) 在……旁边，沿着……的
dedicated [ˈdedikeitid] *adj.* 专注的，献身的
gradient [ˈgreidiənt] *n.* 梯度，倾斜度，坡度，陡坡
accompany [əˈkʌmpəni] *vt.* 陪伴，伴奏
cargo [ˈkɑːgəu] *n.* 船货，(车、船、飞机等运输的) 货物
accident [ˈæksidənt] *n.* 意外事件，事故
epidemic [ˌepiˈdemik] *n.* 流行病

point out 指出

Notes to the Text

1. Many light rail systems—even fairly old ones—have a combination with both on-road and off-road sections.
   译文 许多轻轨系统，甚至相当老的那种，将专有路段和并用路段结合起来。
2. AirTrain JFK，肯尼迪国际机场快线
3. The River Line，新泽西特拉华河线
4. Light rail systems are almost universally operated by electricity delivered through overhead lines, although several systems are powered through different means, such as AirTrain JFK, which uses a third rail for its electrical power, and the River Line in New Jersey which uses diesel powered vehicles; such as the Docklands Light Railway, which uses a standard third rail for its electrical power, and trams in Bordeaux, France which use a special third-rail configuration in which the rail is only powered while a tram is on top of it.
   译文 尽管一些系统用不同的方式提供动力，轻轨系统一般通过高架电路所传送的电流进行营运。例如，JFK气垫列车，采用第三轨作为电源，新泽西的特拉华河线采用内燃机动力车辆；道克兰轻轨，采用标准的第三轨提供电力。法国的波尔多有轨电车采用专门的第三轨配置，在这种配置中，仅当有轨电车在该第三轨配置上方时，才能够产生动力。
5. In addition, light rail has none of the negative connotations of being a system used by the "transit dependent" that can plague bus-rapid-transit ridership levels.
   译文 此外，轻轨作为"运输依赖者"所使用的一种交通系统，无任何降低乘坐公交高速交通乘客人数的负面影响。
6. This fact gives some systems built-in right of way; besides the built-in right of way, the hardware generally operates more quietly than commuter rail or metro systems, and noise mitigation is easier to design.
   译文 这一事实给予某些系统规定的优先通行权，除了规定的优先通行权外，通常其硬件比通勤列车或地铁运行得更安静、更舒适，而且噪音问题也更容易解决。

Exercises to the Text

Ⅰ. Translate the following terms into Chinese.
   (1) heavy rail (2) rapid transit (3) industrial rail
   (4) people mover (5) grade separation (6) electrical power
   (7) street intersections (8) frequent service

Ⅱ. Decide whether each of the following statements is true or false according to the text.
   (1) The light rail belongs to "heavy rail". (　　)
   (2) Light rail systems can handle steeper inclines than heavy rail systems. (　　)
   (3) Light rail systems aren't almost universally operated by electricity. (　　)
   (4) Light rail systems are generally more expensive than heavy rail systems, and cheaper than subway. (　　)
   (5) Modern light rail projects can use abandoned industrial rail lines. (　　)

Ⅲ. Answer the following questions according to the text.

(1) What are the advantages of light rail systems compared to heavy rail?

(2) By what means are light rail systems operated?

(3) Light rail systems are generally cheaper to build than heavy rail systems. Why?

(4) What is the characteristic of Docklands Light Railway?

(5) Light rail trolleys are heavier per pound of cargo carried than heavy rail cars or monorail cars. Why?

Reading Material

The Categeories of the Light Rail

The light rail is generally powered by electricity, usually by means of overhead wires, but sometimes by a live rail, also called third rail(a high voltage bar alongside the track), requiring safety measures and warnings to the public not to touch it. In some cases, particularly when initial funds are limited, diesel-powered versions have been used, but it is not a preferred option. Some systems, such as the AirTrain JFK in New York City, are automatic, dispensing with the need for a driver; however, such systems are not what are generally thought of as light rail. Automatic operation is more common in smaller "people mover" systems than in light rail systems, where the possibility of grade crossings and street running make driverless operation of the latter inappropriate for safety/security reasons. However, this is obviously not true in completely separated light rail systems such as the Kelana Jaya Line in Kuala Lumpur, Malaysia.

A growing area of interest is systems which are described as ultra light rail. Ultra light rail schemes are designed to offer high cost effectiveness and also easy deployment by using modern techniques and materials to dramatically reduce the weight of the vehicles. Ultra light vehicles cannot as a result co-exist with heavy rail or even most light rail systems as the light construction, comparable to that of a car or bus, is insufficiently strong to take an impact with a conventional train. It is however perfectly adequate in the event of collisions with road vehicles or other ultra light rail vehicles. Keeping the weight down allows for energy efficiency comparable with or better than a bus and regular stopping points using nothing more than a cheap petrol engine and flywheel. In addition, the low weight reduces the cost of track and civil engineering and thus the otherwise high initial construction costs.

New Words and Expressions

by means of　依靠
option ['ɔpʃən] *n*.　选项，选择权
automatic[ˌɔːtə'mætik] *adj*.　自动的
dispense [dis'pens] *vt*.　分发，分配
grade crossing　平面交叉
ultra ['ʌltrə]　(前缀)表示"超"，"过"
cost effectiveness　成本效率
flywheel ['flaiwiːl] *n*.　调速轮
civil engineering　土木工程
in the event of　如果……发生

Exercises to the Material

Answer the following questions according to the Material.
(1) Why are some light rail systems diesel-powered?
(2) Where can that automatic operation in light rail systems be adopt?
(3) What light rail system are people interested in?
(4) What is the advantage of ultra light rail after reducing the weight of the vehicles?

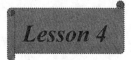

Lesson 4 Maglev Train (磁悬浮列车)

Magnetic levitation transport, or maglev, is a form of transportation that suspends, guides and propels vehicles via electromagnetic energy. This has advantages in terms of speed and ride comfort compared to wheeled mass transit systems — potentially, maglevs could reach velocities comparable to turboprop and jet aircraft(500 to 580 km/h)—but although the idea is decades old, technological and economic limitations have caused relatively few full-scale systems to be built. Maglev technology has minimal overlap with wheeled train technology and is not compatible with conventional railroad tracks.

Because they cannot share existing infrastructure, maglevs must be designed as complete transportation systems. The term "maglev" refers not only to the vehicles, but to the vehicle/guideway interaction; each being a unique design element specifically tailored to the other to create and precisely control magnetic levitation.[1]

The various technological approaches to maglev can be very similar or very different, depending upon the manufacturer. World leader in maglev technology is Germany's Siemens and ThyssenKrupp with its Transrapid system.

Due to the lack of physical contact between the track and the vehicle, the only friction exerted is that between the vehicles and the air. Consequently maglevs can potentially travel at very high speeds with reasonable energy consumption and noise levels. Systems have been proposed to operate at up to 650 km/h, which is far faster than that is practical with conventional rail transport. The very high maximum potential speed of maglevs makes them competitors to airline routes of 1 000 kilometers or less. The world's first commercial application of a high-speed maglev line is the initial operating segment demonstration line in Shanghai that transports people 30 km to the airport in just 7 minutes 20 seconds(top speed of 431 km/h, average speed 250 km/h). Other maglev applications worldwide are being investigated for feasibility.

There are three primary types of maglev technology:
- one that relies on feedback controlled electromagnets;
- one that relies on superconducting magnets;
- and a newer, potentially more economical system that uses permagnets.

A newer, perhaps less-expensive, system is called "Inductrack". The technique has a load-carrying ability related to the speed of the vehicle, because it depends on currents induced in a passive electromagnetic array by permanent magnets. In the prototype, the permanent magnets are in a cart; horizontally to provide lift, and vertically to provide stability. The array of wire loops is in the track. The magnets and cart are unpowered, except by the speed of the cart. Inductrack was originally developed as a magnetic motor and bearing for a flywheel to store power. With only slight design changes, the bearings were unrolled into a linear track.[2]

Inductrack uses Halbach arrays for stabilization. Halbach arrays are arrangements of permanent magnets that stabilize moving loops of wire without electronic stabilization. Halbach arrays were originally developed for beam guidance of particle accelerators. They also have a magnetic field on the trackside only, thus reducing any potential effects on the passengers.

Japan and Germany are active in maglev research, producing several different approaches and designs. In one design, the train can be levitated by the repulsive force of like poles or the attractive force of opposite poles of magnets. The train can be propelled by a linear motor on the track or on the train, or both.[3] Massive electrical induction coils are placed along the track in order to produce the magnetic field necessary to propel the train.

Static magnetic bearings using only electromagnets and permagnets are unstable because of Earnshaw's theorem; on the other hand, diamagnetic and superconducting magnets can support a maglev stably. Some conventional maglev systems are stabilized with electromagnets that have electronic stabilization. This works by constantly measuring the bearing distance and adjusting the electromagnet current accordingly.[4]

New Words and Expressions

magnetic [mæg'netik] adj. 磁的，有磁性的
levitation [ˌlevi'teiʃən] n. 轻轻浮起，升在空中
suspend [səs'pend] v. 悬，悬浮
guide [gaid] n. v. 指导，支配，管理，操纵
propel [prə'pel] v. 推进，推动
via ['vaiə] prep. 经，通过，经由
velocity [vi'lɔsiti] n. 速度
decade ['dekeid] n. 十年，十
turboprop ['tɜːbəuprɔp] n. 涡轮螺旋桨发动机
jet [dʒet] v. 喷出，喷射
compatible [kəm'pætib(ə)l] adj. 兼容的
interaction [ˌintər'ækʃən] n. 相互作用

physical ['fizikəl] *adj.* 物质的，自然的，物理的
tailor ['teilə] *vt.* 适合，适应
approach [ə'prəutʃ] *n.* 方法，途径
friction ['frikʃən] *n.* 摩擦力，摩擦
exert [ig'zɜːt] *vt.* 施加，努力，发挥，竭尽全力
consumption [kən'sʌmpʃ(ə)n] *n.* 消费，消费量
application [ˌæpli'keiʃən] *n.* 应用，运用，施用
investigate [in'vestigeit] *v.* 调查，研究
current ['kʌrənt] *n.* 电流
induce [in'djuːs] *v.* 引诱，引起，感应
passive ['pæsiv] *adj.* 被动的，消极的
array [ə'rei] *v.* 配置，排列
prototype ['prəutətaip] *n.* 原型，模范
cart [kɑːt] *n.* 大车，小车
levitate ['leviteit] *v.* 升空，将……悬置
repulsive [ri'pʌlsiv] *adj.* 排斥的
diamagnetic [ˌdaiəmæg'netik] *adj.* 抗磁的，反磁性的
superconducting [ˌsjuːpəkən'dʌktiŋ] *adj.* 超导
unstable [ʌn'steibl] *adj.* 不稳定的，不牢固的
bearing ['bεəriŋ] *n.* 轴承
stably ['steibli] *adv.* 稳定地，坚固地，坚定地

Notes to the Text

1. The term "maglev" refers not only to the vehicles, but to the vehicle/guideway interaction; each being a unique design element specifically tailored to the other to create and precisely control magnetic levitation.

   译文 "磁悬浮"这一术语不单指车体，还指车体与导轨之间的相互作用，车体和导轨都必须精心设计以致能互相作用来产生磁悬浮，并且准确控制。

2. Inductrack was originally developed as a magnetic motor and bearing for a flywheel to store power. With only slight design changes, the bearings were unrolled into a linear track.

   译文 磁性轨道最初开发成一磁性电动机和轴承来为飞轮储存能量。轴承只具有细微的设计变化，就可被展开成为直线型的轨道。

3. In one design, the train can be levitated by the repulsive force of like poles or the attractive force of opposite poles of magnets. The train can be propelled by a linear motor on the track or on the train, or both.

   译文 一种设计是使列车可以通过同极磁体的排斥力或异极磁体的吸引力使列车悬浮，而且可以通过置于轨道或列车，或在两者上的直线电动机来推动。

4. Some conventional maglev systems are stabilized with electromagnets that have electronic stabilization. This works by constantly measuring the bearing distance and adjusting the

electromagnet current accordingly.

译文 一些常规的磁悬浮系统通过具有电子稳定性的电磁体来进行稳定。可以通过不断测量轴承间距，并进行相对应地调整电磁体的电流来达到此目的。

Exercises to the Text

I. **Translate the following terms into Chinese.**

(1) wheeled mass transit systems   (2) electromagnetic energy

(3) load-carrying ability   (4) magnetic field

(5) particle accelerator

II. **Decide whether each of the following statements is true or false according to the text.**

(1) Maglev technology is compatible with conventional railroad tracks. (　)

(2) Maglev mustn't be designed as complete transportation systems. (　)

(3) All the maglev technological approaches are the same. (　)

(4) Maglev can be operated at up to 650 km/h. (　)

(5) Inductrack technique has a load-carrying ability related to the speed of the vehicle. (　)

(6) There are a magnetic field on the trackside for Inductrack technology. (　)

(7) Static magnetic bearings using only electromagnets and permagnets are stable. (　)

III. **Answer the following questions according to the text.**

(1) What advantage dose maglev have compared to wheeled mass transit systems?

(2) Who is the world leader in maglev technology?

(3) What dose friction refer to as the vehicles run?

(4) Which is the world's first commercial application of a high-speed maglev line?

(5) How many primary types of maglev technology are there? And point out.

(6) Who are active in maglev research?

(7) How can the maglev train be levitated?

Reading Material

Shanghai Maglev Train

Shanghai Maglev Train (Shanghai Transrapid) (上海磁悬浮示范运营线) is the first commercial high-speed maglev line in the world. Construction began in March, 2001, and trial public service commenced on January 1, 2003.

Introduction

The line is operated by Shanghai Maglev Transportation Development Co., Ltd. The train can reach almost 321.87 km/h in 2 minutes, with a maximum speed of 431km/h. The Shanghai Transrapid project took 1.2 billion dollars (10 billion Yuan) and 2.5 years to complete the 19 miles track.

The train runs from Longyang Road station on the Shanghai subway line 2 to Pudong International Airport, and the total track length is about 30 kilometres. The train takes 7 minutes and 20 seconds to complete the journey, and its top speed is 431km/h.

As of June 2005, the one way ticket price is 50 RMB (about 6 US dollars) and 40 RMB for airline passengers with proof of an airline ticket purchase. A round-trip ticket costs 80 RMB.

- Operate time: 7:00 to 21:00.
- Highest speed: 430 km/h (normal times) or 300 km/h (extend times).
- Run time: 7 mins and 20 sec. in normal times, while 8 mins and 10 sec. in extend times.
- Normal time is 8:30-17:00, extend time is 7:00-8:30 and 17:00-21:00.
- Interval: 15mins.

Future

Maglev ridership has been below expectations, due to limited operating hours, the short line, the high price of the tickets and the inconvenient location of the Longyang Road terminus. There is significant local criticism that the project was showy and wasteful, delivering no practical benefit to residents.

Various extension plans have been mooted. In January 2006, the Shanghai Urban Planning Administrative Bureau proposed an extension to Hongqiao Airport via Shanghai South Railway Station and the Expo 2010 site, with a possible continuation towards Hangzhou. If built, the line would allow transferring between the airports, which are located 55 km apart, in about 15 minutes. The plan to Hangzhou was approved by the central government in February 2006, with construction set to start by the end of 2006 and completion by 2010.

New Words and Expressions

as of 到……时为止，从……时起
the one way ticket 单程票
round-trip ticket 往返票，双程票
normal time 正常时间
extend time 加班时间
showy [ˈʃəui] adj. 浮华的,(过分) 艳丽的，炫耀的，卖弄的
moot [mu:t] vt. 提出……供讨论
the Expo 2010 site 2010年世界博览会场馆
continuation [kənˌtinjuˈeiʃən] n. 继续，续集，延长
the central government 中央政府

Exercises to the Material

Decide whether each of the following statements is true or false according to the material.

(1) Maglev ridership is more than expectations. (   )
(2) It takes airline passengers 40RMB to buy the one way ticket. (   )
(3) Limited operating hours, the short line, the high price of the tickets and the inconvenient location of the Longyang Road terminus resulted in low passenger flow. (   )
(4) The plan to Hangzhou was approved by the central government in February 2006. (   )
(5) There are several extension plans which have been mooted. (   )

Lesson 5   Subway (地铁)

A metro system is a railway system, usually in an urban area, that usually has high capacity and frequency, with large trains and total or near total grade separation from other traffic.

There is no single term in English that all speakers would use for all rapid transit or metro systems. This fact reflects variations not only in national and regional usage, but in what characteristics are considered essential.

One definition of a metro system is as follows:
- an urban, electric mass transit railway system;
- totally independent from other traffic;
- with high service frequency.

But those who prefer the American term "subway" or the British "underground" would additionally specify that the tracks and stations must be located below street level.

The volume of passengers a metro train can carry is often quite high, and a metro system is often viewed as the backbone of a large city's public transportation system.

In some cities, the urban rail system is so comprehensive and efficient that the majority of city residents go without an automobile.[1] Paris and London arguably have the best metro systems in the world, while New York City is the only American city on the same level. Chicago, Washington D.C., and Boston follow New York distantly, while the rest of the cities in the United States only have partial or poorly used systems, such as Saint Louis or Detroit. In the Western Hemisphere, Mexico City also has a large system. In Canada, only Toronto has extensive metro networks serving its urban centres; Vancouver's Sky Train also provides high-grade service, but at present acts primarily as a connection between Vancouver and the surrounding areas.

Most underground systems are for public transportation, but a few cities have built freight or postal lines. One example is the Post Office Railway, which transported mail underground between sorting offices in London from 1927 until it was abandoned in 2003.[2] Similarly, in its early days the London Underground's Metropolitan Line transported goods as well as running passenger trains. Another example is the Chicago Freight Subway, which has a dense grid of tunnels under downtown

Chicago.

During the Cold War, an important secondary function of some underground systems was to provide shelter in case of a nuclear attack.

Urban rail systems have often been used to showcase economical, social, and technological achievements of a nation, especially in the Soviet Union and other socialist countries. With their marble walls, polished granite floors and splendid mosaics, the metro systems of Moscow and St. Petersburg are widely regarded as some of the most beautiful in the world. Modern metro stations in Russia are usually still built with the same emphasis on appearance. Similarly, the Independent Subway System in New York City was built to compete with the private systems, and succeeded in running them out of business.[3]

Metro stations, more so than railway and bus stations, often have a characteristic of artistic design that can identify each stop. Some have sculptures or frescos. For example, London's Baker Street station is adorned with tiles depicting Sherlock Holmes. Every metro station in Valencia, Spain has a different sculpture on the ticket-hall level.

In some stations, especially where trains are fully automated, the entire platform is sometimes screened from the track by a wall, typically of glass, with automatic platform-edge doors.[4] These open, like elevator doors, only when a train is stopped, and thus eliminate the hazard that a passenger will accidentally fall or deliberately jump onto the tracks and be run over or electrocuted. Control over ventilation of the platform is also improved, allowing it to be heated or cooled without having to do the same for the tunnels. The doors, however, add cost and complexity to the system, and trains may have to approach the station more slowly so they can stop in accurate alignment with them.

New Words and Expressions

rapid ['ræpid] adj. 迅速的，飞快的
transit ['trænsit] n. 运输，转运，通过
elevated ['eliveitid] adj. 提高的
separation [ˌsepə'reiʃən] n. 分离，分开
reflect [ri'flekt] v. 反射，反映，表现，反省，细想
capacity [kə'pæsiti] n. 能力，容量
frequency ['friːkwənsi] n. 频率，次数
specify ['spesifai] vt. 指定，详细说明，列入清单
usage ['juːsidʒ] n. 使用，用法
characteristic [ˌkæriktə'ristik] n. 特征，特性
definition [ˌdefi'niʃən] n. 定义
electric [i'lektrik] adj. 电的，导电的
independent [ˌindi'pendənt] adj. 独立自主的，不受约束的
frequency ['friːkwənsi] n. 频率，周次，发生次数
prefer [pri'fɜː] vt. 提到，涉及，提交，谈及
specify ['spesifai] vt. 提定，详细说明
backbone ['bækbəun] n. 脊柱，主脊
comprehensive [ˌkɔmpri'hensiv] adj. 全面的，广泛的

efficient [i'fiʃənt] adj. 有效率的，生效的
go without 没有……也行
arguably ['ɑ:gjuəbli] adj. 可论证的
postal ['pəustəl] adj. 邮政的
sorting office 邮件分拣处
high-grade 高级的
grid [grid] n. 格栅
dense [dens] adj. 密集的，浓厚的
tunnel ['tʌnl] n. 地道，隧道
downtown ['dauntaun] n. 商业区，闹市区
shelter ['ʃeltə] n. 躲避，掩避
nuclear ['nju:kliə(r)] n. 核武器
attack [ə'tæk] v. 攻击
achievement [ə'tʃi:vmənt] n. 成就，功绩
showcase ['ʃəukeis] v. 使……展现
economical [,i:kə'nɔmikəl] adj. 节约的，经济的
polish ['pɔliʃ] v. 擦亮，磨光
emphasis ['emfəsis] n. 强调，重点
appearance [ə'piərəns] n. 出现，外观，外貌
sculpture ['skʌlptʃə] v. 雕刻
adorn [ə'dɔ:n] v. 装饰
depict [di'pikt] v. 描绘，描画，描写
fragment ['frægmənt] n. 碎片
artistic [ɑ:'tistik] adj. 艺术的，有美感的
scheme [ski:m] n. 计划，安排，配置
eliminate [i'limineit] vt. 排除，消除，除去
tile [tail] n. 瓦片，瓷砖
mural ['mjuərəl] n. 壁画
artwork ['ɑ:twɜ:k] n. 插图，艺术作品
run over 在……上压过
electrocute [i'lektrəkju:t] v. 使……触电身亡
ventilation [,venti'leiʃən] v. 通风，公开讨论
accurate ['ækjurit] adj. 准确的
alignment [ə'lainmənt] n. 结盟
Chicago [ʃi'kɑ:gəu] 芝加哥
Washington D.C. 华盛顿
Boston ['bɔstən] 波士顿
Saint Louis 圣路易
Detroit [di'trɔit] 底特律
Toronto [tə'rɔntəu] 多伦多
Mexico City 墨西哥城

Vancouver [væn'ku:və]　温哥华
Soviet Union　苏联
Sherlock Holmes　夏洛克·福尔摩斯
Valencia [və'lenʃiə]　巴伦西亚
Los Angeles　洛杉矶

Notes to the Text

1. In some cities, the urban rail system is so comprehensive and efficient that the majority of city residents go without an automobile.
   译文　在一些城市,城市轨道系统非常发达、高效,以至于大部分的城市居民出行时无需私人汽车。

2. One example was the Post Office Railway, which transported mail underground between sorting offices in London from 1927 until it was abandoned in 2003.
   译文　例如,邮政铁路,从1927年开始伦敦分拣中心就是用地铁来运送邮件,直到2003年废弃。

3. Similarly, the Independent Subway System in New York City was built to compete with the private systems, and succeeded in running them out of business.
   译文　类似地,纽约独立地铁系统修建得可与私人汽车系统相竞争,并且成功取得了多数市场份额。

4. In some stations, especially where trains are fully automated, the entire platform is sometimes screened from the track by a wall, typically of glass, with automatic platform-edge doors.
   译文　在一些车站,特别是列车完全自动化运作的车站,有时整个站台通过一面装有自动化站台端门的玻璃墙与轨道屏蔽。

Exercises to the Text

Ⅰ. **Translate the following terms into Chinese.**
   (1) grade separation　　　(2) mass transit　　　(3) the volume of passenger
   (4) service frequency　　　(5) high-grade service

Ⅱ. **Decide whether each of the following statements is true or false according to the text.**
   (1) Subway often is built in urban area. (　　)
   (2) Paris and New York arguably have the best metro systems in the world. (　　)
   (3) All subway are for public transportation. (　　)
   (4) Urban rail systems have often been used to display economical, social, and technological achievement of socialist countries.(　　)
   (5) Subway system in New York competed with the private systems, then gained much market share. (　　)
   (6) Metro stations are less than railway and bus stations. (　　)
   (7) The platform-edge doors add cost and complexity to the system. (　　)

Ⅲ. **Answer the following questions according to the Text.**
   (1) How to define the subway?
   (2) What characteristics does the subway have?

(3) Except the public transportation, what services can the subway also provide?
(4) Which cities have the most beautiful metro systems in the world?
(5) Why does each metro station have different artistic design?
(6) What function does the glass wall with platform-edge doors have?

Reading Material

Underground Transit Systems throughout the World

There are some beautiful, modern, and vast rapid transit systems throughout the world. The most popular and diverse international underground transit systems are listed below, but are merely a sample of the quite eye-catching transit systems that exist throughout the world.

1. London, England

The London Underground is Europe's largest metro subway system and is the world's oldest underground system (it was inaugurated in 1863). It covers 253 miles of track and transports 976 million people yearly. The Underground is also connected to a variety of rail services to London's surrounding areas. Among these services is the Docklands Light Railway (DLR), a popular driverless light rail extension, which offers many scenic views of the Thames River and surrounding areas.

Highlights: Cushioned seats. LED time displays hanging from the ceiling in stations indicate the number of minutes you need to wait before the next train. Eclectic station artwork. Oyster cards allow you to touch against a subway turnstile and go—and you can pay as you ride.

2. Paris, France

The Paris subway system is the second oldest in the world (the initial system was completed in 1900) and aids roughly 1.365 billion people with their daily commutes. Running over 133.7 miles of track and stopping at 380 stations, it has a great amount of coverage throughout the city.

Highlights: Excellent coverage: every building in the city is within 500 meters (1 600 feet) of a subway station. Many stations were designed with the distinctive unique art nouveau style. Modest fares.

3. Moscow, Russia

The Moscow subway system has the biggest ridership of all metro systems throughout the world, with 3.2 billion riders annually traveling on 12 subway lines to 172 stations. In total, the Moscow Metro covers approximately 178 miles. On an average weekday, the subway itself carries about 8.2 million passengers. While most of the Moscow trains run underground, some lines cross bridges and provide scenic views of the Moskva River and the Yauza River.

Highlights: Ornate architecture (at least 44 of these stations are rated as architectural sights). The system has many trains that stop frequently (trains stop at stations approximately every 90 seconds during peak hours). Fastest worldwide system (120 km/h).

4. Madrid, Spain

The Madrid Metro is the second largest underground system in Europe and the sixth largest system in the world. It has 182 miles of track. The Madrid Metro is the densest metro network in the world.

Highlights: Very clean and is implementing an ecologic cleaning system. Fast rides. Affordable fares. Great progress in system expansion (47 miles of new subway lines were built between 1999 and 2003). Modern stations.

5. Tokyo, Japan

The Tokyo subway system carries approximately 2.8 billion people per year to 282 subway stations. In addition to underground subways, the Tokyo transit system consists of the Toden Arakawa light rail line and the Ueno Zoo Monorail.

Highlights: Extremely clean. Trains are on time. Trains always stop in the same place alongside markers. Subway stops are announced in both Japanese and English. Modern system. The system has underground malls and customer amenities.

6. Seoul, Korea

The Seoul Metropolitan Subway is one of the most heavily used subway systems in the world with more than 8 million daily trips. It is also one of the biggest subway stations worldwide, running 179.4 miles in length. The trains mostly run underground, but 30% of the system is above ground.

Highlights: Beautiful architecture. Growth of the system has been incredible over the past few years. Utilizing T-money, a prepaid transportation card for transport throughout the city.

7. New York City, USA

The New York City rapid transit system is one of the most extensive public transit systems worldwide. It has grown from 28 stations when it was founded in October of 1904 to 462 stations presently. The subway carries 4.9 million people daily.

Highlights: Offers express services that run on separate tracks from local trains. The MTA (Metropolitan Transportation Authority) is currently testing out LED displays in subway stations to let commuters know when the next train is expected to arrive. 24 hour service. Unique and distinct artwork throughout the system.

8. Montreal, Canada

The Montreal Metro is a modern system that was inaugurated in 1966. It is a small (37.8 miles reaching 65 stations on four lines) yet unique and modern system that was inspired by the Paris Metro.

Highlights: Diverse, beautiful architecture and unique station art (each station is designed by a different architect). Pleasant riding experience (smooth rides: the trains run on a rubber surface to reduce the screech of train cars). Trains are frequent and fairly comfortable.

9. Beijing, China

The Beijing Subway is a relatively new subway system that opened in 1969 and serves Beijing and the surrounding suburbs. It was expanded for the 2008 Olympic Games. The expansion project brings the length of the subway station from approximately 71 miles to nearly 300 miles.

Highlights: Fairly easy subway to navigate (especially if you're a foreigner). Cheap fare (3 Yuan for most trips). Interesting architecture on the newer subway lines.

10. Hong Kong

The Hong Kong subway, also known as the MTR (Mass Transit Railway), was established in 1979. Despite its relatively small size compared (56 miles) to other transit systems, the MTR transports an average of 2.46 million rides per day. The Hong Kong system is based on a British design.

Highlights: Efficient. Frequent service, high-capacity cars. Extremely affordable. Clean and modern system with air-conditioned cars. Using the Octopus contactless smart card for subway currency, allowing travelers to swipe their card near the turnstile for easy access to train platforms.

New Words and Expressions

scenic ['si:nik] *adj.* 自然景色的；景色优美的
eclectic [i'klektik] *adj.* (人)兼收并蓄的；(方法、思想等)折中的
coverage ['kʌvərɪdʒ] *n.* 覆盖范围
distinctive [dis'tiŋktiv] *adj.* 有特色的，与众不同的
affordable [ə'fɔːdəbl] *adj.* 付得起的，不太昂贵的
incredible [in'kredəbl] *adj.* 不能相信的，不可信的，难以置信的
oyster card   伦敦旅游专用卡
art nouveau style   新艺术时期风格
T-money   一种在韩国首尔及邻近城市使用的公共交通智能卡系统

Exercises to the Material

Answer the following questions according to the material.
(1) Which is Europe's largest metro subway system?
(2) Which is the world's oldest underground system?
(3) Which subway system has the biggest ridership of all metro systems throughout the world?
(4) Which is the densest metro network in the world?

Multiple Units (动车组)

The term Multiple Unit or MU is used to describe a self-propelling train unit capable of coupling with other units of the same or similar type and still being controlled from one cab.[1] The term is commonly used to denote passenger trainsets that consist of more than one carriage, but single self-propelling carriages, can be referred to as Multiple Units if capable of operating with other units.

Multiple Units are of three main types:
- Electric Multiple Unit(EMU)
- Diesel Multiple Unit(DMU)
- Diesel Electric Multiple Units(DEMU).

Multiple Unit trainset has the same power and traction components as a locomotive, but instead of the components concentrating in one carbody, they are spread out on each car that makes up the set.[2] Therefore these cars can only propel themselves when they are part of the set; thus making them semi-permanently coupled. For example, a DMU might have one car carry the prime mover and traction motors, and another the engine for head end power generation; an EMU might have one car carry the pantograph and transformer, and another car carry the traction motors.

Advantages

Multiple Units have several advantages over locomotive-hauled trains.
- Energy efficiency—MUs are more energy efficient than locomotive-hauled trains. They are more nimble, especially on grades, as much more of the train's weight(sometimes all of it)is carried on power-driven wheels, rather than suffer the dead weight of unpowered hauled coaches.[3] In addition, they have a lower weight-per-seat value than locomotive-hauled trains since they do not have a bulky locomotive that does not itself carry passengers but contributes to the total weight of the train. This is particularly important for train services that have frequent stops, since the energy consumed for accelerating the train increases significantly with an increase in weight.
- No need to turn locomotive—Most MUs have cabs at both end, resulting in quicker turnaround times, reduced crewing costs, and enhanced safety. The faster turnaround time and the reduced size(due to higher frequencies)as compared to large locomotive-hauled trains, have made the MU a major part of suburban commuter rail services in many countries. MUs are also used by most rapid transit systems.
- Composing can be changed mid journey—MUs may usually be quickly made up or separated into sets of varying lengths. Several multiple units may run as a single train, then be broken at a junction point into smaller trains for different destinations.[4]
- Reliability—Due to having multiple engines the failure of one engine does not prevent the train from continuing its journey. A locomotive drawn train typically only has one power unit whose failure will disable the train. Some locomotive hauled trains may contain more than one power unit and thus be able to continue at reduced speed after the failure of one.
- Safety—Multiple Units normally have completely independent braking systems on all cars meaning the failure of the brakes on one car does not prevent the brakes from operating on the other cars.
- Axle load—Multiple Units have lighter axle loads, allowing operation on lighter tracks, where locomotives are banned. Another side effect of this is reduced track wear, as traction forces can be provided through many axles, rather than just the four or six of a locomotive.
- Easy and quick driving—Multiple Units generally have rigid couplers instead of the flexible ones on locomotive hauled trains. That means brakes or throttle can be more quickly applied without excessive amount of jerk experienced in passenger coaches.

Disadvantages

Multiple Units do have some disadvantages as compared to locomotive hauled trains.
- Maintenance—It may be easier to maintain one locomotive than many self-propelled cars.
- Safety—In the past it was often safer to locate the train's power systems away from passengers. This was particularly the case for steam locomotives, but still has some relevance for other power sources. A head on collision involving a Multiple Unit is likely to result in more casualties than one with a locomotive.
- Easy replacement of motive power—Should a locomotive fail, it is easily replaced. Failure of a Multiple Unit train-set will often require a whole new train or time-consuming switching.
- Efficiency—Idle trains do not waste expensive motive power resources. Separate locomotives mean that the costly motive power assets can be moved around as needed.

- Flexibility—Large locomotives can be substituted for small locomotives where the gradients of the route become steeper and more power is needed.[5] Also, different types of passenger cars can be easily added to or removed from a locomotive hauled train. However, it is not so easy for a Multiple Unit since individual cars can be attached or detached only in a maintenance facility.
- Noise and vibration—The passenger environment of a Multiple Unit is often noticeably noisier than that of a locomotive-hauled train, due to the presence of underfloor machinery. The same applies to vibration. This is a particular problem with DMUs.
- Obsolescence cycles—Separating the motive power from the payload-hauling cars means that either can be replaced when obsolete without affecting the other.
- It is difficult to have gangways between coupled sets, and still retain an aerodynamic leading front end.

Features

It is not necessary for every single car in a MU set to be motorized. Therefore MU cars can be motor units or trailer units. Instead of motors, trailing units can contain some supplemental equipment such as air compressors, batteries, etc.

In some MU trains, every car is equipped with a driving console and other controls necessary to operate the train. Therefore every car can be used as a cab car whether it is motorised or not. However, other EMUs can be driven/controlled only from dedicated cab cars.

Well-known examples of MUs are the Japanese Shinkansen and the last generation German ICE. Most trains in the Netherlands and Japan are MUs, making them suitable for use in areas of high population density. A new high-speed MU was unveiled by France's Alstom on February 5th, 2008. It has a claimed service speed of 360 km/h.

New Words and Expressions

Multiple Unit   动车组
denote [di'nəut] *vt.*   指示，表示
turnaround ['tɜːnəraund] *n.*   回车场
axle load   轴载重，轴负重
ban [bæn] *vt.*   禁止，取缔(书刊等)
track wear   轨道磨损
coupler ['kʌplə] *n.*   连结者，配合者；耦合器
motive power   动力
console [kən'səul] *n.*   [计]控制台
supplemental [ˌsʌpli'mentl] *adj.*   补足的，追加的
trailing unit   挂车组

Notes to the Text

1. The term Multiple Unit or MU is used to describe a self-propelling train unit capable of coupling with other units of the same or similar type and still being controlled from one cab.

   译文 动车组这一术语用于描述自力推进的列车组，该列车组可以与其他车或类似的列车组

连接起来，并且受同一司机室控制。

2. Multiple Unit trainset has the same power and traction components as a locomotive, but instead of the components concentrating in one carbody, they are spread out on each car that makes up the set.

   译文 动车组固定编组列车虽然具有与机车一样的动力和牵引力，但不是将构件集中在单节车体上，而是分散在组成列车组的每一节车厢上。

3. They are more nimble, especially on grades, as much more of the train's weight(sometimes all of it)is carried on power-driven wheels, rather than suffer the dead weight of unpowered hauled coaches.

   译文 动车组更敏捷，特别是在斜坡上，因为大部分列车的重量被传送至电力驱动的车轮上，而无需承受无动力拖动车厢的固定负载。

4. Several multiple units may run as a single train, then be broken at a junction point into smaller trains for different destinations.

   译文 几个动车组可作为单辆列车运行，即在枢纽站可分开成数截，分别开向不同的目的地。

5. Large locomotives can be substituted for small locomotives where the gradients of the route become steeper and more power is needed.

   译文 在坡度越来越陡的路线上，以及需要更多动力时，大型机车可以被小型机车取代。

Exercises to the Text

Ⅰ. **Translate the following words and phrases into English.**

   (1) 动车组　　　　　　(2) 固定编组列车　　　　(3) 自力推进车厢
   (4) 电力动车组　　　　(5) 内燃动车组　　　　　(6) 导电弓
   (7) 牵引电机　　　　　(8) 机车拖动普通列车　　(9) 轨道磨损
   (10)拖车组　　　　　　(11) 轴重　　　　　　　　(12) 市郊通勤铁路
   (13)固定负载

Ⅱ. **Decide whether each of the following statements is true or false according to the text.**

   (1) A bulky locomotive can increase the total weight of the train.　(　)
   (2) When the train weight increases, then the energy consumed for accelerating the train increases significantly.　(　)
   (3) In many countries, MUs are a major part of suburban commuter rail services, but are not used by most rapid transit systems.　(　)
   (4) Failure of a Multiple Unit train-set must be required a whole new train to replace.　(　)
   (5) Different types of passenger cars can be easily added to or removed from a Multiple Unit train-set.　(　)

Ⅲ. **Answer the following questions according to the text.**

   (1) How to define Multiple Units?
   (2) How many types of Multiple Units are there? Please make a list.
   (3) What are the same characteristics between Multiple Units and locomotive?
   (4) Why can every car of some MU trains be used as a cab car whether it is motorized or not?
   (5) What areas are MUs suitable for use?

Reading Material

Electric Multiple Unit

An Electric Multiple Unit or EMU is a Multiple Unit train consisting of many carriages using electricity as the motive power.

The cars that form a complete EMU set can usually be separated by function into four types: power car, motor car, driving car, and trailer car. Each car can have more than one function, such as a motor-driving car or power-driving car.

- A power car carries the necessary equipment to draw power from the electrified infrastructure, such as shoes for third rail systems and pantograph for overhead lines systems, and transformers.
- Motor cars carry the traction motor to move the train.
- Driving cars are similar to a cab car, containing a driver's cab for controlling the train. An EMU usually has two driving cars, with one at each end of the train.
- Trailer cars are any car that carries no traction or power related equipments, and is similar to a passenger car in a locomotive-hauled train.

Some of the more famous Electric Multiple Units in the world are high speed trains: the Shinkansen in Japan, the TGV in France, and ICE3 in Germany.

EMUs are also popular on commuter and suburban rail networks around the world due to their fast acceleration, pollution free operation and quietness. Being quieter than DMU (Diesel Multiple Unit) and locomotive-drawn trains, EMUs can operate later at night and more frequently without disturbing residents living near the railway lines. In addition, tunnel design for EMU trains is simpler as provisions do not need to be made for diesel exhaust fumes.

Exercises to the Material

Answer the following questions according to the material.
(1) How to define EMU?
(2) What types can the cars that form a complete EMU set usually be separated by function into?
(3) What functions does each type have?
(4) What are the famous Electric Multiple Units in the world?
(5) Why are EMUs also popular on commuter and suburban rail networks around the world?

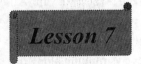 Lesson 7　Beijing West Terminal（北京西站）

In Beijing West Terminal (BWT), the principal railway projects include the construction of multipurpose terminal buildings with a total area of $17 \times 10^4 \, m^2$, a passenger operation yard with nine passenger platforms, a technical station for the service and repair of passenger trains, and a 28-km line from BWT to Changyangcun. In addition, manufacturing and residential areas cover $40 \times 10^4 \, m^2$. Municipal projects cover plazas in front of the south and north terminal buildings, the widening of six

streets, and underground railway line, converting open waterways into covered ditches, and a number of buildings to house municipal administrations, post and telecommunications services, and other public utilities and commercial setups.

The main terminal building (north building) is on the north side of the passenger operation yard. The south building is on the south side of the yard. The passenger operation yard is west of Beifengwo Avenue and east of West Sanhuan Avenue. The technical station serving passenger trains is between West Sanhuan Avenue and West Sihuan Avenue in line with the terminal building. The station is divided into a passenger train service area and a technical service area, with a car-washing setup between the two. A locomotive depot is on the south side of the train service area and a car depot is on the north side of the technical service area. A total of 113 km of track will be laid.

Terminal buildings

The main part of the multipurpose north terminal building will include ticket windows, VIP waiting room, commercial areas and a hostel for train crews. Flanking the main part will be areas for checking baggage and parcel, a hotel, a public security office, a dormitory for single workers, and part of the hostel. The total building area covers $20 \times 10^4 \text{ m}^2$, including $3.0 \times 10^4 \text{ m}^2$ for overhead waiting halls. The south building comprises a main building, a baggage and parcel building and signal tower. The main building's passenger areas, booking center and extended passenger services occupy about $5.5 \times 10^4 \text{ m}^2$.

Terminal plazas

The plaza in front of the north terminal building is 660 m from east to west and is divided into a central plaza and two flanking plazas. The east plaza will be a bus terminal and the west one a parking lot for groups and VIPs, with a special passageway, an underground parking area, $1.4 \times 10^4 \text{ m}^2$, will accommodate 570 automobiles, and a $4 \times 10^4 \text{ m}^2$ mezzanine will accommodate bicycles[1].

Platforms and waiting halls

Six elevated passengers waiting halls, totaling $2.4 \times 10^4 \text{ m}^2$ floor space[2], will span platforms 1 to 6 across the 217-m-wide passenger train yard between the south and north terminal buildings.

Attached to the north building is a platform area of 550 m×25 m×1.1 m, and to the south building a platform area of 550 m×9 m×1.1 m. The eight platforms each measure 550 m ×12 m×0.5 m. All platforms except those in the south area are long enough to receive 20-car passenger trains.

The platforms will be covered by light rain sheds. Over the platforms there will be a 38-m-wide elevated central passageway, which will be connected to two 4-m wide passageways running along the east and west side of the elevated waiting halls.[3] This arrangement will facilitate boarding trains from the waiting rooms.

A long concourse, 214 m long, 86.2 m wide and 2.8m high, will be constructed under the platforms. It will connect with a 10-m-wide, 2.8-m-high exit underpass on the east side of the terminal, so arriving passengers can leave the terminal or move to subway platforms.

Passenger operation yard

This yard is east of the service yard. It will have 20 tracks including main-line tracks. Two separate locomotive tracks are between platforms 2 and 3, 5 and 6. The west passage has seven parallel tracks, including two man-line tracks, four tracks connecting the terminal and depots and one special-duty track. From the east passage five tracks lead out, i.e., three main-line tracks and two locomotive service tracks.

Design feature of the BWT project

BWT is Beijing's second principal terminal, and its design has the following features.

Free flow paths of incoming passengers are smooth and direct, and those of outgoing passengers clearly defined, so that passengers have to walk only the shortest possible distance in the building with the help of an updated guiding system.

Baggage and parcels pass through an exclusive subway connecting the platforms with the baggage and parcel building and postal distribution building, so that they do not interfere with the flow of passengers.

Servicing and technical service for passenger cars will be executed in a flow fashion in separate areas of the yard, enabling passenger trains to go through the terminal passages at raised speeds.

Ingenious design details

The entrance to the main part of the north terminal is a portal with a 40 m span. At the center of the facade, it gives prominence to the building that will serve as the capital's west gate.

Square pavilions with glazed-tile roofs stand on top of the building in the center and at each corner, adding a touch of traditional Chinese architecture.[4]

The south and north walls of the north terminal are covered with jumbo plate glass, and other new materials and technologies have been introduced, adding a touch of modernity.

The portal entrance of the north terminal building is designed to straddle the subway structure, enabling simplification of the latter and making it easier for passengers to change trains.

Benefits of the project

Operation of the completed BWT will have the following socio-economic benefits.

With an overall capacity of 60 pairs of train, the new terminal will be able to handle 30 million passengers a year. This means an increase of over 50% in the junction's gross passenger traffic capacity. Passengers' current difficulty in procuring ticket is expected to be greatly relieved.

Since some passenger trains will transfer from BT (Beijing Terminal) to BWT, BT's departure and arrival intervals can be lengthened, enhancing train operation safety and reducing the crowds in the terminal area.

The strained carrying capacity of the Beijing-Guangzhou line will improve somewhat, and the strain on passenger and freight traffic capacity in the Fengtai Station can be alleviated.

Along with upgrading railway passenger service, the municipal environment will be improved and embellished, contributing to the capital as a political and cultural center.

New Words and Expressions

project ['prɔdʒekt] *n.* 设计，方案，工程
principal ['prinsip(ə)l] *adj.* 主要的，首要的
multipurpose ['mʌltipɜːpəs] *adj.* 多种用途的

residential [ˌrezi'denʃ(ə)l] adj.　住宅的
manufacturing [ˌmænju'fæktʃəriŋ] adj.　生产的，制造的
municipal [mju(:)'nisipəl] adj.　市政的
plaza ['plɑ:zə] n.　广场
ditch [ditʃ] n.　沟，沟渠，壕沟
telecommunication [ˌtelikəmju:ni'keiʃ(ə)n] n.　电信
utility [ju:'tiliti] n.　公用事业，效用
hostel ['hɔstəl] n.　宿舍，招待所
include [in'klu:d] vt.　包含，包括
flank [flæŋk] v.　位于……的侧面
overhead [ˌəuvə'hed] adj.　在上头的，高架的
mezzanine ['mezəni:n] n.　底层
accommodate [ə'kɔmədeit] v.　接纳，使适应
check [tʃek] v.　托运，寄存，检查
span [spæn] n.　跨度
extended [ik'stendid] adj.　扩展的，延伸的
facilitate [fə'siliteit] v.　使便利
concourse ['kɔŋkɔ:s] n.　车站大厅
house [hauz] v.　容纳
passageway ['pæsidʒwei] n.　走廊，过道
measure ['meʒə] n.　尺寸，方法，测量
shed [ʃed] n.　棚，小屋
move [mu:v] v.　移动，离开
parallel ['pærəlel] adj.　平行的，类似的
underpass ['ʌndəpɑ:s] n.　地道，地下过道
updated [ʌp'deitid] adj.　最新的
facade [fə'sɑ:d] n.　正面，外观
jumbo ['dʒʌmbəu] adj.　特大的，巨大的
portal ['pɔ:təl] n.　入口，大门
strain [strein] v. n.　(使)紧张
alleviate [ə'li:vieit] v.　减轻，缓和
embellish [im'beliʃ] v.　装饰，美化
procure [prə'kjuə] v.　获得
ingenious [in'dʒi:njəs] adj.　有独创性的，巧妙的
pavilion [pə'viljən] n.　亭子
jumbo ['dʒʌmbəu] adj.　巨大的
socio-economic adj.　社会经济的
be attached to　附属于
give prominence to　突出
a touch of　一点，少许
in line with　一致，成一直线

arrival [əˈraivəl] *n.* 到站
departure [diˈpɑːtʃə(r)] *n.* 离开，出发，起程
convert…to   把……转换

Notes to the Text

1. The east plaza will be a bus terminal and the west one a parking lot for groups and VIPs, with a special passageway, an underground parking area, 1.4×10^4 m^2, will accommodate 570 automobiles, and a 4×10^4 m^2 mezzanine will accommodate bicycles.
   译文 东边广场将是汽车总站，而西边广场将是为团体和贵宾服务的停车场，并且东西广场间有一条专门通道。地下停车场有 1.4 万平方米，可停车 570 辆，另外还有一个 4 万平方米的大厦底层可停放自行车。
   这是一个并列句，第二个分句中的 one 指代 plaza，相当于 the west plaza，其谓语动词 will be 省略。

2. floor area 与 floor space 的含义不同，前者指占地面积，后者则是指楼面面积。

3. Over the platforms there will be a 38-m-wide elevated central passageway, which will be connected to two 4 m wide passageways running along the east and west side of the elevated waiting halls.
   译文 站台上方将有一条 38 米宽的高架中心通道，该通道连接着两条 4 米宽、连通高架候车厅东西两侧的过道。
   这是一个复合句，主句后面是一个由 which 引导的定语从句修饰 a 38-m-wide elevated central passageway，在定语从句中，现在分词短语 running along the east and west side of the elevated waiting halls 用作后置定语，说明前面的名词短句 two 4 m wide passageways。

4. Square pavilions with glazed-tile roofs stand on top of the building in the center and at each corner, adding a touch of traditional Chinese architecture.
   译文 覆盖着琉璃瓦的方形塔楼耸立在大楼的中央和每个角上，增添了中国传统建筑的色彩。

Exercises to the Text

Ⅰ. **Translate the following terms into Chinese.**

(1) passenger operation yard   (2) locomotive depot   (3) car depot
(4) passenger train   (5) ticket windows   (6) VIP waiting room
(7) baggage and parcel building (8) booking center   (9) parking lot
(10) main-line track   (11) waiting hall   (12) outgoing passengers
(13) the junction's gross passenger traffic capacity   (14) procuring ticket
(15) signal tower   (16) terminal building

Ⅱ. **Decide whether each of the following statements is true or false according to the text.**

(1) The main terminal building is on the south side of the passenger operation yard. (   )
(2) There are six elevated passengers waiting halls in Beijing West Terminal. (   )
(3) All platforms can receive 20-car passenger trains. (   )
(4) Passenger operation yard have 20 tracks. (   )
(5) With the construction of Beijing West Terminal, passengers' current difficulty in procuring ticket is expected to be greatly relieved. (   )

Ⅲ. **Answer the following questions according to the text.**

(1) Where is the main terminal building?

(2) What areas is Beijing West Terminal divided into?

(3) What will the main part of the multipurpose north terminal building include?

(4) Where is the passenger operation yard?

(5) How many parallel tracks does the west passage have?

Reading Material

The Form of a Passenger Station

Most large passenger stations are popularly referred to "terminals" even though strictly speaking. they actually are not terminals.

A passenger station may be divided into three sections: the building which is to contain the booking and other offices necessary for the comfort of the business of the railway staffs, the platform by which the passengers enter or leave the train and the track layout at the platforms and in the yard outside the station. From the railway point of view the last is the most important, for upon it hinges the capacity of the station to deal with the maximum number of trains especially at the hours of greatest traffic pressure.

A very important feature of a large modern station is the concourse. It is the place where most of the services and conveniences required by the traveler are found. It gives access to the train platforms and communication from one platform to another.

The platforms vary in height from rail to car floor level. Where rapid exit of passengers from cars is required, the high or car level platform is used. British platforms are of car floor level. They are some three feet or so above rail level, so that the passenger steps into or out the train on the same level, rather than having to climb up into his compartment.

Usually one platform serves two tracks, one at either side, the passenger, baggage and mail traffic, all being handle thereon. At some stations, however, separate baggage platforms are provided. The train platforms are usually protected from weather by a continuous roof, which sometimes extend over the adjacent tracks.

When the tracks are at different level from the station and streets, stairways are generally used to connect them, additional elevators or lifts and escalators are used, and in recent stations the incline or ramp has been introduced.

The size and accessories of waiting rooms are influenced by local traffic necessities, such as the proportion of passengers changing from one train to another and the relative volume of suburban or long distance traffic.

The tickets windows and counters should be set back from the main current of traffic, affording room for lines at windows so that they do not interfere with the general circulation.

The lines leading into a terminal are often 6 or 8 in number, but 4 are more usual. It is normal practice to place the lines between two platforms with the necessary cross-over lines so that an engine may run round its train.

The yard where carriages may be stored, cleaned and examined should be as close to the station as possible.

New Words and Expressions

passenger station 客运站
hinge[hindʒ] v. 装以铰链，依……而转移
track layout 轨道配置
give access to 接见，准许出入
step into 进入
climb up 爬上
compartment [kəm'pɑːtmənt] n. 间隔间，车厢
thereon [ðeər'ɔn] adv. 在其上，在那上面，……之后立即
continuous [kən'tinjuəs] adj. 连续的，持续的
stairway ['steəwei] n. 楼梯
ramp [ræmp] n. 斜坡，坡道
accessory n. 附件
set back 使退步
interfere with 妨碍，干涉，干扰

Exercises to the Material

Answer the following questions according to the material.
(1) What sections may a passenger station be divided into?
(2) What is the most important section?
(3) What is the very important feature of a large modern station?
(4) Which platforms are of car floor level?
(5) Which can influence the size and accessories of waiting rooms?
(6) Why should the tickets windows and counters be set back from the main current of traffic?

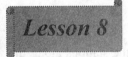

Lesson 8　Passenger Rail Transport in China (中国铁路客运)

　　Rail is one of the principal means of transport in Mainland China, with over 1.2 billion railway trips taken each year. The Spring Festival Travel Season is the peak railway travel season of the year. In 2006, more than 144 million people traveled by rail during this 40 day festival period.

Passenger train route identifiers
　　Every train route has an identification number of two to four characters. The first character can be alphabetic or numeric, while the second to fourth characters are all numeric.
　　Trains are classified as up trains or down trains. Since Beijing is seen as the center of the network, the train from Beijing is the down service, while the train towards Beijing is the up service. Trains that do not go to Beijing are designated up or down based on the railway they are traveling on.[1] Railways that do not go to Beijing are up or down based on their directions: south and east are up, north and west

are down. Train routes that change from up service to down service while traveling in a certain direction might use two different route numbers.

First character

The first character of the route identifier usually indicates the class of the passenger train, often determined by the speed and the relative number of stops the train makes along the way. There are five alphabetic prefixes.

D (*EMU train*)

This series will be available after the sixth rise in speed of the railway in April 18, 2007. All will have soft beds or seats. The top speed will be 250 km/h. These trains will be powered using Electric Multiple Units (EMUs).

Z (*direct express*)

Though its name in Chinese technically implies a "non-stop" train, some of these trains have several stops between the two stations. The majority have sleepers, while very few have not sleepers. As of August, 2006, all but one of the Z-series trains have either Beijing Railway Station or Beijing West Terminal as their destination or origin.

T (*express*)

This series of trains have a limited number of stops along their routes, only in major cities, or in some instances stops for switching the driver or locomotive. The standard pronunciation on the railway system is "Te" in Chinese, which most people spell as "T" in English.

K (*fast*)

This series of trains stop at more stations than T-series, and normally have a slower travel speed than the T-series in the same corridor. The standard pronunciation on the railway system is "Kuai" in Chinese, which most people spell as "K" in English.

All K-series trains travel on lines operated by more than one railway bureau.

N (*fast train within one railway bureau*)

Similar to a K train, but this series of trains travel exclusively within one railway bureau. The standard pronunciation on the railway system is "Nei" in Chinese, which most people spell as "N" in English.

- 1-5 general fast train

General fast trains are slower passenger trains that stop at around half of the stations along the way, resulting in a longer travel time than the fast trains. Route numbers are always four numeric digits—a numeric prefix from 1-5 followed by a 3-digit route number.

- 6-9 general train

The general train often simply referred to as slow train has as many stops as possible, and is often the preferred choice for rural workers to visit their home villages. This is the slowest type of train and has the lowest priority in the fixed train timetable.

Route identifiers for general trains are always 4 digits—a numeric prefix from 6-9 followed by a 3-digit route number.

L (*temporary train*)

This series of trains are temporary—They are not listed in the official train schedule, but are added when necessary. Many of these trains only operate at peak passenger travel season such as during the spring festival period. In addition, many new train services are originally added as L-series before train schedules are readjusted and later become regular services.

The standard pronunciation on the railway system is "Lin" in Chinese, which most people spell as "L" in English.

A (*train meeting needs*)

This series is similar to the L-series, but is used when a number is taken by a regular train.

The standard pronunciation on the railway system is "An" in Chinese, which most people spell as "A" in English.

S (*suburb train*)

Used for commuter traffic, they generally have a short route—for example, S801, from Meilong in Shanghai to Jiashan in Zhejiang, has a route of only 59 km.

Numeric portion (Digits 2-4)

Down trains use odd numbers, while up trains use even numbers. For example, the T103 travels from Beijing to Shanghai, and the N522 travels from Hangzhou to Meilong.[2]

Some examples of double train numbers that switch up and down during their route. The Shanghai to Harbin train is the K56/57—it uses K56 before Tangshan, and uses K57 after Tangshan.

The Shanghai to Chengdu is the K290/291—it uses K290 before Xuzhou(towards Beijing on the Beijing-Shanghai Railway), and uses K291 after Xuzhou(east to west on the Longhai Railway and north to south on the Baoji-Chengdu Railway).

Accommodation and fares

There are four types of tickets that may be purchased.

- Hard seat is the basic fare, somewhat similar to the economy class on an airplane. On busier routes, passengers who cannot arrange for better seats because of overcrowding must also purchase this type of ticket.[3]
- Soft seat is one level above the hard seat, and has comfortable seating similar to business class on airplanes.
- Hard sleeper is the basic accommodation for an overnight train. Despite the name, the bunks comfortably accommodate anyone below six feet. Bunks are arranged three on a side in a compartment—indicated by up, middle and bottom on the ticket.
- Soft sleeper contains a larger bunk bed in an enclosed cabin, two bunks to a side. These tickets are usually reserved more than a week prior to departure.

A few trains will have a kind of accommodation more expensive than a soft bed, named "Advanced Cab".

The fares are different between trains with or without air-conditioning.

Combined transportation

Combined transportation trains allow passengers to remain on a single train during two routes, without transferring to a different train at the station where the route changes.[4]

Guangzhou-Kowloon

No.T97/98(Beijing-Kowloon)and No.K99/100(Shanghai-Kowloon)are combined transportation trains. Passengers can complete all formalities in their departure station, and no longer need to alight at Dongguan.

International combined transportation

A few trains can transport passengers out of China to places such as Ulaanbaatar in Mongolia, Moscow in Russia, Almaty in Kazakhstan, Pyongyang in D.P.R.Korea, Hanoi in Vietnam and so on.

Since Chinese railways and those of its neighbours sometimes have different gauges of rail track, passengers in some trains may need to alight at a border city and wait for a train of a different gauge to continue their journey.

New Words and Expressions

identifier [aiˈdentifaiə] n.　检验人，标识符
up train　上行车
down train　下行车
designate [ˈdezigneit] vt.　指明，指出，任命，指派
alphabetic [ˌælfəˈbetik] adj.　照字母次序的，字母的
prefix [ˈpriːfiks] n.　前缀
instance [ˈinstəns] n.　实例，情况，场合
railway bureau　铁路局
train schedule　列车明细表
commuter traffic　通勤交通
overnight [ˌəuvəˈnait] adj.　通宵的，晚上的，前夜的
bunk [bʌŋk] n.　(轮船，火车等)铺位
cabin [ˈkæbin] n.　小屋，船舱
combined transportation　联合运输
formality [fɔːˈmæliti] n.　拘谨，礼节，仪式，正式手续，拘泥形式
departure station　旅客出发站
general train　普通旅客列车
general fast train　普通旅客快车，普快
Advanced Cab　高级软卧包厢
soft seat　软座
hard sleeper　硬卧
soft sleeper　软卧
hard seat　硬座

Notes to the Text

1. Trains that do not go to Beijing are designated up or down based on the railway they are traveling on.

   译文　不到达北京的列车根据其行车的铁路方向被指定为上行或下行。

2. Down trains use odd numbers, while up trains use even numbers. For example, the T103 travels from Beijing to Shanghai, and the N522 travels from Hangzhou to Meilong.

   译文　下行列车采用奇数，而上行列车采用偶数。例如，T103 是从北京驶往上海，N522 是从杭州驶往梅隆。

3. On busier routes, passengers who cannot arrange for better seats because of overcrowding must also

purchase this type of ticket.

译文　在较繁忙线路上，由于过度拥挤不能安排更好座位的旅客必须购买硬座车票。

4. Combined transportation trains allow passengers to remain on a single train during two routes, without transferring to a different train at the station where the route changes.

译文　联合运输列车允许旅客在两个线路期间乘坐同一列车，在线路交汇车站无需换乘。

Exercises to the Text

Ⅰ. Translate the following terms into Chinese.

(1) the peak railway travel season　(2) up train　(3) down service

(4) fast train　(5) general train　(6) general fast train

(7) train schedule　(8) regular services　(9) suburb train

(10) combined transportation

Ⅱ. Decide whether each of the following statements is true or false according to the text.

(1) Trains are classified as up trains and down trains. (　　)

(2) Railways that do not go to Beijing are up or down based on their directions: south and east are down, north and west are up. (　　)

(3) The first character must be alphabetic, while the second to fourth characters are all numeric. (　　)

(4) Down trains use even numbers, while up trains use odd numbers. (　　)

(5) Combined transportation trains allow passengers to remain on a single train during two routes, without transferring to a different train at the station where the route changes. (　　)

Ⅲ. Answer the following questions according to the text.

(1) What does the first character of the route identifier usually indicate?

(2) There are eight alphabetic prefixes for the first character, please make a list of it.

(3) When will EMU trains be available?

(4) What types of tickets can be purchased?

(5) Why do some trains need to alight at a border city for international combined transportation?

Reading Material

The Overview of China Railway

With Beijing as its hub, the railway links all the provincial capitals providing a network that serves all parts of China. There are sixteen trunk lines crisscrossing the country. Of these the Beijing-Kowloon line is the longest covering more than 2 500 kilometers. Other notable long distance routes link Beijing with Guangzhou, Shanghai, and Harbin. The very latest and probably the most exciting development has been the already world-famous Tibet Railway, a quarter of which is electrified. Opened in July 2006, the traffic along the line has already covered a total of some 80 000 kilometers. The railway operates at the highest land altitudes ever and the passenger compartments are pressurized in the same manner as civil aircraft.

With the passenger transport capacity of about one billion a year, China's railway is always very busy; the trains and train stations are usually very crowded. In order to alleviate the congestion and improve efficiency, steps have been taken to increase speeds, thus reducing journey times and allowing faster turn round, while ensuring high standards of safety. This means the modern trains can operate at speeds between 160 and 200 kilometers per hour.

Almost all the Chinese cities have their own railway stations, some have more than one. These stations provide passenger related facilities and services such as a dining hall, coffee house, shops, phone booths and newsstands. Tickets can be purchased in the ticket booking hall. Actually, train tickets are difficult to buy in China, especially during the high travel season or at the start and finish of national holidays such as the Spring Festival, May Day, and the National Day as well as the summer or winter vacation. There are many ticket agencies throughout the city where a 24 hour service is available. However, a fee of 5 yuan is added to the ticket price at these outlets. Normally, train tickets can be booked between 3 to 15 days ahead of travel time subject to variations depending upon the city or time of year.

Exercises to the Material

Decide whether each of the following statements is true or false according to the material.
(1) The Beijing-Kowloon line is the longest covering more than 2 500 kilometers. (　)
(2) A quarter of Tibet Railway is electrified. (　)
(3) The modern trains can operate at speeds between 160 and 200 kilometers per hour in China. (　)
(4) Almost all the Chinese cities have only one railway station. (　)
(5) A fee of 5 yuan is added to the ticket price, when buying ticket from ticket agencies. (　)

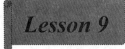

Lesson 9　Railroad Car (铁路车厢)

hard seat car　　　　　　　　　　　　dining car

A railroad car is a vehicle on a railroad. That is not a locomotive—one that provides another purpose than purely haulage, although some types of cars are powered.[1] Cars can be coupled together into a train, either hauled by a locomotive (s) or self-propelled.

Most cars carry a revenue load, although non-revenue cars exist for the railroad's own use, such as for maintenance-of-way purposes. "Revenue" cars are basically of two types: passenger cars and freight cars.

Passenger cars

Passenger cars vary in their internal fittings.

In standard gauge cars, seating is usually three, four, or five seats across the width of the car, with an aisle in between (resulting in 2+1, 2+2 or 3+2 seats) or at the side. Tables may be present between seats facing one another. Alternatively, seats facing the same direction may have access to a fold-down ledge on the back of the seat in front.

- If the aisle is located between seats, seat rows may face the same direction, or be grouped, with twin rows facing each other. Sometimes, for example on a commuter train, seats may face the aisle.
- If the aisle is at the side, the car is usually divided in small compartments, each with two seat rows opposite to each other, with 6 or 8 seats.

Cars usually have either air-conditioning or windows that can be opened. Toilet facilities are also usual, though the setup varies.

Other types of passenger cars exist, especially for long journeys, such as the dining car, parlor car, disco car, and in rare cases theater car. Observation cars were built for the rear of many famous trains to allow the passengers to view the scenery. These proved popular, leading to the development of dome cars, multiple units of which could be placed mid-train, and featured a glass-enclosed upper level extending above the normal roof to provide passengers with a better view.[2]

Sleeping cars generally outfitted with small bedrooms allow passengers to sleep through their night-time trips, while couchette cars provide more basic sleeping accommodation. Long-distance trains often require baggage cars for the passengers' luggage. Historically in European practice it was common for day coaches to be formed of compartments seating 6 or 8 passengers, with access from a side corridor. Corridor coaches fell into disfavor in the 1960s and 1970s partially because open coaches are considered more secure by women traveling alone.

Another distinction is between single-deck and double-deck train cars. An example of a double decker is the Amtrak superliner.

A "trainset" (or "set") is a semi-permanently arranged formation of cars. These are only broken up and reshuffled "on shed" in the maintenance depot. Trains are then built of one or more of these "sets" coupled together as needed for the capacity of that train.

Often, but not always, passenger cars in a train are linked together with enclosed, flexible gangway connections that can be walked through by passengers and crew members.[3] Some designs incorporate semi-permanent connections between cars and may have a full-width connection, making in essence one longer, flexible "car". In North America, passenger equipment also employs tightlock couplings to keep a train reasonably intact in the event of a derailment or other accident.

Many multiple unit trains consist of cars which are semi-permanently coupled into sets; these sets may be joined together to form larger trains, but generally passengers can only move around between cars within a set. This "closed" nature allows the separate sets to be easily split to go separate ways. Some multiple-unit trainsets are designed so that corridor connections can be easily opened between coupled sets; this generally requires driving cabs either set off to the side or above the passenger compartment.

Freight cars

Freight cars exist in a wide variety of types, adapted to the ideal carriage of a whole host of different things.[4] Originally there were very few types of car; the boxcar, a closed box with side doors, was among the first.

Common types of freight cars include the following.
- Autoracks—specialized multi-level cars designed for transportation of unladen automobiles.
- Boxcars—box shape with roof and side or end doors.
- Refrigerator cars—a refrigerated subtype of boxcar.
- Flatcars for larger loads that don't load easily into a boxcar. Specialised types such as the depressed-center flatcar exist for truly outsize items or the Schnabel car for even larger and heavier loads. With the advent of containerised freight, special types of flatcar were built to carry standard shipping containers and semi-trailers. Some (well cars) allow containers to be stacked two high (double stacked).
- Gondolas, railroad cars with an open top but enclosed sides and end, for bulk commodities and other goods that might slide off.
- Hopper cars, gondolas with bottom dump doors for easy unloading of things like coal, ore, grain, cement, track ballast and the like. Two varieties: open top and closed top.
- Tank cars for the carriage of liquids.
- Stock cars for the transport of livestock.
- Well cars—specialized cars designed for carrying shipping containers. These have a very low bottom floor to allow double stacking, and articulated 3-car and 5-car sets are common.
- CargoSprinter—a self propelled container flatcar.

Non-revenue cars
- Cabooses (or guard's vans or brake vans) which are attached to the rear of freight trains to order to watch the train and assist in shoving moves.
- Maintenance of way (MOW) cars, for the maintenance of track and equipment.
- Handcars, which are powered by their passengers.
- Railroad cranes.

New Words and Expressions

haulage ['hɔːlidʒ] *n.* 托运，牵引力
locomotive [ˌləukə'məutiv] *n.* 机车
revenue ['revənjuː] *n.* 收入
maintenance ['meintinəns] *n.* 维修
coach [kəutʃ] *n.* 四轮大马车，长途汽车
fitting ['fitiŋ] *n.* 装配，装置
width [widθ] *n.* 宽度
present [pri'zent] *vt.* 呈现，提出
ledge [ledʒ] *n.* 壁架

parlor ['pɑːlə] n. 客厅,会客室
view [vjuː] v. 观察，观看
scenery ['siːnəri] n. 风景，景色
upper ['ʌpə] adj. 上面的，上部的
outfit ['autfit] n. 配备，装备
dome [dəum] n. 圆屋顶
aisle [ail] n. 坐席之间的纵行通道
railroad car   列车车厢
commuter train   通勤列车
compartment [kəm'pɑːtmənt] n. 隔间
couchette [kuːˈʃet] n. 坐卧两用车厢
accommodation [ə,kɔmə'deiʃən] n. 住处，预定铺位
baggage ['bægidʒ] n. 行李
luggage ['lʌgidʒ] n. 行李
access ['ækses] n. 通路，入门
distinction [dis'tiŋkʃən] n. 区别，差别，级别
reshuffle [riːˈʃʌfl] v. 改组
baggage car   行包车厢
corridor ['kɔridɔː] n. 走廊，车厢走廊
couple ['kʌpl] v. 联合，连接
link [liŋk] n. v. 连接，联合
enclose [inˈkləuz] vt. 装入，环绕
flexible ['fleksib(ə)l] adj. 灵活的，可变形的
connection [kəˈnekʃən] n. 连接
incorporate [inˈkɔːpəreit] v. 包含
equipment [iˈkwipmənt] n. 装备，装置，铁路车辆
employ [imˈplɔi] vt. 雇用，使用
nature ['neitʃə] n. 本性，天性
split [split] v. 分裂，分离
unlade [ʌnˈleid] vt. 卸下，卸货
with the advent of   随着……到来
containerize [kənˈteinəraiz] vt. 用集装箱装
stack [stæk] v. 堆叠
slate [sleit] n. 石板，石片
break up   分解，分裂

Notes to the Text

1. That is not a locomotive—one that provides another purpose than purely haulage, although some types of cars are powered.

   译文 虽然有些类型的铁路车厢能提供动力，但还有一些铁路车厢并不提供动力，而是有其

他用途，这种铁路车厢就不是机车。

2. These proved popular, leading to the development of dome cars, multiple units of which could be placed mid-train, and featured a glass-enclosed upper level extending above the normal roof to provide passengers with a better view.

译文 这些均被证明非常受欢迎，从而导致了可置于列车中间的观光车厢动车组的发展，装有玻璃的上顶延伸到整个车顶，这使旅客能更好地欣赏风景。

3. Often, but not always, passenger cars in a train are linked together with enclosed, flexible gangway connections that can be walked through by passengers and crew members.

译文 列车的旅客车厢通常通过封闭、灵活的过道连接，便于旅客和乘务员通过。

4. Freight cars exist in a wide variety of types, adapted to the ideal carriage of a whole host of different things.

译文 货运车厢种类繁多，能适应不同货物的大批量装运。

Exercises to the Text

Ⅰ. Translate the following terms into Chinese.

(1) passenger car (2) freight car (3) dining car
(4) parlor car (5) disco car (6) theater car
(7) dome car (8) sleeping car (9) couchette car
(10) maintenance depot (11) well car (12) tank car
(13) stock car (14) hopper car (15) boxcar
(16) flatcar (17) refrigerator car

Ⅱ. Decide whether each of the following statements is true or fasle according to the text.

(1) Revenue cars can be divided into passenger cars and freight cars. (　)

(2) The internal fitting of most passengers are the same. (　)

(3) The aisle can only be located between seats. (　)

(4) There are many types of passenger cars for long journeys. (　)

(5) All sleeping and couchette cars allow passenger to sheep at night. (　)

(6) Corridor coaches have disappeared now. (　)

(7) There are single-deck and double-deck train cars now in the world. (　)

(8) Different train sets which have different destinations can be joined together to form large trains. (　)

(9) The boxcars have side doors. (　)

(10) Hopper cars can load granular materials. (　)

Ⅲ. Answer the following questions according to the text.

(1) What types can "revenue" cars be divided into?

(2) What are the functions of observation cars?

(3) Why did corridor coaches fall into disfavor in the 1960s and 1970s?

(4) How many types do freight cars include? Give a concrete example.

Reading Material

The New Type of Double-Decker Passerger Train

The new type of double-decker passenger train for medium-distance and long-distance operation is composed of six types of coaches:double-decker cushioned-berth sleeping car, double-decker semicushioned-berth sleeping car, double-decker semicushioned seat coach, double-decker buffet coach, single-decker baggage van and dynamo van.

Characteristics of the new type of double-decker coaches are as follows.

First, carrying capacity has increased, thus passenger traffic capacity has also increased.

Compared with single-decker coaches, the new double-decker coaches for short-distance and medium-distance operation, for Guangzhou-Shenzhen quasi-high-speed operation and for medium-distance and long-distance operation have greatly increased carrying capacity, thus greatly increasing passenger traffic capacity as well. This not only relieves the shortage in railway capacity, but produces economic gains for the railway.

Second, the riding comfort for passengers has greatly improved, mainly owing to the adoption of air spring suspended model 209 PK bogies with good kinetic properties that enable the coach to run smoothly with minor noise. The coaches are air-conditioned, so the interior is warm in winter and cool in summer.

Third, a great deal of new technology, structure and material has been adopted for the coaches. For instance, model 209 PK bogie, by using new technology and a structure of air spring suspension and disc brake, not only makes the train run smoothly, with less impact when applying brakes, but also guarantees reliable stops; weather-resistant steel is adopted for the body structure, which has not only high strength, but also long life. New materials of reinforced fiber-glass and plastic are used for the coaches' interior decoration. Which are not only beautiful and dignified but also light in weight and saving of wood.

Fourth, a totally closed under-frame structure is employed for the car body, giving small clearance to the rail top and thus reducing resistance and saving energy.

Exercises to the Material

Answer the following questions according to the material.

(1) What types of coaches compose the new type of double-decker passenger train for medium-distance and long-distancc operation?
(2) Compared with single-decker coaches, what is the advantage of the new double-decker coaches for short-distance and medium-distance operation?
(3) Why has the riding comfort for passengers greatly improved?
(4) What new technology, structure and material have been adopted for the coaches?
(5) Why is a totally closed under-frame structure employed for the car body?

Lesson 10 Freight Traffic (货运)

Freight traffic constitutes the bulk of the railroad business and source of revenue. Some railroads haul nothing but freight. Freight statistics are reported in carloads, tons, or ton miles. The last unit, which represents one ton moved a distance of one mile, is used most often, since it combines two factors—the quantity handled and the distance moved.[1] There are several possible freight classifications.

Carload (CL) freight moves in sufficient quantities to require one or more fully loaded cars. Tariffs specify the minimum tonnage of a commodity the consignor must offer to obtain the low carload rate. Most bulk commodities and large manufactured products move in carload lots or, when in great quantities, in trainload lots based on a minimum number of cars in the shipment (20,30,50,etc.).

Less than carload (LCL) freight includes all freight in quantities smaller than that required for a carload minimum. Individual shipments must be brought to the freight house either in the consignor owe truck or in the railroad's pickup and delivery vehicle. Shipments to the same city or terminal destination are combined into cars billed to these common points. Because of the costs of additional handling, railroads are permitted to charge more per ton LCL than for CL freight.

Interstate Commerce Commission (ICC) commodity categories established for statistical purposes contain some 35 items of freight traffic. The largest of these categories are the granular bulk: coal, ore, aggregate and grain. Chemicals, motor vehicles and forest products also provide high volumes.

The commodity classification can be consolidated into smaller groupings based on the service requirements, special equipment, and handling facilities of each group.

Granular bulks: coal, ore, grains, aggregate and phosphates.

Liquid bulks: petroleum and its products and chemicals.

Livestock: cattle, sheep and so on for market.

Perishables: fresh fruits and vegetables, fish, meat, dairy products, frozen foods, and so on.

Manufactured goods: automobiles and trucks, farm, electrical, plant machinery, and so on.

Merchandise: small lot shipments of manufactured goods.

Freight handling methods vary considerably according to the country concerned. A limited number of bogie wagons are in use in Great Britain for various special purposes. These include flat wagons for the carriage of 60 feet steel rails, steel sections and other lengthy consignments, 50-ton capacity brick wagons, tank wagons and various other types. Of four-wheel wagons there is an enormous variety. Coal and mineral wagons are built for discharge either through side doors or end doors, or hoppers on their undersides, the last-mentioned being particularly suitable for use on the elevated tracks in ironworks and steelworks, where their contents are emptied speedily into the large storage bins below.[2] "Bolster" wagons are the long flat wagons provided for carrying steel rails and similar loads, which are supported above the wagon floors on transverse bolsters, so that chains can pass underneath to lift the loads with cranes.

For loads which require protection from weather, covered or "box" wagons are used, and it is chiefly wagons of this type that compose the vacuum-braked express freight trains, loaded with miscellaneous merchandise.[3] Foodstuffs and other perishables require vans fitted with ice containers for refrigeration purposes, or, for certain types of traffic, the simpler "ventilate" vans. Cement is another material needing protection from weather. A large proportion of the heavy tonnage of this material required for concrete manufacture is now transported in completely enclosed container wagons of a special type, which are loaded and unloaded by air pressure; in effect the cement is "blown" into and out of the containers, without any shoveling of hand manipulation. For fragile consignments, special wagons are now available which are fitted internally for cushioning their loads against shock.

Such loads as bananas have to be carried in steam-heated vans preserving an even temperature. This is a reminder of the heavy traffic in fruit and vegetables which are concentrated into certain seasons of the year and required very rapid transit, all carried in special trains.[4] Then there are cattle wagons, roofed over but with sides partly open for ventilation, and with adjustable interior partitions, so that the standing animals may be kept sufficiently close together to prevent the possibility of their being thrown over by a jerky start or stop; these wagons also are often marshaled into special trains, run in connection with markets or cattle sales. In recent years also an extensive business has developed on the mainland of Europe, and to some extent in Great Britain, in the movement of new cars from manufacturers' works to the cities in which they are to be sold, so avoiding the necessity for driving the cars over long distances by road, a practice to which the purchaser of a nominally new car often objects. Special wagons carrying up to four cars are used for this purpose.

One advantage possessed by road vehicles over these on rails is door-to-door transport. The first attempt by the railways to meet this door-to-door competition was the introduction of the container system of transport. The containers are large box-shaped receptacles, which can be carefully packed at the originating point and then transferred on lorries to the railway depot for loading, usually in pairs, on to four-wheel flat wagons. The transfer by crane and the securing on the wagons is a task of a few minutes, and equally the transfer back to a road lorry at the end of the journey; the actual transport by rail is of course, cheaper than a correspondingly long journey by road, seeing that the single train crew may be working from 60 to 100 containers or even more, whereas few road lorries would be able to carry the contents of more than two or three containers at most.

In the United States this principle is now being carried a great deal further by what is known as "piggyback" transport. At specially equipped depots located at the main traffic centers, the road lorries are driven in a procession on to a long line of bogie flat wagons. When loading is complete, the "piggyback" train, which has a scheduled starting time, sets out on an overnight run at a speed but little inferior to that of a passenger express, and at a definite time on the following day the lorries are able to run under their own power direct off train to the consignees. This method gives door-to-door delivery at guaranteed time, and on long journeys provides far faster transport than anything possible by road haulage throughout.

A large development of the "piggyback" method is the use of lorries supported at one end on four-wheel tractors and at the other on a normal rear axle; at the loading depot the lorry and tractor move on the flat rail wagon, which accommodates the rear pair of lorry wheels in ordinary way, while the front end is carried on a specially designed cradle, so enabling the tractor to be withdrawn before the lorry is in transit. In some cases the flat wagons are provided rather than end-loading only on a special platform. This arrangement, though requiring more expensive wagon equipment, avoids the immobilization of the tractors while the lorries are in course of rail transport.

  Many other ways modern methods are being applied to the movement of freight in such a way as to reduce to a minimum manual labour and the individual handling of small articles. One such method is known as "palletization". A pallet is, in effect, a large tray lifted off the ground on four short legs, so that the arms of a mechanically propelled fork-lift truck can be passed underneath. The pallet is loaded with a consignment, and is wheeled by the fork-lift truck into a box wagon; at the destination another fork-lift truck runs into the wagon, lifts the pallet and its load bodily and transfers both to the goods shed. Or the pallets can be loaded at the works where the articles have been made, transferred by fork-lift truck direct from lorry to wagon, with the same process in reverse at destination to the consignee. Wider doors have been fitted to many wagons in order to facilitate the entry of the fork-lift trucks. Each box wagon can carry a number of loaded pallets simultaneously. Also in order to cut down handling, some modern goods stations are equipped with endless moving bands on which the loads are moved along the loading platform from the road lorries to the railway wagons, or vice versa.

New Words and Expressions

tariff ['tærif] *n.* 关税率，关税，收费表
shipment ['ʃipmənt] *n.* 运送，发送，运送的货物
handle ['hændl] *v.* 处理
aggregate ['ægrigət] *n.* 集合物，填料，集料
phosphate ['fɔsfeit] *n.* 磷酸盐，磷肥
perishable ['periʃəbl] *n.* 易腐品
consignment [kən'sainmənt] *n.* 托运的货物，托运，委托
consignor [kən'sainə(r)] *n.* 发货人
consignee [ˌkɔnsai'ni:] *n.* 收货人
discharge [dis'tʃɑ:dʒ] *v.* 卸货，释放
underside ['ʌndəsaid] *n.* 下面，底面
ironworks ['aiənwɜ:ks] *n.* 炼铁厂
steelworks ['sti:lwɜ:ks] *n.* 炼钢厂
bolster ['bəulstə] *n.* 承枕，支承架
underneath [ˌʌndə'ni:θ] *adv.* 在下面，向下面
miscellaneous [ˌmisə'leiniəs] *adj.* 杂的，各种各样的
merchandise ['mɜ:tʃəndaiz] *n.* 商品
ventilate ['ventileit] *v.* 通风，排气
manipulation [məˌnipju'leiʃən] *v.* 操作，操纵
partition [pɑ:'tiʃən] *n.* 隔板，间壁
nominally ['nɔminəli] *adv.* 标称地，名义上地
receptacle [ri'septəkl] *n.* 容(贮)器
secure [si'kjuə] *v.* 固定，紧固
delivery [di'livəri] *n.* 运送，交付
haulage ['hɔ:lidʒ] *n.* 运输，牵引

throughout [θru(:)'aut] *adv.* 一直，自始至终
piggyback ['pigibæk] *n.* 在平车上的背负式(运输)
procession [prə'seʃən] *n.* 行列，一排
cradle ['kreidl] *n.* 托架，支架
immobilization [i,məubilai'zeiʃən] *n.* 无机动性，固定不动
pallet ['pælit] *n.* 托盘
tray [trei] *n.* 托盘，托架
bodily ['bɔdili] *adv.* 整个地，完全地
simultaneously [,siməl'teiniəsli] *adv.* 同时
in effect   实际上，事实上
cushion…against   把……加以衬垫以防
be inferior to   次于，低于
in reverse   反过来

Notes to the Text

1. The last unit, which represents one ton moved a distance of one mile, is used most often, since it combines two factors—the quantity handled and the distance moved.

   译文 吨英里表示一吨货物运送一英里的距离，因为该单位包含了两个因素，即货物的数量和运送货物移动的距离，所以被经常采用。

   该句为复合句，主语为 the last unit，谓语为 is used，which 引导的定语从句修饰 the last unit，since 引导的状语从句解释主句的原因。

2. Coal and mineral wagons are built for discharge either through side doors or end doors, or hoppers on their undersides, the last-mentioned being particularly suitable for use on the elevated tracks in ironworks and steelworks, where their contents are emptied speedily into the large storage bins below.

   译文 煤矿车可以通过边门、端门或车底的漏斗卸货。漏斗车特别适用于钢铁厂的高架轨道上，它们能迅速把煤或矿石卸入轨道下面的大型储料仓内。

3. …it is chiefly wagons of this type that compose the vacuum-braked express freight trains, loaded with miscellaneous merchandise.

   译文 主要使用棚车这类带真空制动的货车组成的快运列车，来装运零担货物。

   该句为 It is…that…强调句型，强调 wagons of this type。

4. This is a reminder of the heavy traffic in fruit and vegetables which are concentrated into certain seasons of the year and required very rapid transit, all carried in special trains.

   译文 这点提醒我们注意水果、蔬菜的大量运输。水果、蔬菜是时令商品，要求用专门列车进行快速运输。

Exercises to the Text

Ⅰ. Translate the following terms into Chinese.

(1) box wagon   (2) cattle wagon   (3) less-than-carload freight
(4) pick-up and delivery service   (5) freight house   (6) elevated track
(7) loading platform   (8) door-to-door transport   (9) in transit

(10) moving band (11) piggyback transport (12) tank wagon
(13) end door (14) storage bin (15) goods shed
(16) flat wagon (17) bogie wagon (18) container wagon
(19) fork-lift truck (20) express freight train

Ⅱ. **Decide whether each of the following statements is true or false according to the text.**

(1) Ton mile is used more often. (   )

(2) Less than carload freight includes all freight in quantities smaller than that required for a carload minimum. (   )

(3) There are some 35 items of freight traffic. (   )

(4) Cement are loaded and unloaded by air pressure. (   )

(5) Fruit and vegetables have to be transited rapidly. (   )

(6) New cars often can be transported by special wagons which may carry up to four cars. (   )

(7) The advantage of road transport is door-to-door transport. (   )

(8) The railway have introduced the container system of transport to compete with highway transport. (   )

(9) Palletization can reduce manual labour and the individual handling of small articles. (   )

(10) Piggyback train can arrive at destination in time. (   )

Ⅲ. **Answer the following questions according to the text.**

(1) How many types of railway wagons are there?

(2) What is "piggyback" transport? And what is the advantage of it?

(3) What is "palletization" in the movement of freight? How does it work?

Reading Material

Freight Cars

Freight cars are seldom all alike, they are usually of many sizes and perhaps many colors, and there are different kinds of cars for different kinds of freight.

The most common type of car is the box car, the car which is used to haul grain, groceries, drygoods, furniture, hardware, automobiles and all kinds of ordinary merchandise. The body of this car is merely a huge box, with a sliding door on each side.

Box cars are made in many different sizes. Very large ones are used for automobiles and furniture. Box cars that carry grain in bulk must be fitted with "grain door" in addition to the ordinary doors.

The stock cars, in which railroads transport horses, cattle hogs, sheep and other live animals, have roofs, but the sides are slatted, to give plenty of light and air. Stock cars which carry hogs and sheep are usually built with double decks, that is, they have an extra floor halfway between the roof and the bottom floor of the car. Double-deck cars can carry twice as many animals as cars with a single floor. Stock cars used in transporting chickens and ducks and other kinds of poultry are covered with wire netting.

Liquid freight, such as oil, acid, wine or mineral water, may be transported in tank cars. A great deal of liquid freight is carried in wooden or steel barrel, but when large shipments are made, tank cars are more economical. The tanks are built of steel. At the top of a tank is a dome with an opening, through which the tank is filled and emptied. There is also a valve at bottom of the tank, through which the liquid contents of the tank may be drawn off.

Another type of car is the container car. It is a flat car, carrying several removable containers which may be lifted from the car and set upon a dray or a motor truck. Goods are packed into a container at a factory or warehouse, the container is carried by truck to the car, hauled by rail, and taken by truck to the final destination. The container car reduces the work of loading and unloading cars at freight stations and lessens the danger of loss and breakage of the goods which they carry.

Exercises to the Material

Decide whether each of the following statements is true or false according to the material.
(1) All freight cars are alike. (   )
(2) The most common type of car is the box car. (   )
(3) Double-deck cars can carry twice as many animals as cars with a single floor. (   )
(4) When large shipments are made, tank cars are more economical. (   )
(5) The container car reduces the work of loading and unloading cars at freight stations and lessens the danger of loss and breakage of the goods which they carry. (   )

The Railroad Track (铁路轨道)

Rail tracks are used on railroads, which, together with railroad switches, guide trains without the need for steering. Tracks consist of two parallel steel rails, which are laid upon cross ties that are embedded in ballast to form the railroad track.[1] The rail is fastened to the ties with rail spikes, lag screws.

The type of fastener depends partly on the type of sleeper, with spikes being used on wooden sleepers, and clips being used more on concrete sleepers.

Usually, a baseplate tie plate is used between the rail and wooden sleepers, to spread the load of the rail over a larger area of the sleeper. Sometimes spikes are driven through a hole in the baseplate to hold the rail, while at other times the baseplates are spiked or screwed to the sleeper and the rails clipped to the baseplate.

Steel rails can carry heavier loads than any other material. Railroad ties spread the load from the rails over the ground and also serve to hold the rails a fixed distance apart.

Rail tracks are normally laid on a bed of coarse stone chippings known as ballast, which combines resilience, some amount of flexibility, and good drainage.[2] Steel rails can also be laid onto a concrete slab. Across bridges, track is often laid on ties across longitudinal timbers or longitudinal steel girders.

Alternative view of track joints

There are different ways of joining rails together to form tracks. The traditional method was to bolt rails together in what is known as jointed track. In this form of track, lengths of rail, usually around 20 metres (60 feet) long, are laid and fixed to crossties, and are joined to other lengths of rail with steel plates known as joint bars.

Joint bars are usually 60 centimetres (2 feet) long, and are bolted through each side of the rail ends with bolts (usually four, but sometimes up to six). Small gaps known as expansion joints are deliberately left between the rails to allow for expansion of the rails in hot weather. The holes through which the fishplate bolts pass are oval to allow for expansion.

Because of the small gaps left between the rails, when trains pass over jointed tracks, they make a "clickety-clack" sound. Unless it is well maintained, jointed track doesn't have the ride quality of welded rail, and is unsuitable for high speed trains. A major problem is cracking around the bolt holes, which can lead to the rail head breaking.[3] Jointed track is still extensively used in poorer countries due to the lower construction cost and lack of modernization of their railway systems.

Continuous welded rail

Most modern railways use continuous welded rail (CWR); in this form of track, the rails are welded together by utilizing the thermite reaction or flash butt welding to form one continuous rail that may be several kilometres long. Because there are few joints, this form of track is very strong, gives a smooth ride, and needs less maintenance. Welded track has become common on main lines since the 1950s.

Because of the increased strength of welded track, trains can travel on it at higher speeds and with less friction. Welded rails are more expensive to lay than jointed tracks, but have much lower maintenance costs.

Rails expand in hot weather and shrink in cold weather. Because welded track has very few expansion joints, if no special measures are taken it could become distorted in hot weather and cause a derailment.

To avoid this, welded rails are very often laid on concrete or steel sleeper, which are so heavy they hold the rails firmly in place. After new segments of rail are laid, or defective rails replaced, the rails are artificially stressed. Great attention is paid to compact the ballast effectively, particularly the shoulder over the ends of the sleepers, to prevent them from moving. Even so, in extreme weather, foot patrols monitor sections of track known to be problematic.[4]

The stressing process involves either heating the rails causing them to expand, or stretching the rails with hydraulic equipment.[5] They are then fastened to the sleepers in their expanded form. This process ensures that the rail will not expand much further in subsequent hot weather. In cold weather the rails try to contract, but because they are firmly fastened, they cannot do so. In effect, stressed rails are a bit like a piece of stretched elastic firmly fastened down.

Joints are used in continuously welded rail when necessary; instead of a joint that passes straight across the rail, producing a loud noise and shock when the wheels pass over it, two sections of rail are sometimes cut at a steep angle and put together with a gap between them.

New Words and Expressions

steer [stiə] *v.* 驾驶，掌舵
crosstie ['krɔstai] *n.* 枕木
embed [im'bed] *vt.* 使插入，使嵌入，嵌入
fasten ['fɑːsn] *vt.* 扎牢，扣住，闩住，拴紧，使固定
　　　　　　　 vi. 扣紧，抓住
spike [spaik] *n.* 长钉，道钉
lag screw　方头螺钉
sleeper ['sliːpə] 轨枕，枕木
clip [klip] *vt.* 夹住
baseplate ['beispleit] *n.* 基础板，基板
coarse [kɔːs] *adj.* 粗糙的，粗鄙的
chipping ['tʃipiŋ] *n.* 碎屑，破片
ballast ['bæləst] *n.* 压舱物，沙囊，道碴
resilience [ri'ziliəns] *n.* 弹力，恢复力，顺应力
drainage ['dreinidʒ] *n.* 排水，排泄，排水装置
concrete slab　混凝土板
longitudinal [,lɔndʒi'tjuːdinl] *adj.* 经度的，纵向的
joint bar　钢轨连接板
gap [gæp] *n.* 缺口，裂口，间隙，缝隙
expansion joint　伸缩接头，膨胀节
deliberately [di'libəritli] *adv.* 故意地
continuous welded rail　无缝钢轨
thermite ['θɜːmait] *n.* 铝热剂，灼热剂
flash butt welding　闪光对接焊
shrink [ʃriŋk] *v.* 收缩，(使)皱缩，缩短
distort [dis'tɔːt] *vt.* 扭曲，歪曲(真理、事实等)
compact [kəm'pækt] *v.* 压紧，(使)坚实
patrol [pə'trəul] *n.* 巡逻，巡查
hydraulic [hai'drɔːlik] *adj.* 水力的，水压的
stretch [stretʃ] *v.* 伸，拉伸，伸长[展]
problematic [,prɔblə'mætik] *adj.* 成问题的，有疑问的

Notes to the Text

1. Tracks consist of two parallel steel rails, which are laid upon cross ties that are embedded in ballast to form the railroad track.
   译文　轨道由两条平行钢轨组成，而钢轨置于嵌入道碴的枕木上形成铁轨。

2. Rail tracks are normally laid on a bed of coarse stone chippings known as ballast, which combines resilience, some amount of flexibility, and good drainage.

   译文 铁轨通常置于名为道碴的一层粗糙石屑上,道碴具有弹性、灵活性及良好的排水性。

3. A major problem is cracking around the bolt holes, which can lead to the rail head breaking.

   译文 主要的问题是螺栓孔附近的裂缝,将导致轨头破裂。

4. Great attention is paid to compact the ballast effectively, particularly the shoulder over the ends of the sleepers, to prevent them from moving. Even so, in extreme weather, foot patrols monitor sections of track known to be problematic.

   译文 为防止其移动,人们有效地压紧道碴,特别是枕木两端的路肩。虽然如此,在极端天气情况下,还是要步行巡逻检测有问题的轨道部件。

5. The stressing process involves either heating the rails causing them to expand, or stretching the rails with hydraulic equipment.

   译文 加固过程包括加热钢轨而导致其膨胀,或采用液压设备拉伸钢轨。

Exercises to the Text

Ⅰ. Decide whether each of the following statements is true or false according to the text.

(1) Rail tracks can guide trains without the need for steering. ( )

(2) Spikes can be used on concrete sleepers. ( )

(3) Steel rails can carry heavier loads than any other material. ( )

(4) The traditional method was to bolt rails together in what is known as jointed track. ( )

(5) Most modern railways use jointed track. ( )

Ⅱ. Answer the following questions according to the text.

(1) How to define tracks?

(2) Why is a baseplate tie plate used between the rail and wooden sleepers?

(3) What function does that ballast have?

(4) Why do they make a "clickety-clack" sound when trains pass over jointed tracks?

(5) Why can trains travel on welded track at higher speeds and with less friction?

Reading Material

Main Functions of Tracks

Track has three main functions. It must support the load, provide a smooth surface for easy movement and guide the wheels of the train.

The railroad line should be as a level and straight as can be achieved because grades and curves increase the burden on the locomotive and the wear on the track. The tractive effort required to pull a load up a 1% grade is about five times what is required on straight level track and a curvature of 1 degree requires an increase of from 12.5% to 25% in tractive effort.

Road-bed is the subgrade on which the ballast, ties and rails are laid. There are two types of it. It should be firm, well drained and of adequate dimensions.

Steel rails support the load which locomotives and cars impose on the track.

Ties support the rail and ballast supports the ties. Today, rail weighing as much as 60 kilogrammes is in use on lines handling heavy traffic. The use of the so-called T-rail (from its shape) has persisted because experience has shown it is the most practical and economic form of rail.

The ties keep the rail the proper distance apart, support them and transmit the load to the ballast cushion beneath. For the saving of timber and other reasons, concrete ties have developed so rapidly that concrete is now considered to be the ideal material for railway ties.

To reduce mechanical wear from impact of loads transmitted through the rail, metal tie plates are inserted between the rail and the tie. These plates spread the rail burden over a wide tie area, and thus help to protect the tie from the cutting and wearing effect of the rail base. Wheel friction causes a tendency for rails "to creep" longitudinally on multiple tracks where the trains generally run in the same direction on each track. Small anchors applied to the rail and bearing against the edge of the tie are used to check this movement.

Ballast, usually of crushed rock, cinder, gravel or mine waste, supports and cushions the ties and helps to keep them in proper position as well as to distribute the track load over the road-bed. It also facilitates drainage, thereby promoting firmness and smooth riding qualities of track.

As a train enters a curve, its natural tendency is to continue going straight ahead. It turns only because the outside rail forces it to do so. To permit trains to traverse curve with safety and greater smoothness, the outer rail is super-elevated, or raised above the height of the inner rail so as to balance the forces when the movement of the train is diverted from a straight line by the rails of a curve. The right amount of superelevation for a given curve depends on the rail speeds.

Exercises to the Material

Answer the following questions according to the material.
(1) What main functions do tracks have?
(2) Why should the railroad line be as level and straight as can be achieved?
(3) What is the road-bed?
(4) Why has the use of the so-called T-rail (from its shape) persisted?
(5) What functions do ballast have?

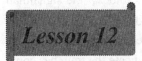

Lesson 12　Railway Signaling (铁路信号)

Railway signaling is a safety system used on railways to prevent trains from colliding. Trains are uniquely susceptible to collision because of running on fixed rails. They are not capable of avoiding a collision by steering away, and as can a road vehicle;[1] furthermore, trains cannot decelerate rapidly, and are frequently operating at speeds where by the time the driver can see an obstacle, the train cannot stop in time to avoid colliding with it.

Most forms of train control involve messages being passed from those in charge of the rail network or portions of it to the train crew; these are known as "signals" and from this the topic of train control is known as "signaling".

Timetable and train order operation has some significant flaws, such as an over-reliance on the ability of the crew of a stranded train to let other trains know of the problem, and a general intolerance for human error. When everything goes perfectly, it works well, but mistakes are easy and deadly.

Timetable or train order is only suitable for railway lines which carry relatively little traffic, and is unworkable on busy rail lines, because it requires great separation between trains. Where this is the case, physical signals need to be used to show the train crew whether the line ahead is occupied and to ensure that sufficient space is kept between trains to allow them to stop.[2]

If two trains can't be running on the same section of track at the same time, then they cannot collide. This notion forms the basis of most signaling systems.

The rail network is divided into sections, known as blocks. Two trains are not allowed to be in the same block at the same time. A train cannot enter a block until it is permitted, generally by a signal that the block ahead is empty.

On high-speed railways, block signaling has disadvantages. Because the required block length to safely stop a train would severely decrease the line's capacity. Also, signals become increasingly hard to spot and recognize at higher speeds. Several cab signaling systems have been developed to overcome those disadvantages. The European Train Control System will feature moving blocks that allow trains to follow each other at exact braking distance. Historically, some lines operated rules, where certain large high speed trains were signaled under different rules and only given the right of way if two blocks in front of the train were clear.[3]

There are two distinct forms of block signaling. Absolute block signaling is operated in a manner designed to ensure two trains may not occupy the same block at once. Telegraph codes are used to communicate between signal boxes, each of which controls a block. The signalman only allows entry to a given block, when no train occupies the block. When the train traverses the block, the signalman signals ahead to the next block who will accept the train if they have space or delay it otherwise. As an additional safety check all trains have tail lamps.[4] If no tail lamp is seen, the signalman assumes his block is not empty, after the train has passed. As the lack of a tail lamp may indicate the train has come apart. Instead the block remains occupied and the signalman telegraphs the next signal box to halt the train and investigate.

In a permissive block system, trains are permitted to pass signals indicating the line ahead is occupied, but only to do so in a manner where they can stop safely driving by sight.[5] This allows improved efficiency in some situations and is mostly used in the USA.

An absolute block system is itself not entirely absolute. Multiple trains may enter a block, given specific authorization. This is necessary in order to join trains together, split trains, rescue failed trains and the like. The signalman in giving authorization also ensures the driver knows precisely what to expect ahead, and the driver must operate the train in a safe manner considering this information.

New Words and Expressions

collide [kəˈlaid] v.　碰撞
susceptible [səˈseptəb(ə)l] adj.　易受感动的，敏感的
avoid [əˈvɔid] vt.　避免，消除
steer [stiə] v.　指导，驾驶
decelerate [diˈseləreit] v.　减速
in charge of　负责
timetable [ˈtaimteib(ə)l] n.　时间表
flaw [flɔː] n.　缺点，缺陷
stranded [ˈstrændid] adj.　束手无策的，进退两难的
intolerance [inˈtɔlərəns] n.　不容忍
error [ˈerə] n.　误差，过失，错误
deadly [ˈdedli] adj.　致命的，极度的，必定的
relatively [ˈrelətivli] adv.　相关地
unworkable [ʌnˈwɜːkəbl] adj.　难运转的，不能实行的
separation [ˌsepəˈreiʃən] n.　分离，分开
occupy [ˈɔkjupai] vt.　占用，占领，占据
section [ˈsekʃən] n.　区
notion [ˈnəuʃən] n.　概念，观念，想法，主张
divide [diˈvaid] v.　划分，分开，隔开
ensure [inˈʃuə] vt.　保证，担保
spot [spɔt] v.　认出，发现
block [blɔk] n.　区间，闭塞
disadvantage [ˌdisədˈvɑːntidʒ] n.　不利，劣势
severely [siˈviəli] adv.　严格地，激烈地
decrease [diˈkriːs] vi., vt.　减少
overcome [ˌəuvəˈkʌm] vt.　战胜，克服，征服
distinct [disˈtiŋkt] adj.　清楚的，明显的，独特的
telegraph [ˈteligrɑːf] v.　发电报，打电报说
code [kəud] n.　代码，代号，编码
communicate [kəˈmjuːnikeit] v.　沟通，通信，传达
indicate [ˈindikeit] vt.　指出，显示，象征，预示
halt [hɔːlt] vt.　使停止，使立定
permissive [pəˈmisiv] adj.　许可的
entirely [inˈtaiəli] adv.　完全地，全然地，一概地
multiple [ˈmʌltipl] adj.　多样的，多重的
authorization [ˌɔːθəraiˈzeiʃən] n.　授权，认可
traverse [ˈtrævɜːs] v.　横过
be capable of　能够

Notes to the Text

1. Trains are uniquely susceptible to collision because, running on fixed rails; they are not capable of avoiding a collision by steering away, and as can a road vehicle.

   译文 列车运行在固定铁轨上,对碰撞特别敏感。它们不能像路上的车辆那样避开碰撞。

2. Where this is the case, physical signals need to be used to show the train crew whether the line ahead is occupied and to ensure that sufficient space is kept between trains to allow them to stop.

   译文 在此情况下,需用物理信号来显示前方线路是否有车占用,并确保列车间有足够间距以允许停车。

3. Historically, some lines operated rules, where certain large high speed trains were signaled under different rules and only given the right of way if two blocks in front of the train were clear.

   译文 历史上,某些线路按规章运行,在这些线路上,某些大型高速列车在不同的规章下发信号,并且,只有在列车运行前方的两个区间都开通时,才会给予列车通行权。

4. As an additional safety check all trains have tail lamps.

   该句为一倒装句。正确顺序为:All trains have tail lamps as an additional safety check.

5. In a permissive block system, trains are permitted to pass signals indicating the line ahead is occupied, but only to do so in a manner where they can stop safely driving by sight.

   译文 在一个容许闭塞系统中,允许列车传送信号以显示前方线路有车占用,但仅当通过视觉能够判断列车能安全停靠时才采用这一方式。

Exercises to the Text

Ⅰ. **Translate the following terms into Chinese.**

(1) railway signaling (2) rail network (3) busy rail line
(4) physical signal (5) block signaling (6) cab signaling systems
(7) moving block (8) braking distance (9) absolute block signaling
(10) signal boxes

Ⅱ. **Decide whether each of the following statements is true or false according to the text.**

(1) Trains are capable of avoiding a collision by steering away. (   )
(2) A train can't enter a block until it is permitted. (   )
(3) There are three distinct forms of block signaling. (   )
(4) Each signal box controls a block. (   )
(5) An absolute block system is entirely absolute. (   )

Ⅲ. **Answer the following questions according to the text.**

(1) How to define a block?
(2) What disadvantages has block signaling on high-speed railways?
(3) What is the basis of most signaling?
(4) When are trains permitted to pass signal in a permissive block system?
(5) What significant flaws does timetable or train order operation have?

Reading Material

The Development of Railway Signal

In the very early days of railways, on double-tracked railway lines, where trains traveled in one direction on the same stretch of track, a means was needed to space out the trains to ensure that they did not collide. In the very early days of railways, men were employed to stand next to the line at certain intervals with a stop watch, these men used hand signals to signal to train drivers that a preceding train had passed more or less than a certain number of minutes ago, this was called "time interval working". If a train had passed the man only a short while ago, the following train was expected to slow down or stop to allow sufficient space to develop between the trains, to prevent a collision.

This system was flawed, however, as the watchman had no way of knowing whether the preceding train had cleared the tracks ahead. And so if the preceding train broke down or stopped for some reason, the following train would have no way of knowing, and collide with it rear-on. Accidents of this type were common in the early days of railways. However, with the invention of the electrical telegraph, it became possible for the station or signal box ahead to send message back to confirm that a train had passed and that the line ahead was clear; this was called the "block system".

Mechanical semaphore signals replaced hand signals in the early 1840s. When the all-clear message was received, a signalman in a signal box would pull a lever which would move the signal into the all-clear position. This required the placing of signal boxes at regular intervals along the line.

The block system came into use gradually during the 1850s and 1860s but became mandatory in the United Kingdom after parliament passed legislation in 1889 as a response to numerous railway accidents. This required block signaling for passenger railways, along with interlocking and most of the practices still required and used today. Similar legislation was passed by the United States around the same period.

New Words and Expressions

space out　留间隔，把……拉开距离
interval ['intəvəl] *n.*　间隔
preceding train　先行列车
the following train　后行列车
semaphore signals　臂板信号

Exercises to the Material

Answer the following questions according to the material.
(1) How to space out the trains to ensure that they did not collide in the very early day of railways?
(2) Why did it become possible for the station or signal box ahead to send a message back to confirm that a train had passed and that the line ahead was clear?
(3) When did mechanical semaphore signals replace hand signals?
(4) When did the block system come into use gradually?
(5) Where did the block system become mandatory?

Part 3

Rail Signal System（轨道信号）

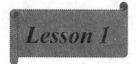

Railroad Switch (铁路道岔)

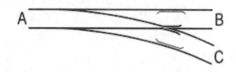

Figure 1 A diagram of a right-hand railroad switch

Introduction

A railroad switch is a mechanical installation enabling trains to be guided from one track to another.[1]

In Figure 1, rail track A divides into two: track B (the straight track) and track C (the diverging track). The switch consists of the pair of linked tapering rails, known as points (switch rails or point blades) lying between the diverging outer rails (the *stock rails*). These points can be moved laterally into one of two positions so as to determine whether a train coming from A will be led towards B or towards C.[2] A train moving from the A direction towards either B or C is said to be executing a facing-point movement.

Unless the switch is locked, a train coming from B or C will be led to A regardless of the position of the points, as the vehicle's wheels will force the points to move. Passage through a switch in this direction is known as a trailing-point movement.

A switch can be described by the direction in which the diverging track leaves the straight track. A right-hand switch has track C to the right of a straight track formed by A and B. A left-hand switch has track C to the left.

A straight track is not always present, however both tracks may curve, one to the left and one to the right or both tracks may curve, with differing radii, in the same direction.

The operation of a railroad switch

In Figure 2, the track is the one travelled during a facing-point movement. The switch mechanism, shown in black, may be operated remotely using an electric motor or lever from a nearby ground frame.

A railroad car's wheels are guided along the tracks by coning of the wheels. Only in extreme cases does it rely on the flanges located on the insides of the wheels. When the wheels reach the switch, the wheels are guided along the route determined by which of the two points is connected to the track facing the switch. In the illustration, if the left point is connected, the left wheel will be guided along the rail of that point, and

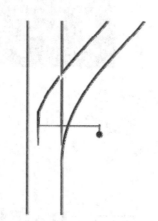

Figure 2 The operation of a railroad switch

the train will diverge to the right. If the right point is connected, the right wheel's flange will be guided along the rail of that point, and the train will continue along the straight track. Only one of the points may be connected to the facing track at any time; the two points are mechanically locked together to ensure that this is always the case.

A mechanism is provided to move the points from one position to the other (change the points). Historically, this would require a lever to be moved by a human operator, and some switches are still controlled in this way.[3] However, most are now operated by a remotely controlled electric motor or by pneumatic or hydraulic actuation.

In a trailing-point movement, the wheels will force the points to the proper position. This is sometimes known as running through the switch. If the points are rigidly connected to the switch control mechanism, the control mechanism's linkages may be bent, requiring repair before the switch is again usable.[4] For this reason, switches are normally set to the proper position before performing a trailing-point movement.

Components
Points

The points (switch rails or point blades) are the movable rails which guide the wheels towards either the straight or the diverging track. They are tapered on most switches. In the UK and Commonwealth countries, the term point refers to the entire mechanism, whereas in North America the term refers only to the movable rails.

Frog

The frog (common crossing) refers to the crossing point of two rails. This can be assembled out of several appropriately cut and bent pieces of rail or can be a single casting.[5] A frog forms part of a railroad switch, and is also used in a level junction (flat crossing).

On lines with heavy and/or high-speed traffic, a swingnose crossing is often used.[6] As the name implies, there is a second set of points located at the frog. This effectively eliminates the gap in the rail that normally occurs at the frog, so long as trains are moving in the direction that the switch is aligned to. This use of the word "frog" derives from the appearance of the triangular assemblage of rails which recalls the frog of a horse's hoof.

Guard rail (check rail)

A guard rail (check rail) is a short piece of rail placed alongside the main (stock) rail opposite the frog. These exist to ensure that the wheels follow the appropriate flange through the frog and that the train does not derail. Generally, there are two of these for each frog, one by each outer rail. Guard rails are not required with a "self-guarding cast manganese" frog, as the raised part of the casting serves the same purpose. These frogs are for low-speed use and are common in rail yards.

Switch motor

A switch motor is an electric or pneumatic mechanism that aligns the points with one of the diverging routes.

Point lever

A point lever and accompanying linkages are used to align the points of a switch manually. This lever and its accompanying hardware are usually mounted to a pair of long sleepers that extend from the switch at the points. They are often used in a place of a switch motor. In some places, may be operated from a ground frame.

Joints

Joints are used where the moving points meet the fixed rails of the switch. They allow the points to hinge easily between their positions.

New Words and Expressions

railroad switch　铁路道岔
diverge [daiˈvɜːdʒ] vi.　分开；偏离；分歧
taper [ˈteipə] vt., vi.　(使)一端逐渐变细
point blades　尖轨
stock rails　基本轨
trailing [ˈtreiliŋ] adj.　拖尾的，曳尾的，被拖动的
passage [ˈpæsidʒ] n.　通过，经过
lateral [ˈlætərəl] adj.　侧面的，从旁边的，至侧面的
execute [ˈeksikjuːt] vt.　处决，执行，实现
right-hand switch　右开道岔
left-hand switch　左开道岔
radii [ˈreidiai] n.　半径
flange [flændʒ] n.　(机械等的)凸缘，(火车的)轮缘
illustration [ˌiləsˈtreiʃən] n.　插图，说明，图解
electric motor　电机
pneumatic [njuː(ː)ˈmætik] adj.　充气的，由压缩空气操作[推动]的，风动的
hydraulic [haiˈdrɔːlik] adj.　液力的，液压的
trailing direction　背向
linkage [ˈliŋkidʒ] n.　结合；联系；联动装置
guard rail (check rail)　护轨
align [əˈlain] vt.　使结盟，使成一行，使成一线
manually [ˈmænjuəli] adv.　用手地
hinge [hindʒ] vt., vi.　用铰链连接(某物)，给(某物)装上铰链
derail [diˈreil] vt., vi.　出轨
regardless of　不管，不顾
so long as　只要
derive from　由……起源
out of　由……制成
be used to　过去习惯于
divide into　分成；分为
whether...or　或者……或者

Notes to the Text

1. A railroad switch is a mechanical installation enabling trains to be guided from one track to another.

   译文　铁路道岔是一个使火车由一个股道转入另一个股道的连接设备。

   enabling 引导的部分是现在分词作定语，后置，修饰 a mechanical installation。

   如：The farmers working here are very busy.

2. These points can be moved laterally into one of two positions so as to determine whether a train coming from A will be led towards B or towards C.

译文　这两个尖轨能从侧面移动到两个位置中的任何一个，从而确定火车是由轨道 A 驶向轨道 B，还是由轨道 A 驶向轨道 C。

3. A mechanism is provided to move the points from one position to the other (change the points). Historically, this would require a lever to be moved by a human operator, and some switches are still controlled in this way.

译文　为使尖轨从一个位置移到另一个位置而设置了一种机械装置。但历史上，则是由人使用一个操作手柄来移动尖轨，如今仍有一些道岔是采用这种方法。

4. If the points are rigidly connected to the switch control mechanism, the control mechanism's linkages may be bent, requiring repair before the switch is again usable.

译文　如果尖轨与道岔控制装置紧密地连接在一起，那么控制装置的连接部分会弯曲变形，在道岔再次使用之前需要维修。

5. The frog (common crossing) refers to the crossing point of two rails. This can be assembled out of several appropriately cut and bent pieces of rail or can be a single casting.

译文　辙叉(公共交叉部分)是指两轨交叉的部分。辙叉可以由几段经过适当切割和弯曲的钢轨组装而成，也可以是一个单个的铸件。

out of 在这里表示"由……制成"。

如：She made a hat out of bits of old material. 她用旧的零碎材料做了一顶帽子。

6. On lines with heavy and/or high-speed traffic, a swingnose crossing is often used.

译文　在重载或者高速运输线路上，经常使用活动心轨道岔。

a swingnose crossing 是指 The crossing has flexibly moving point and splice rails。

Exercises to the Text

Ⅰ. Translate the following terms into Chinese.

(1) railroad switch　　　　(2) the straight track　　　　(3) the diverging track
(4) switch rails or point blades　(5) a facing-point movement　(6) a trailing-point movement
(7) right-hand switch　　　(8) left-hand switch　　　　(9) guard rail(check rail)
(10) frog (common crossing)　(11) switch motor

Ⅱ. Decide whether each of the following statements is true or false according to the text.

(1) From the text we know the point blades can be moved laterally into one of two positions so as to determine whether a train coming from A will be led towards B or towards C. （　　）

(2) A train moving from the A direction towards either B or C is said to be executing a trailing-point movement in Figure 1. （　　）

(3) A right-hand switch has track C to the right of a straight track formed by A and B. （　　）

(4) From the text we can conclude that some switches are still require a lever to change the points by a human operator today. （　　）

Ⅲ. Answer the following questions according to the text.

(1) What's the function of the joints?
(2) Where are points lever and its accompanying hardware usually mounted?
(3) Is the check rail a short piece of rail placed alongside the main rail opposite the frog?
(4) Which does a railroad switch consist of?

Ⅳ. **Translate the following passage into Chinese.**

Classification

The divergence and length of a switch is determined by the angle of the frog (the point in the switch where two rails cross) and the curvature of the switch blades. The length and placement of the other components are determined from this using established formulas and standards. This divergence is measured as the number of units of length for a single unit of separation. In North America this is generally referred to as a switch's "number". For example, on a "number 12" switch, the rails are one unit apart at a distance of twelve units from the center of the frog. In the United Kingdom points and crossings using chaired bullhead rail would be referred to using a letter and number combination. The letter would define the length (and hence the radius) of the switch blades and the number would define the angle of the crossing (frog). Thus an A7 turnout would be very short and likely only to be found in dockyards etc. whereas a E12 would be found as a fairly high speed turnout on a mainline.

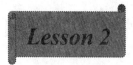

D-C Track Circuits（直流轨道电路）

Introduction

A track circuit is a track clear detection device consisting of an electrical circuit fed through the running rails of a section of track. Each section is electrically isolated from others. It is not only used to detect the presence or absence of a train on a railroad track, but also used to inform signalmen and control relevant signals.

The track circuit is fundamental to most of signaling systems. There are many different arrangements of the track circuit used today, but they are alike in their basic principle of operation.

Fundaments of D-C track circuits

The simplest form of track circuit is an insulated section of track with a relay on one end and with a battery, or some other source of energy on the other end.[1]

Figure 3 shows an elementary track circuit. It consists of the following:

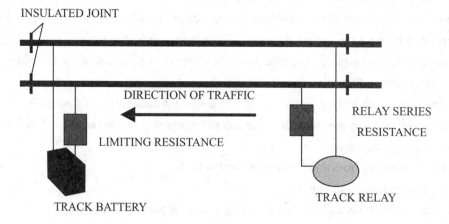

Figure 3　Simplified diagram of a track circuit

- A source of energy—for example, a battery.
- A limiting resistance, so called because it limits the current from the battery.
- Rails and rail bonding, both offering resistance.
- Ties and ballast, both offering a path for current leakage from rail. This path has resistance, referred to as "ballast resistance".
- Relay series resistance (resistance placed in series with the relay).
- A track relay.

The arrows show the direction of current flow. Starting from positive post of the battery, the current flows through the limiting resistance, the one rail, the relay windings, the relay series resistance, and the other rail, then back to the negative post of the battery.[2] With the relay energized, it closes a contact to light the lamps (or to control mechanism).

As the wheels and axles of a train move onto the track circuit, they provide a path from rail to rail through which the battery current flows, thus robbing the relay of its current and causing it to open the contact.

In other words, when no train is present, the relay is energized by the current flowing from the power source through the rails. When a train is present, its axles shorten (shunt) the rails together, the current to the track relay coil drops, and the relay is de-energized. Therefore circuits through the relay contacts report whether or not the track is occupied.

Track circuits allow railway signaling systems to operate semi-automatically, by displaying signals for trains to slow down or stop when track ahead is occupied. They help prevent dispatchers and operators from causing accidents, both by informing track occupancy and by preventing signals from displaying unsafe indications.

Resistance of the track circuit

The resistance of the track circuit includes: rail resistance, ballast resistance, limiting resistance. In common track circuits, the resistance of the rails may vary from 0.015 to 0.05 ohm per 1000 feet of the track, the ballast resistance may vary from one to hundreds of ohms per 1000 feet of track. For example, a 4000-foot circuit may have a total rail resistance of 0.1 ohm and a total minimum ballast resistance of 0.25 ohm in wet weather. In dry weather, or in zero weather, this ballast resistance may increase to hundreds of ohms.

The maximum distance over which a track circuit can operate properly is dependent on several factors, principally on ballast leakage.[3]

Because there is a limiting resistance in the battery feeding to the track, the track voltage and, in turn, the relay voltage vary path consisted of the various conducting paths through the ballast and ties and, when the track is occupied, the path also consists of the wheels and axles of the train. Thus we have a widely varying resistance across the rails and a widely varying voltage across the relay.

Figure 4 shows how relay current varies as the resistance across the rails is varied. To simplify our example, we have chosen a relay that picks up at 100 milliamperes and drops away at 50 milliamperes. Pickup means the relay is sufficiently energized to attract its armature and close its contacts. In signalmen's language we would say this relay has 100 mills pickup and 50 mills release.

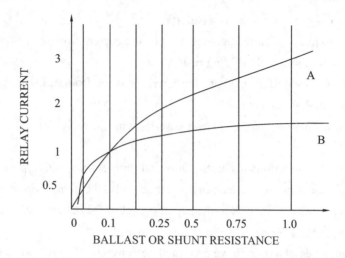

Figure 4 Relay current variation with varying resistance across the rails

Looking at curve B in Figure 4, as we move shunt resistance across the rails from zero to 0.25 ohm, the relay current increases 100 mills, picking up this relay. In other words, this circuit will not operate unless the ballast resistance is 0.25 ohm or more.[4] Now moving backward along curve A toward zero resistance, we find the current of this relay releases below 50 mills at 0.1 ohm. This is well above the 0.06-ohm shunt required by the Federal Railroad Administration to ensure the proper sensitivity of track circuit shunting.

The picture is varied by many factors: percent release of the track relay, relay resistance changed with temperature, "off" and "on" charge voltage of the track battery, type of battery, rail resistance changed with temperature, etc.

New Words and Expressions

arrangement [ə'reindʒmənt] n. 布局，安排
principle ['prinsəpl] n. 法则，原则，原理
insulated section　绝缘区段
relay ['riːlei] n. 继电器
resistance [ri'zistəns] n. 电阻
rail bonding　钢轨引接线
ballast resistance　轨间电阻
tie [tai] n. 轨枕
leakage ['liːkidʒ] n. 漏，泄漏，渗漏
positive post　正极
negative post　负极
contact ['kɔntækt] n. 节点
wheel and axle　轮轴
voltage ['vəultidʒ] n. 电压
attract [ə'trækt] vt. 吸引
armature ['ɑːmətjuə] n. 衔铁

exert [ig'zɜ:t] v.　施加
shunting sensitivity　　分路灵敏度
be fundamental to　　对……很重要
consist of　　由……组成
refer to as　　称为
in series with　　与……串联
rob of　　使……失去
be dependent on　　视……而定
vary with　　随……而变化

Notes to the Text

1. The simplest form of track circuit is an insulated section of track with a relay on one end and with a battery or some other source of energy on the other end.
   译文　轨道电路最简单的形式是一段绝缘钢轨，在其一端有一个轨道继电器，在另一端有一个蓄电池或其他类型的电源。

2. Starting from positive post of the battery, the current flows through the limiting resistance, the one rail, the relay windings, the relay series resistance, and the other rail, then back to the negative post of the battery.
   译文　电流从电源的正极开始，流经限流电阻、其中一根钢轨、继电器线圈、继电器串联电阻，最后经由另外一根钢轨回到电源的负极。
   Starting from positive post of the battery 为现在分词作状语，the current 为句子的主语。

3. The maximum distance which a track circuit can operate properly is dependent on several factors, principally on ballast leakage.
   译文　保证轨道电路正常工作的最大距离取决于若干因素，尤其是镇流漏电。
   The maximum distance 为句子的主语 which a track circuit can operate properly 修饰主语。

4. In other words, this circuit will not operate unless the ballast resistance is 0.25 ohm or more.
   译文　换句话说，除非轨间电阻达到 0.25 欧姆或 0.25 欧姆以上，否则电路不会工作。
   not...unless　　除非……才

Exercises to the Text

Ⅰ. **Translate the following terms into Chinese.**
   (1) track circuits　　　　(2) an insulated section of track　　　(3) a limiting resistance
   (4) ballast resistance　　(5) the negative post of the battery　　(6) in turn
   (7) sensitivity of track circuit shunting　　(8) picks up　　(9) drop away

Ⅱ. **Decide whether each of the following statements is true or false according to the text.**
   (1) When the train is present, the relay is energized. (　　)
   (2) In Figure 4, as we move shunt resistanle across rails from zero to 0.25 ohm, the relay current increases 100 mills. (　　)
   (3) When the relay is energized, its contacts will be closed. (　　)
   (4) With the relay energized, its contacts will be opened to light the lamps or to control mechanism. (　　)

(5) The maximum distance of a track circuit is dependent on several factors, principally on ballast leakage. (　)

Ⅲ. **Answer the following questions according to the text.**

(1) What does a simplest track circuit consist of ?

(2) How does the relay current vary as the resistance across the rails is varied?

(3) How does the resistance of the rails may vary in common track circuits?

(4) When we say this relay had 100 mills pickup, what does it mean?

Reading Material

Track Circuit Data and Calculations

In the earlier discussion of D-C track circuits, it was pointed out that track circuits and the shunting of track circuits are not as simple as might appear from schematic diagrams. A-C track circuits introduce further considerations involving frequency discrimination and phase relationship which make additional complexity. High-frequency track circuits involve circuit parameters which are negligible in D-C or A-C track circuits but which become important at audio frequencies controlling.

Nevertheless, given characteristic data on a track, it is possible to apply mathematical methods to design track circuits for that track, including series rail resistance and inductance, also shunt leakage and capacitance. Measurements made on the track, according to input impedance of the open-circuited and short-circuited track at a remote point, are helpful to obtain the necessary data.

GRS (General Railway Signal) has developed a number of computer programs used in track circuit design which are applicable to track with a variety of physical and electrical characteristics. Track circuit performance predicated by these programs has been substantiated by extensive observations on actual track circuits.

The computer programs are used by GRS for signal system work in which GRS has responsibility for track circuit design. The programs are also used by GRS to provide consulting service to railroad signal engineers engaged in track circuit design.

Exercise to the Material

Choose the best answer according to the material.

(1) The word "Nevertheless" in line 7 is closest in meaning to "_____".

　　A. However　　　　　　B. Because　　　　　C. So　　　　　　D. Though

(2) GRS has developed the computer programs to _____.

　　A. design track circuits

　　B. provide consulting service to railroad workers

　　C. measure track circuits

　　D. simplify track circuits

(3) The word "which" in line 6 refers to _____.

　　A. track circuits　　　　　　　　　　B. circuit parameters

　　C. audio frequencies　　　　　　　　D. further considerations

(4) Which of the following can be inferred from the passage? _____.

A. D-C track circuits are as simple as might appear from schematic diagrams

B. A-C track circuits are simpler than D-C track circuits

C. A-C track circuits involve more parameters which make for complexity

D. A-C track circuits involve some parameters which are negligible in D-C track circuits

(5) What do we not need to apply mathematical methods to assist in the design of track circuits for that track? _____ .

A. Series rail resistance and inductance   B. Shunt leakage

C. Capacitance track   D. The relay resistance

Lesson 3 A-C Track Circuits (交流轨道电路)

What is A-C

A-C stands for "Alternating Current". This is a term used to describe one of the two common forms of supplying electrical power. The other common form is "Direct Current" (D-C). Current is a measure of electron flow rate. Direct Current describes current that flows in one direction. Alternating Current describes current which flow direction alternates. It flows in one direction, then reverses to the other direction.

The outlines of A-C track circuits

In a previous article, the operation of D-C track circuits was described. Those track circuits use D-C to power track circuit relays. An A-C track circuit uses the same principle. A-C track circuits use alternating current signals instead of D-C signals. In signal terminology, A-C track circuits are energized at "power" (relatively low) frequencies, such as 60 Hz or 100 Hz. These circuits arrangement are very similar to D-C track circuits arrangement, although A-C relays and reactors are used in A-C track circuits by transformers, batteries and resistors are utilized in D-C track circuits.

High-frequency (also called audio-frequency) track circuits are a more updated development. These also utilize A-C energy, frequencies range from about 600 Hz to over 10 kHz, equipment for high-frequency circuits is largely electronic, and their characteristics differ substantially from that of D-C and A-C track circuits.

On electrified railroads, the rails typically serve as return conductors for propulsion, which may be A-C or D-C. Track circuits on such roads must function in the presence of propulsion currents which can be hundreds of times greater than the track circuit current flowing in the same rail.[1] D-C track circuit cannot operate properly in this environment. This prevents from using the basic D-C track circuit because the substantial traction currents overwhelm the very small track signal currents.

A-C track circuits and relays were developed essentially concurrently with the growth of electric propulsion. By utilizing induction affect associated with A-C, A-C track relays were immune to D-C propulsion. By using track circuit energy with a frequency different from that of A-C, A-C track circuits which operated reliably in the presence of the A-C propulsion were developed.

A-C track circuits are also used in classification yards. In such applications the reason for using A-C may improve track shunting by using the high peak voltage of the A-C wave, or may be economical to use commercial power served as track energy source.[2] A-C circuits are sometimes used in areas where conditions introduce stray currents which interfere with D-C track circuits.

Track circuit apparatus used in A-C track circuits

A-C track circuits are energized by track transformer, usually with a primary rated input for a standard commercial input, such as 120 vots, 60 Hz. Secondary windings are tapped to permit track voltage choice.

Adjustable impedances (reactors or resistors) are used between track transformers and track. They are used to adjust the current of the track circuit when the track circuit is shunted by a train.

A balancing impedance, an impedance of special design, is used across the track phase of two-element track relays on single-rail track circuits of D-C electrified railroads in order to prevent magnetization of the relay magnetic circuit if any D-C enters the relay winding.

Fuses are used between track and transformer secondary winding to protect the apparatus if excessive direct current continue to flow.

Impedance (reactor) bonds are large reactors connected between the rails at each end of double-rail track circuit on both D-C electrified and A-C electrified railroads. Their purpose is to permit propulsion current flow from one track circuit to the adjoining one. The size of impedance bonds is determined by the amount of propulsion return current.

Propulsion voltages are typically higher in A-C than those in D-C propulsion systems. For given propulsion power, higher propulsion voltages require less current. Thus impedance bonds for A-C propulsion are usually smaller than those for D-C propulsion.

New Words and Expressions

outline ['əutlain] *n.* 摘要
terminology [ˌtɜːmi'nɔlədʒi] *n.* 术语
utilize ['juːtilaiz] *v.* 利用
transformer [træns'fɔːmə(r)] *n.* 变压器
reactor [ri'æktə] *n.* 反应堆，电抗器
resistor [ri'zistə] *n.* 电阻器
audio-frequency *n.* 声(音)频
characteristic [ˌkæriktə'ristik] *adj.* 特有的，表示特性的，典型的
substantially [səb'stænʃ(ə)li] *adv.* 实质上；本质上
electrified railroad *n.* 电气化铁路
typically ['tipikəli] *adv.* 一般
propulsion current *n.* 牵引电流
essentially [i'senʃəli] *adv.* 实质上；基本上
concurrent [kən'kʌrənt] *adj.* 并发的，协作的，一致的
induction affect *n.* 感应效应
classification yard *n.* 编组场
peak [piːk] *n.* 峰值
commercial power *n.* 市电

apparatus [ˌæpəˈreitəs] n. 装置；设备
track transformer n. 轨道变压器
primary [ˈpraiməri] adj. 初级的
secondary [ˈsekəndəri] adj. 次级的
rated input n. 额定输入
tap [tæp] vt. 开发，利用
adjust [əˈdʒʌst] v. 调节；调整
impedance [imˈpiːdəns] n. 阻抗
two-element track relay 二元轨道继电器
single-rail track circuit 单轨条轨道电路
magnetization [ˌmægnitaiˈzeiʃən] n. 磁化
magnetic circuit 磁化电路
excessive [ikˈsesiv] adj. 过大的；过量的
impedance bond 阻抗联结器
adjoining [əˈdʒɔiniŋ] adj. 邻接的
be similar to... 与……相似；类似
differ from 不同于；与……有区别
serve as 用作；供作……之用
in the presence of 在……的情况下
be associated with 与……有关联
be immune to 不受……影响

Notes to the Text

1. Track circuits on such roads must function in the presence of propulsion currents which can be hundreds of times greater than the track circuit current flowing in the same rail.

   译文 电气化铁路区段的轨道电路必须在牵引电流的情况下工作，牵引电流能比相同区段的轨道电流大数百倍。

   such roads 指上文提到的 electrified railroads，which 引导的从句修饰 propulsion currents。

2. In such applications the reason for using A-C may improve track shunting by using the high peak voltage of the A-C wave, or may be economical to use commercial power served as track energy source.

   译文 一方面是因为利用交流的较高峰值电压可以提高轨道分路灵敏度，另外一个方面是因为使用市电比较经济。

   句子的主语为 the reason，for using A-C 修饰主语。

Exercises to the Text

Ⅰ. **Translate the following terms into Chinese.**

  (1) audio-frequency track circuits (2) electrified railroad (3) in the presence of
  (4) propulsion current (5) adjustable impedance (6) impedance (reactor) bond

Ⅱ. **Decide whether each of the following statements is true or false according to the text.**

  (1) Impedance bonds for A-C propulsion are usually bigger than those for D-C propulsion.(   )

(2) The rails can be used to serve as return conductors for propulsion on electrified railroads. (   )

(3) Propulsion currents can be hundreds of times greater than the track circuit current flowing in the same rail. (   )

(4) Secondary windings of the track transformer are tapped to permit track voltage choice.
(   )

(5) The size of impedance bonds is determined by the amount of propulsion return current.
(   )

Ⅲ. **Answer the following questions according to the text.**

(1) What are the reasons for using A-C in classification yards?

(2) What is high-frequency track circuits called?

(3) Which apparatus is used in A-C Track Circuits?

(4) Are propulsion voltages typically higher in A-C than those in D-C propulsion systems?

Reading Material

Circuit Failures

The circuit is designed so that most failures will cause a "track occupied" indication. For example:

- A broken rail or wire will break the circuit between the power supply and the relay, de-energizing the relay.
- A failure in the power supply will de-energize the relay.
- A short across the rails or between adjacent track sections will de-energize the relay.
- On the other hand, failure modes which prevent the circuit from detecting trains are possible. Examples include:
- Mechanical failure of the relay, causing the relay to be stuck in the "track clear" position even when the track is occupied.
- Conditions which partially or completely insulate the wheels from the rail, such as rust, sand, or dry leaves on the rails. This is also known as "poor shunting" ("failure to shunt" in North America).
- Conditions in the roadbed which create stray electrical signals, such as muddy ballast (which can generate a "battery effect") or parasitic electrical currents from nearby power transmission lines.
- Equipment which is not heavy enough to make good electrical contact (shunt failure) or whose wheels must be electrically insulated.
- A rail break between the insulated rail joint and the track circuit wiring would not be detected.

Failure modes that result in an incorrect "track clear" signal may allow a train to enter an occupied block, creating the risk of a collision. They may also cause the warning systems at a grade crossing to fail to activate.

Different means are used to respond to these types of failures. For example, the relays are designed to a very high level of reliability. Equipments being less susceptible to interference are used in some areas where stray electrical signals of track circuits exist. Speeds may be restricted when and where fallen leaves are at issue. The other equipments may be embargoed in order to let traffic pass, and the traffic cannot reliably shunt the rails.

Of course, sabotage is possible. In the 1995 Palo Verde derailment saboteurs connected sections of rail which they had displaced in order to cover up the breaks in the track they had made. Therefore, the track circuit did not detect the breaks and indication to stop wasn't given to the engineer.

Exercises to the Material

Choose the best answer according to the material.

(1) How many conditions referred in the text will de-energize the relay when no train is present? _____.
    A. 3   B. 4   C. 5   D. 6

(2) How many failure modes referred in the text prevent the circuit from detecting trains? _____.
    A. 3   B. 4   C. 5   D. 6

(3) An incorrect "track clear" signal may result in _____.
    A. a train to enter a clear block
    B. creating the risk of a collision
    C. the warning systems at a grade crossing to activate
    D. a train to leave a occupied block

(4) The word "reliability" in paragraph 7 is closest in meaning to _____.
    A. feasibility   B. ability   C. security   D. capability

(5) From the last paragraph we cannot say that _____.
    A. the breaks of the track circuit were not detected
    B. the train derailed
    C. the engineer was given no indication to stop the train
    D. nobody sabotaged the track circuits

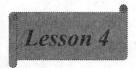

Lesson 4 Electronic-Coded Track Circuits (电码化轨道电路)

Introduction

The coded track circuit is not essentially different from the steady-energy track circuit. It is not so much a new kind of track circuit as it is an important track circuit since it retains all the advantages and has, in addition, other desirable attributes.[1] Among these additional advantages are: improved shunting sensitivity, improved broken-rail detection, increased average track-circuit length, improved protection against the effects of foreign current or failure of insulated joints, and elimination of cut sections.

Because of the improved shunting sensitivity of the coded track circuit and the efficiency of the code-responsive track relay, it is possible to increase the length of a coded track circuit well beyond the length that would operate satisfactorily with a steady-energy track circuit, assuming similar conditions for each.[2] Thus coded track circuits do not need as many cut sections as steady-energy track circuits.

The same factors that contribute to improve shunting sensitivity also contribute to improve broken-rail detection. The shunting sensitivity of the coded track circuit is affected directly by the relay's pickup value rather than by its release value. Furthermore, the code-responsive track relay requires more current than the steady-energy track relay.[3] Therefore, the leakage resistance around a broken rail does not have to be as high as it would with a steady-energy track circuit to effect a stop indication with a coded track circuit.[4]

By interrupting or "coding" the current to the rails at different rates in accordance with the condition of the next track circuit ahead, and by providing appropriate apparatus at the relay end of the track circuit that will respond selectively to the code being received, multiple proceed aspects may be controlled through the rails, thus eliminating signal-control line wire.

Elementary principles

Figure 5 illustrates an elementary coded track circuit. Code transmitter CT at the battery end of the circuit interrupts the energy to the rails 75 times per minute so that the energy in the rails pulses in alternate "on" and "off" periods.

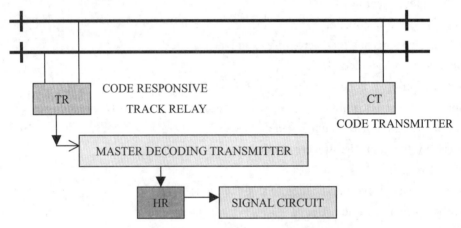

Figure 5　Simplified diagram of coded track circuit

At the other end of the track circuit, code-responsive track relay TR alternately picks up and releases in response to those impulses of energy and controls the flow of local energy to the master decoding transformer.

The signal circuits are controlled by HR, a steady-energy repeater of the code-responsive track relay. HR is controlled through the contacts of TR and by the master transformer that it will release unless TR is coding.

When a train enters such a track circuit, the value of the train shunt needs only be sufficient to reduce the energy in the coils of TR relay to a point below its pickup value to cause track-detector relay HR to drop.

In the steady-energy D-C track circuit, the value of the train shunt must be sufficient to reduce the energy in the track relay to a point below its release value. In as much as it takes less energy to hold a relay in its picked-up position than it does to cause a relay to pick up from its released position, the coded track circuit has a correspondingly higher shunting sensitivity. Furthermore, if the code-responsive track relay should remain in either the energized or the de-energized position, HR would drop.

Recently there are many types of coded track circuits used in railway signaling, such as A-C counting code track circuit, polar-impulse track circuit, asymmetrical high voltage impulse track circuit, polar-frequency coded track circuit, FSO track circuit, HF track circuit and so on.

As the name implies, frequency-shift overlay (FSO) track circuits may be "overlaid" on the track circuits installed for other purposes without disturbing the function of the original circuits.[5]

Track frequencies in the audio range are not restricted to application in overlay circuits. They also may be used for basic track circuits in a block signal systems, and are usually referred to as high-frequency track circuits.

High-frequency track circuits are suitable for general application. They are particularly adapted to electric rapid transit system, where the maximum track circuit length of 2 000 feet is adequate, and where the elimination of insulated joints simplifies the use of the rails for propulsion current return. With welded rail, there is additional benefit of elimination breaks in the continuous rail structure.

New Words and Expressions

introduction [ˌintrəˈdʌkʃən] n. 介绍，序言，导言
retain [riˈtein] v. 保留
advantage [ədˈvɑːntidʒ] n. 优点
desirable [diˈzaiərəbl] adj. 所希望的；想要的
attribute [əˈtribjuːt] n. 属性，特性
broken-rail detection 断轨检测
insulated joint failure 绝缘节破损；绝缘不良
elimination [iˌlimiˈneiʃən] n. 消除
cut section n. 分割区段
efficiency [iˈfiʃənsi] n. 性能
satisfactorily [ˌsætisˈfæktərili] adv. 满意地
assume [əˈsjuːm] v. 假定
condition [kənˈdiʃən] n. 条件
factor [ˈfæktə] n. 因素
contribute [kənˈtribjuːt] v. 促使，有助于
release value 释放值
pickup value 吸起值
furthermore [ˌfɜːðəˈmɔː(r)] adv. 此外
interrupt [ˌintəˈrʌpt] v. 间断
appropriate [əˈprəupriit] v. 合适的，适当的
multiple proceed aspects 多显示
illustrate [ˈiləstreit] v. 举例说明
code transmitter 电码发送器
decoding transformer 译码器
repeater [riˈpiːtə] n. 复示器

coil [kɔil] *n.* 线圈，绕组

remain [ri'mein] *v.* 保持

A-C counting code track circuit　交流计数电码轨道电路

polar-impulse track circuit　极性脉冲轨道电路

asymmetrical high voltage impulse track circuit　不对称脉冲轨道电路

polar-frequency code track circuit　极频轨道电路

FSO track circuit　移频重叠轨道电路

HF track circuit　高频轨道电路

(be) different from　与……不同；不同于

in addition　另外还有；此外

protect…against…　保护……以防(免遭)……

in accordance with　按照；根据

in response to　响应

(be) sufficient to　足够(做)……

in as much as　因为；由于

Notes to the Text

1. It is not so much a new kind of track circuit as it is an important track circuit since it retains all the advantages and has, in addition, other desirable attributes.

    译文　与其说它是一个新型的轨道电路，不如说它是一个重要的轨道电路，因为它保留了恒源轨道电路所有的优点，另外，它还具有其他具有应用前景的特性。

    not so much...as..., 意思是"与其说……不如说……"。

    since 意思是"因为"，相当于 because 或 as。

2. Because of the improved shunting sensitivity of the coded track circuit and the efficiency of the code-responsive track relay, it is possible to increase the length of a coded track circuit well beyond the length that would operate satisfactorily with a steady-energy track circuit, assuming similar conditions for each.

    译文　因为电码化轨道电路提高了分路灵敏度，同时电码化轨道继电器性能优良，所以增加电码化轨道电路的传输长度是有可能的。这个长度会远远超过同等条件下恒源轨道电路正常工作的传输长度。

    it 是形式主语，to increase the length of a coded track circuit 是真正的主语。

    Because of the improved shunting sensitivity of the coded track circuit and the efficiency of the code-responsive track relay 作并列的原因状语。

    that would operate satisfactorily with a steady-energy track circuit—assuming similar conditions for each 作定语从句，修饰 the length。

3. The shunting sensitivity of the coded track circuit is affected directly by the relay's pickup value rather than by its release value.

    译文　电码化轨道电路的分路灵敏度是直接受继电器的吸起值影响的，而不是受继电器释放值影响。

    rather than 表示"而不是"。

4. Therefore, the leakage resistance around a broken rail does not have to be as high to effect a stop indication with a coded track circuit as it would with a steady-energy track circuit.

译文　所以，电码化轨道电路断轨周围的漏泄电阻不需要像恒源轨道电路那么高就可实现停车显示。

the leakage resistance around a broken rail 为句子的主语。

not... as...as...意思是"与……不一样"。

5. As the name implies, frequency-shift overlay (FSO) track circuits may be "overlaid" on the track circuits installed for other purposes without disturbing the function of the original circuits.

译文　顾名思义，移频重叠轨道电路是可以叠加在为其他目的而安装的轨道电路之上的，且不影响原轨道电路的功能。

installed for other purposes 过去分词作定语，修饰 the track circuits。

without disturbing the function of the original circuits 作状语，说明 frequency-shift overlay (FSO) track circuits。

Exercises to the Text

I. **Translate the following terms into Chinese.**

(1) electronic-coded track circuits　(2) not so much...as　(3) in addition

(4) shunting sensitivity　(5) elimination of cut sections　(6) broken-rail detection

(7) average track-circuit length　(8) sensitivity of track circuit shunting

(9) protection against the effects of foreign current　(10) failure of insulated joints

(11) in accordance with　(12) in response to

II. **Decide whether each of the following statement is true or false according to the text.**

(1) The coded track circuit differs from the steady-energy track circuit. (　)

(2) The coded track circuit retains all the advantages of the steady-energy track circuit and has other desirable attributes. (　)

(3) The coded track circuit cannot increase the average length of the track-circuit. (　)

(4) The coded track circuits do not need as many cut sections as steady-energy track circuits. (　)

(5) The code-responsive track relay requires less current than the steady-energy track relay. (　)

III. **Answer the following questions according to the text.**

(1) Which factors contribute to improve broken-rail detection?

(2) Does the coded track circuit have a correspondingly higher shunting sensitivity?

(3) Which types of coded track circuits are used in railway signaling?

(4) How many times per minute does code transmitter CT at the battery end of the circuit interrupt the energy to the rails in Figure 5?

(5) A coded track circuit can increase the average track circuit length. Why?

Reading Material

Frequency-Shift Overlay Track Circuits

FSO circuits of different frequency may also be superimposed on each other. Thus two FSO circuits may be overlapped to provide a track section in which both circuits respond simultaneously to occupancy in the overlapped section while responding independently to occupancy outside the overlapped section.

The detailed electronic technology of FSO transmitters, receivers and related equipment is beyond the scope of this discussion. It is feasible, however, to present the general features of FSO track circuits without such details.

The basic units of FSO apparatus are the transmitter and receiver.

In the transmitter, the carrier signal generated by the oscillator is frequency shifted at a relatively low audio-frequency rate by the modulator. The output is fed to the amplifier, where the power level is increased, and through the coupling unit to the track.

At the receiving end of the circuits, the signal feeds to an integrated circuit amplifier through the coupling unit and the input section (a carrier filter). The amplifier raises the signal level sufficiently to drive the detector. With sidebands (frequency-shifting signal) present, the detector produces output to operate the relay driver, the output of which in turn picks up the biased-neutral track relay.

Exercises to the Material

Choose the best answer according to the material.

(1) The word "which" in line 5 refers to _____.
  A. two FSO circuits   B. a track section
  C. audio frequencies   D. different frequency

(2) The word "overlaid" in line 7 is closest in meaning to _____.
  A. impulse   B. overlap   C. imposed   D. overlapped

(3) Which of the following is true about FSO track circuits? _____.
  A. Two FSO circuits cannot be overlapped on a same track section
  B. Two FSO circuits may be overlapped on a same track section
  C. FSO circuits of same frequency may also be superimposed on each other
  D. Two FSO circuits respond simultaneously to occupancy outside the overlapped section

(4) Where is the carrier signal level generated in the transmitter? _____.
  A. In the oscillator   B. In the modulator
  C. In the amplifier   D. In the coupling unit

(5) Where is the carrier signal level increased at the receiving end of the circuits? _____.
  A. The input section   B. In the detector
  C. In the amplifier   D. In the coupling unit

 **Basic Automatic Block Signals** (自动闭塞信号)

Definition

The Association of American Railroad's Standard Code defines automatic block system as: "A series of consecutive blocks governed by block signals, cab signal, or both, and actuated by a train, or engine, or by certain conditions affecting the use of a block".

Automatic block signal, or ABS, consists of a series of signals that govern blocks of track between the signals. The signals are automatically activated by the conditions of the block beyond the signal. If a train is currently occupying a block, that block's signal will not allow a train in the previous block to proceed into the block, or will only allow it to proceed at a speed which allows the train to stop before colliding with the train or another object (also known as restricted speed).

Automatic block signals also detect the status of a following signal. If a signal is displaying a stop indication, the preceding signal will display an aspect that warns the train crew that the following signal may require the train to stop.

ABS systems detect track occupancy by passing a low-voltage current through the track between the signals and detecting whether the circuit is closed, open, or shortened. A train's metal wheels and axles will pass current from one rail to the other, thereby shortening the circuit. If the ABS system detects that the circuit is shortened between two signals, it understands that a train is occupying that block and will "drop" the signals (display a stop indication) on either side of that block to prevent another train from entering. ABS system electronics are also able to detect breaks in the rail or improperly-lined switches, which result in an open circuit. These will also cause the signal's aspect to drop, and prevent any trains from entering the block and running the risk of bending, breaking, or overturning the rail and derailing or running through an improperly-lined switch.

Signal space

Figure 6 shows a piece of railroad which has been divided into blocks AB, BC, CD. The lengths of blocks are planned according to the density of traffic that is to be handled and the braking distance of the trains.[1] Where traffic is heavy, blocks are relatively short in order to permit trains to follow each other closely and safely. Where traffic is light, blocks can be longer.

For safe operation, the space between signals must not be less than braking distance. Braking distance means the distance it takes to stop the train that is operating at maximum permissible speed.[2] Braking distance is a variable factor, and most railroads have conducted tests to determine what this distance is for their trains. This data is used in determining the minimum lengths of blocks. Of course, compensations must be made for grade. In actual practice, automatic block signal space on mainline railroads varies anywhere from 1/2 mile to 2 miles, while on rapid transit systems, space may be only a few hundred feet.

You may say, "Why not space these signals so far apart that there would be no question of having sufficient braking distance?"[3] This can be and is done in territory where there are few trains, but in places where trains have to follow each other at short intervals, it becomes necessary to make these block as short as possible so as to handle the traffic.

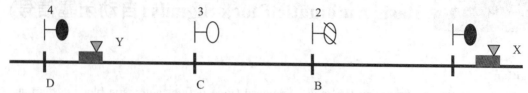

Figure 6 Diagram of 2-block, 3-aspect signaling

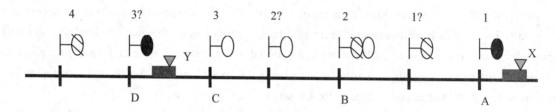

Figure 7 Diagram of 3-block, 4-aspect signaling

Signal aspects and indications

Let us consider the simplest aspects that can be displayed by a signal system protecting this piece of railroad and providing their meaning to an engineman on a train. Each of these signals 1, 2, 3 and 4 is capable of displaying a red, yellow or green light.

These aspects are defined as follows in the book of the rule which governs operation of trains in automatic block territory:

Green—proceed.

Yellow—proceed preparing to stop at next signal.

Red—stop; then proceed at restricted speed.

In order to see how these signals function for train operation, let us assume a train X has stopped in block AB, and a following train Y will continue to operate at normal speed until it approaches signal 3, which will be yellow. Then the train will reduce so as to be able to stop when it has arrived at signal 2, which is red.

To keep trains moving at a high rate of speed and on closer space or headway. 4-aspect signaling is used. On this system, each signal has two heads mounted one above the other. The aspects and their definitions set forth by the AAR Standard Code are:

RR—stop; then proceed at restricted speed.

YR—proceed preparing to stop at next signal.

YG—proceed approaching next signal at medium speed (30 mph).

GG—proceed.

With this system, the signals are no longer spaced braking distance apart. However, the distance from the YG aspect to the RR must be at least braking distance, and the distance from the YR aspect to the RR must be at least braking distance for 30 mph.

Let us take the Figure 7 and modify it to a 3-block, 4-aspect system. Let us assume that in Figure 6 the signals are spaced just braking distance apart. With the aspects as given for this system, another signal can be located between each of the existing signals. With this modification, then the signaling would be illustrated in Figure 7 (For practical purposes such a rough-and-ready method for conversion from 2-block to 3-blok signaling would most likely be quite impractical, but it is used here to simplify our example).

Now let's assume some different conditions for train X and Y in Figure 6 and 7 and see what the advantage of the additional signals are.

With both trains as shown, should X be standing still, Y would reduce speed at signal 2 in both figures.[4]

If X were standing across joint A, Y in Figure 6 would have to reduce speed at signal 2, but Y in Figure 7 could continue at full speed up to signal 2′.[5]

If X were standing just across joint B, Y in Figure 6 would have to reduce speed at signal 3, but Y in Figure 7 could continue at full speed to signal 3′.

If the distance AB is 7500 feet, the distance from red to green is 15 000 feet in Figure 6; but the distance from red/red to green/green in Figure 7 is only 11 250 feet—only 75% of the Figure 6 distance. Thus, if you can get 75 trains in 100miles of the Figure 6 arrangement, you could get 75 trains in 75miles of the Figure 7 arrangement—or 100 trains in 100 miles, the track capacity is increased.

New Words and Expressions

automatic block signaling　自动闭塞信号
definition [ˌdefiˈniʃən] n.　定义
association [əˌsəusiˈeiʃən] n.　协会；学会
consecutive [kənˈsekjutiv] adj.　连续的；依次相连的
govern [ˈgʌvən] v.　控制；调解；管理
cab signal　机车信号
actuate [ˈæktʃueit] v.　动作
engine [ˈendʒin] n.　机车
affect [əˈfekt] v.　影响；对……起作用
density [ˈdensiti] n.　密度
braking distance　制动距离
permissible [pəˈmisəbl] adj.　容许的；许可的
grade [greid] n.　坡度
far apart　离得很远；间距很大
territory [ˈteritəri] n.　区域；区段
interval [ˈintəvəl] n.　间距
display [diˈsplei] v.　显示
engineman [ˈendʒinmæn] n.　司机
restricted [riˈstriktid] adj.　限制的
train operation　行车；列车运行
approach [əˈprutʃ] vt.　接近；逼近
headway [ˈhedwei] n.(前后两车) 车间时距；时间间隔
mount [maunt] v.　安装

medium ['miːdiəm] *adj.* 中等的；中级的
modify ['mɔdifai] *v.* 修改；改进
conversion [kən'vɜːʃən] *n.* 转换；转化
capacity [kə'pæsiti] *n.* 通过能力
define…as… 把……定义为……
a series of 一系列；一连串
be divided into 划分成
according to 按照；根据
of course 当然；自然
make compensation for 补偿
set forth 规定；宣布
no longer 不再；已不

Notes to the Text

1. The lengths of blocks are planned according to the density of traffic that is to be handled and the braking distance of the trains.

   译文 闭塞分区的长度是根据实际的交通密度和列车的制动距离来设置的。

   that is to be handled 是修饰 the density of traffic 的，表示能实现的。

2. Braking distance means the distance it takes to stop a train which is operating at maximum permissible speed.

   译文 制动距离是指列车以最大允许速度运行到安全停止所需要行驶的距离。

   which is operating at maximum permissible speed 定语从句，修饰 a train。

3. Why not space these signals so far apart that there would be no question of having sufficient braking distance?

   译文 为什么不把信号机的间距设得足够大，这样保证足够大的制动距离不就没有问题了吗？

   so … that, 如此……以致。

4. With both trains as shown, should X be standing still, Y would reduce speed at signal 2 in both figures.

   译文 如图所示的两列列车，假设列车 X 继续占用，则列车 Y 在信号机 2 处将减速。

   should 提前倒装，表示假设的含义。

5. If X were standing across joint A, Y in Figure 6 would have to reduce speed at signal 3, but Y in Figure 7 could continue at full speed up to signal 2'.

   译文 如果列车 X 越过绝缘节 A，图 6 中的列车 Y 必须在信号机 3 处减速，但图 7 中的列车 Y 可以全速运行至信号机 2'。

Exercises to the Text

Ⅰ. Translate the following terms into Chinese.

  (1) braking distance   (2) the density of traffic   (3) make compensation for

  (4) automatic block signal   (5) train operation   (6) cab signal

  (7) safe operation   (8) at maximum permissible speed

II. **Decide whether each of the following statement is true or false according to the text.**

(1) The lengths of blocks are planned according to the safe operation. (　)

(2) Figure 7 shows a 3-block, 4-aspect system. (　)

(3) Where traffic is heavy, blocks are relatively short and where traffic is light, blocks can be longer. (　)

(4) 4-aspect signaling system can keep trains moving at a high rate of speed and on closer headway. (　)

(5) The space between signals must not be less than braking distance for safe operation. (　)

III. **Answer the following questions according to the text.**

(1) How are the lengths of blocks planned?

(2) Where must these blocks be as short as possible so as to handle the traffic?

(3) May signal space be only a few hundred feet on rapid transit systems?

(4) What are the advantage of the additional signals in Figure 7?

(5) In territory where there are few trains, can signal space be far away?

IV. **Translate the following passage into Chinese.**

Automatic Block Signaling Control Circuits

Now let's see what circuits we are going to need to make the automatic block signaling work.

In Lecture 2, "D-C Track Circuits", we have a very elementary arrangement where we can get 1-block, 2-aspect signaling. This arrangement has a serious disadvantage. Most block lengths need more than one track circuit, so that they can reach from one signal to the next. We can solve this problem in several ways. For example, we can use as many track circuits as we need and take a pair of line wire to make all the track relay connection in series. Usually, it is also a good way to increase the length of one track circuit by about 50 percent.

Now we can spread our signals as far as we wish, but we still need additional information—"What is the position of the H relay in the next block ahead"?

Let's find this out, by taking another line wire back to control a distant relay, which we shall call D. Now, if we have H up, we know the block ahead is clear; and if we have D up, we know the second block ahead is clear, so we can show a green signal. This circuit needs three line wires.

The next step is to use a three-position polarized relay, thus cutting our line wire requirements to two.

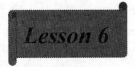

Lesson 6　Interlocking(车站连锁设备)

Introduction

Interlocking is used to facilitate and safeguard the movement of trains at stations, junction points, railroad grade crossing and so on. It is defined as: "An arrangement of signals and appliances is interconnected so that their movements must succeed each other in proper sequence and for which interlocking rules are in effect. It may be operated manually or automatically."

Interlocking types

Interlocking can be categorized as all-mechanical, electrical(relay-based), and electronic/computer-based.

The first interlocking was mechanical. Then electric operation of switches and signals was introduced. In present systems, relay circuits provide the interlocking. Modern interlocking—those installed since the early 1990s—are generally solid state, where the complex wired networks of relays are replaced by computer software logic. The fact that the logic implemented by software rather than hard-wired circuitry greatly facilitates the ability to make modifications when needed by reprogramming rather than rewiring.

When the operator of the interlocking is located within the locality of the interlocked switches and signals, controls are directed by wire, and central energy sources are provided to operate the relays, signals and electric switch machines. Energy sources are common batteries of storage cells, with provision for charging from commercial power which is available. Sometimes standby power sources, such as motor generator sets, are also provided.

When one—or sometimes several—locations are distant from the control center, remote control and indication systems are used.[1] There are many types of remote control systems, some use physical line circuits, some carrier, some microwave, etc.

Computer-controlled interlocking system for a railway installation

A computer-controlled interlocking system for a railway installation which comprises a plurality of sections, each of which has an associated plurality of elements, comprises a plurality of section computers respectively associated with the sections and arranged to be fail-safe in terms of signaling technology.[2] Each section computer is provided with a respective program memory which, in turn, is provided with programs relating to the process of requirements for control, both individual and in relation to routes. Each section computer also has a write/read memory arranged for receiving and storing installation-specific data relating to the railway installation topography and the respective element characterization in terms of type of element, element program, element designation and the arrangement of the elements relative to neighboring elements. An input computer is provided in common to all of the section computers and arranged to be fail-safe in terms of signaling technology.

A typical control panel of all-relay interlocking

Relay interlocking is also controlled via keyboards and video monitors, but the basic relay interlocking circuits remain the same.

The track diagram in the upper portion of the panel represents the track layout. In accordance with interlocking practice, signal 1L is located at the clearance point between the main and branch lines, and signal 1R is located in advance of the switch points. These signals govern train movements in accordance with the route set up and the condition of the block ahead.[3]

Home signals 1L and 1R respectively have two arms. Signal 1LA on the main line governs traffic to the left over the normal switch. Signal 1LB on the branch line governs traffic to the left over the normal switch. Signal 1LB on the branch line governs traffic to the left over the reverse switch. Signal 1RA governs traffic to the right over the normal switch, and signal 1RB governs traffic to the right over the reverse switch onto the branch line. Automatic signals 15 and 44 act as mainline approach signals to the plant, and signal 01 acts as the approach signal from the branch line. The home signals normally display red (stop) aspects, and the approach signals display yellow (approach) aspects.

Three approach lights AE on the panel indicate when their respective approaches are occupied by a train. Track light TE indicates track circuit 2T (at the switch) is occupied.

Switch lever 2 has two positions: normal (N) and reverse (R). This lever is used to control the switch machine. When in horizontal or reverse (R) position, it calls for the switch machine to set up a route for the branch line. Switch lever contacts NC are closed from normal (N) to center position (C). Switch lever contacts RC are closed from reverse (R) to center (C). Contacts N and R are closed only when the lever is in normal or reverse position.

Lock light LE indicates the switch is locked and out of the operator's control.[4] Correspondence light WE indicates when the switch is not in correspondence with the switch lever.

Signal lever 1 has three positions, right, left and stop. When positioned to the left (L), it indicates a control to clear either signal 1LA or 1LB for traffic movement to the left. When positioned to the right (R), it indicates a control to clear signal 1RA or 1RB for traffic movement to the right. In the vertical position, all signals are at stop. Signal-clear lights RGE and LGE indicate when signals are cleared for a traffic movement to the right or left.

New Words and Expressions

all-relay interlocking   继电式电气集中联锁
safeguard ['seifgɑːd] v.   防护
junction point   枢纽
grade crossing   平交道口
appliance [ə'plaɪəns] n.   设备；装置
interconnect [ˌɪntəkə'nekt] v.   互联；相互联系
succeed [sək'siːd] v.   接续；接着……发生
categorize ['kætɪɡəraɪz] v.   把……归类；把……列作
mechanical [mɪ'kænɪkl] adj.   机械的
electric operation switch   电动道岔
locality [ləʊ'kælɪtɪ] n.   地点；位置
interlocked switch   连锁道岔
electric switch machine   电动转辙机
storage cell   蓄电池
charge [tʃɑːdʒ] vt.   使充电
standby ['stændbaɪ] n.   备用的
motor generator set   发电机组
remote control system   遥控
microwave ['maɪkrəʊweɪv] n.   微波
opposing signal   反向信号
route [ruːt] n.   进路
with provision for   考虑到
comprise [kəm'praɪz] v.   包含，包括，由……组成

plurality [pluə'ræliti] *n.* 多元化，多重性，众多
via ['vaiə] *prep.* (经)由；借助于
video monitor　视频监视器
upper portion　上方
represent [ˌrepri'zent] *v.* 代表；表示
layout ['leiaut] *n.* 配置；布局
normal ['nɔ:məl] *adj.* 正常的，正规的，标准的
reverse [ri'vɜ:s] *adj.* 相反的，倒转的，颠倒的
vertical ['vɜ:tikəl] *adj.* 垂直的，直立的，顶点的
horizontal [ˌhɔri'zɔntl] *adj.* 地平线的，水平的
in terms of　就……而言，从……方面说来，根据
provided with　拥有
in relation to　与……有关
set up　建立
act as　充当；起……作用
call for　要求；需要
in correspondence with　和……相一致，与……有通信联系

Notes to the Text

1. When one or sometimes several locations are distant from the control center, remote control and indication systems are used.

   译文　当有一个车站，有时是几个车站，距离控制中心比较远时，就要应用远程控制系统和显示系统。

   locations 是指"铁路沿线车站"。

2. A computer-controlled interlocking system for a railway installation which comprises a plurality of sections, each of which has an associated plurality of elements, comprises a plurality of section computers respectively associated with the sections and arranged to be fail-safe in terms of signaling technology.

   译文　铁路设备计算机联锁系统包含许多个组成部分，每个组成部分都有许多互相关联的元素。根据信号技术设计符合故障-安全原则的要求，铁路设备计算机联锁系统由诸多相对独立又互相联系的计算机构成。

   for...elements 修饰主语 A computer-controlled interlocking system，谓语是句中的第二个 comprises。

   fail-safe 是表示信号"故障-安全原则"。

3. These signals govern train movements in accordance with the route set up and the condition of the block ahead.

   译文　这些信号机根据所建立的进路和前方闭塞分区的状态控制列车运行。

   set up 过去分词修饰 the route，表示"建立好的"或"办理好的"。

4. Lock light LE indicates the switch is locked and out of the operator's control.

   译文　锁闭灯 LE 表示道岔被锁闭，且不受操作员控制。

out of 表示在……之外。

Exercises to the Text

I. **Translate the following terms into Chinese.**

(1) standby power sources (2) the presence of the trains
(3) grade crossing (4) home signals
(5) the main and branch lines (6) in advance of the switch points
(7) lock out opposing signals (8) the switch machine

II. **Decide whether each of the following statements is true or false according to the text.**

(1) When signal lever 1 is positioned to the left, it indicates a control to clear either signal 1LA or 1LB for traffic movement to the left. (   )
(2) When the switch is locked and the operator can control it. (   )
(3) Switch lever 2 is used to control the switch machine. (   )
(4) In present systems, the interlocks are used in relay circuits. (   )
(5) Automatic interlocking requires many operators. (   )

III. **Answer the following questions according to the text.**

(1) What function does a interlocking device have?
(2) How many arms do home signals 1L have?
(3) How many positions does the signal lever 1 have?
(4) Relay interlocking is controlled via keyboards or video monitors, isn't it?
(5) The automatic interlocking is actuated by the presence of the trains on the controlling track circuits, isn't it?

Reading Material

Basic Circuits of the Interlocking

When a train approaches the interlocking plant, the track relays drop and in turn drop approach relay AR, closing its back contact to light the lamp AE.

Detection of a train on the approach is usually arranged so that the control machine operator has time to clear the home and in turn, the approach signal before the engineman has to make a brake application.

Lock indication relay LKR indicates when it is possible to operate the switch machine. Magnetic-stick relay CWZR checks the switch lever, if it is to be effective to control the switch, the switch lever must be corresponded with the position of the switch machine, and agree with the position of magnetic-stick switch to control relay WZR.

With the switch lever in the N position, positive of split battery, BL, is applied to the LKR, CWZR and WZR relays in series to common, CL, of the split battery. A front contact of lock relay L is inserted in the circuit to prevent changing the position of the WZR relay, when the locking in the field is in effect, such as when a signal has been cleared.

To reverse a switch, the operator moves the switch lever to the R position. Negative NL of split battery applied through the RC contact on the lever drops magnetic-stick relay CWZR and WZR, and calls for the switch machine to operate on the reverse position for a move onto the branch line.

If the operator leaves the switch lever in the center position, both sides of split battery, NL, and BL, are applied through lever contacts NC and RC to hold LKR relay energized. Lock indication light LE, controlled over a back contact of the LKR relay, cannot be lit. Correspondence light WE will be lit, indicating that the position of the switch lever does not correspond with the position of the switch machine.

Signal control relays LGZR and RGZR for clearing signals to the left or right are biased-neutral relays. They will pick up only when voltage of the proper polarity is applied to their windings. LGZR and RGZR repeat the left or right position of the signal lever only if the switch lever is in correspondence with the CWZR relay. This check of correspondence between the switch lever and relay CWZR ensure that a signal cannot be cleared over an unintended route.

When signal lever 1 has been positioned to the right to clear signal 1R over the reverse switch for a branch-line move, positive BL of split battery is applied through R contact of the signal lever, R contact of the switch lever and back contact R of CWZR to check the switch lever in the reverse position. Relay RGZR picks up and is stuck up through a circuit which bypasses the switch lever and CWZR contacts, thus preventing putting signal 1R to stop by unintentional operation of switch lever.

When signal 1R has cleared, right red signal repeater relay RRPR drops to close its back contact, and apply EB to right signal indication lamp RGE. Lock indication lamp LE, controlled over a back contact on LKR, is lighted to indicate that the switch cannot now be moved unless the signal is put to stop at first.

When a train has accepted the clear signal, it moves into the interlocking plant. When it just passed the home signal, it arrives on the OS track, then track relay 2TR drops. Lamp energy is thus applied to light lamp TE indicating that a train is on the switch track circuit.

When the train passes the home signal, the signal goes to red, and right red signal repeater RRPR picks up, opening the circuit to lamp RGE.

The circuits discussed and shown here are typical for a small plant and become more complex as the plant increases the size with more functions to be controlled, but the fundamental principles involved remain the same.

Exercises to the Material

Choose the best answer according to the material.
(1) From the facts in the text we cannot safely say that _____.
  A. when a train approaches the interlocking plant, the track relays will drop
  B. when a train approaches the interlocking plant, approach relay AR will drop
  C. when a train approaches the interlocking plant, the lamp AE will be lit
  D. when a train approaches the interlocking plant, all relays will drop
(2) When the train passed the home signal, from the text we can conclude that _____.
  A. the signal goes to red   B. the signal goes to yellow
  B. the signal goes to green   D. the signal goes to blue

(3) The word "arranged" in paragraph 2 is closest in meaning to _____.
   A. planned   B. placed   C. lay   D. considered
(4) Which of the following is false? _____.
   A. The circuits of the relay interlocking that were discussed in the text are simple
   B. The circuits of the relay interlocking will be more complex when the size of the plant is bigger
   C. The circuits of the relay interlocking will be more complex as the plant increases more functions
   D. The circuits of the relay interlocking that were discussed in the text are complex
(5) If the operator leaves the switch lever in the center position, it will happen that _____.
   A. LKR relay is energized
   B. Lock indication light LE cannot be lit
   C. Correspondence light WE will be lit
   D. all of above

Lesson 7 Highway Crossing Warning Signals (道口预警信号)

Introduction

Safety at highway grade crossings has been a concern of railroads, rail-transit properties and government at local, state and federal levels.[1] At issue are impatient motorists who circumvent down crossing gates in an attempt to drive over the crossing before the arrival of a train. This frequently meets with fatal results to motorists and train crews. These concerns are especially acute in high-speed rail territory, where grade separation of highways and railways is not possible and where the speed of the train makes it nearly impossible for the train operator to stop the train once the crossing comes into view and a motor vehicle stalled on the crossing becomes visible.[2]

Typical arrangements

Flashing light signals are available in various arrangements, usually with 4-inch diameter aluminum masts, 13 feet high. The signal mast is usually fifteen feet from the nearest rail, and six feet from the edge of the highway. Lamps commonly used range from 17 to 25 watts. Special windows in each light unit allow personnel passing trains to check whether the lamps are lighting. Bells may be added, as well as signs indicating the number of tracks to be crossed.

At crossings where trains and traffic density is higher, the installation of automatic gates in combination with flashing lights is advisable.[3] Thus, they are the most efficient crossing protection system.

Housings, as a rule, are located about 25 feet from the highway and 15 to 20 feet from the nearest rail or where room is available. Underground cables feed the signals and track circuits, and a 3-inch pipe is typically run under the street to protect them. In addition, warning signs are also installed.

All installation should be in accordance with pertinent railroad and government requirement.

Control circuits

Control circuits crossing warning systems are generally similar but vary widely in detail for individual location because of switching, station stops, multiple tracks, availability of commercial power, and other factors. The basic control circuits for crossing warning systems include: track circuits which can be subdivided into flashing light control circuits and crossing gate control circuits etc.

On tracks where trains are operated in both directions, the track circuit control system must be arranged to clear the crossing signals as soon as the trains are off the highway intersection — regardless of the direction of the train operation.[4]

Lamp lighting circuit for flashing light signal can be designed to operate when the train occupies the approaching track. While the train has cleared the highway, the control circuits clear the warning devices to permit highway traffic to cross the track.

Crossing gate control circuits are similar to flashing lights. The principle difference is in the gate motor control. Before the gates start to descend, the lights and bells should operate three to five seconds. The total descent time including the preliminary time lag is about fifteen seconds, which means that the gate may be down only about five seconds before the train arrives. The gate acts as a physical barrier, while the lights and bells give advance warning.

New Words and Expressions

highway crossing warning　道口预警
flashing light signal　闪光信号机
available [əˈveiləbl] adj.　备有的；通用的
diameter [daiˈæmitə] n.　直径
aluminum [əˈluːminəm] n.　铝
mast [mɑːst] n.　桅杆；支座
watt [wɔt] n.　瓦特
personnel [ˌpɜːsəˈnel] n.　(全体)人员；职员
bell [bel] n.　电铃
sign [sain] n.　标志
automatic gate　自动栏木
advisable [ədˈvaizəbl] adj.　可行的；合理的
underground cable　地下电缆
warning sign　预告标志
pertinent [ˈpɜːtinənt] adj.　相应的；有关的
individual [ˌindiˈvidjuəl] adj.　各个的；特殊的
switch [switʃ] n.　道岔
station stop　车站定点停车
availability [əˌveiləˈbiləti] n.　可用性；现有
both directions　双向
clear a crossing signal　开放道口信号
intersection [ˌintəˈsekʃən] n.　交叉点
lamp lighting circuit　电灯电路
warning device　预警设备
crossing gate　道口栏木

descend [di'send] *v.* 落下
preliminary [pri'liminəri] *adj.* 预备的，初步的
lag [læg] *v.* 滞后；迟延
barrier ['bæriə] *n.* 栅栏
as well as 以及；像……一样
be combination with 配合；和……共同结合
regardless of 不管；与……无关

Notes to the Text

1. Safety at highway grade crossings has been a concern of railroads, rail-transit properties and government at local, state and federal levels.

   译文 平交道口的安全问题已经成为铁路、铁路运输部门以及地方政府，甚至州政府、联邦政府所关注的问题。

2. These concerns are especially acute in high-speed rail territory, where grade separation of highways and railways is not possible and where the speed of the train makes it nearly impossible for the train operator to stop the train once the crossing comes into view and a motor vehicle stalled on the crossing becomes visible.

   译文 在那些公路、铁路不可能分离的高速铁路区段，以及列车速度使司机看到道口及停在道口的机动车辆时几乎不可能停下的高速铁路区段，这些问题就尤其严重。

   两个 where 引导的是并列的状语从句，becomes 的主语省略了，仍然是 These concerns。

3. At crossings where trains and traffic density is higher, the installation of automatic gates in combination with flashing lights is advisable.

   译文 在列车运行密度以及公路交通密度比较大的地方，建议安装自动栏木，并同时安装闪光信号机。

   句子真正的主语是 the installation of automatic gates in combination with flashing lights，为被动语态。

4. On tracks where trains are operated in both directions, the track circuit control system must be arranged to clear the crossing signals as soon as the trains are off the highway intersection—regardless of the direction of the train operation.

   译文 在列车双向运行的区段，无论列车的运行方向如何，轨道电路控制系统必须设计成列车一离开道口时就开放道口信号机。

   as soon as, 一……就。

   off 表示"远的"，从上下文推断应该是快要接近但还没到达的地方。

Exercises to the Text

Ⅰ. **Translate the following terms into Chinese.**

(1) meet with   (2) flashing light signals   (3) crossing protection system
(4) in accordance with   (5) flashing light control circuits   (6) crossing gate

Ⅱ. **Decide whether each of the following statements is true or false according to the text.**

(1) The word "this" in line 4 of the first paragraph refers to safety.　(　　)

(2) The signal mast is usually 15 feet from the nearest rail, and 6 feet from the edge of the highway. (   )

(3) All installation of the highway crossing warning should only be in accordance with pertinent railroad rules. (   )

(4) When the train occupies the approaching track, lamp lighting circuit for flashing light signal can operate. (   )

(5) From the text we know that the flashing light signal gives advance warning. (   )

Ⅲ. **Answer the following questions according to the text.**

(1) Where are flashing light signals installed?

(2) When can lamp lighting circuit for flashing light signal operate?

(3) When are the warning devices cleared to permit highway traffic to cross the track?

(4) What's the difference between crossing gate control circuits and flashing lights circuits?

Reading Material

Four-Quadrant Gate Highway-Crossing Warning System

To attempt to improve grade-crossing safety for both motor vehicles and trains, particularly at high-speed locations, US&S has developed the Four-Quadrant Gate Highway-Crossing Warning System.

The system primarily consists of four highway-crossing signal/gate assemblies, an inductive motor-vehicle detection loop, a vital processor, a cab signal system interface in rail territory equipped with cab signaling, and approach and island track circuits. Gate operation is controlled so that motor vehicles will not be trapped on the crossing during the approach of a train.

Signal/Gate assemblies

Two Model 95 signal/gate assemblies are installed on each side of the track so the highway is completely blocked on both sides of the rail right-of-way when the gates are down and a train is approaching the crossing.

Loop detectors

Loop detectors are buried beneath the crossing surface for detecting motor vehicles. Since the loop detectors' inductance varies whenever a motor vehicle passes over the crossing, the presence of a motor vehicle on the crossing will be detected. The loop output is sent to the warning system's vital/non-vital processor. If a vehicle is on the crossing when a train approaches and activates from the highway-crossing warning system, the exit gates will remain raised to allow the vehicle to exit from the crossing. Once again, this feature provides an exit for the vehicle so it's not trapped on the crossing by all four gates being down.

Vital/non-vital processor

The wayside control system functions as a vital/non-vital processor, and serves as the heart of the control system. It executes the vital logic required for gate operation, motor-vehicle detection, and the locomotive cab indications This processor also tests for loop-detector faults, crossing-system intrusion and broken gates, and, if any of these conditions are detected, it generates a maintenance call.

Track circuits

Track circuits detect the presence of a train within the crossing approaches and on the island (where track and road meet) and initiate operation of the highway crossing warning system.

Operation

With no train approaching the crossing, the gates are vertical, the flashing warning lights on the signal gate assemblies are dark, the warning bell is silent and track-circuit relays are energized. The vital portion of the system constantly monitors the status of the loop detectors that indicate whether a motor vehicle is traveling over or is stopped on the crossing. Loop status information also is passed to the non-vital portion of the processor, which directs the information to a data logger for recording. When a train enters one of the highway-crossing warning systems approach track circuits, the approach track-circuit relay is de-energized, the warning lights begin to flash, the bell begins to ring, and the vital processor checks if the crossing is occupied by a motor vehicle or other obstruction. If the crossing is clear (as determined via input from the motor-vehicle detection loops), the processor will allow the gates to begin their descent seven seconds after the activation of the lights and the bell. If, however, the crossing is blocked by a motor vehicle, for example, the processor will allow the gates guarding the entrance lanes of the crossing to descend, but it will keep the exit gates raised to allow the vehicle to exit from the crossing. At the same time, the locomotive cab signal (in cab signal territory) will be reduced from a clear indication to an approach-medium indication. If the crossing still is not clear 10 seconds later, the cab signal is reduced to an approach indication, and then to a restrictive indication 10 seconds later if the crossing still is obstructed. These cab-signal reduction points are located so the train can stop before reaching the crossing.

Exercises to the Material

Choose the best answer according to the material.

(1) From the facts in the text we cannot safely say that _____.

A. the Four-Quadrant Gate Highway-Crossing Warning System can improve grade-crossing safety

B. the Four-Quadrant Gate Highway-Crossing Warning System consists of four highway-crossing signal/gate assemblies

C. the Four-Quadrant Gate Highway-Crossing Warning System involves four highway-crossing signal/gate assemblies

D. the Four-Quadrant Gate Highway-Crossing Warning System is developed by US&S

(2) Loop detectors are used to _____.

    A. detect motor vehicles   B. allow the vehicle to exit from the crossing

    C. control system   D. detect the presence of a train

(3) A vital/non-vital processor executes the vital logic that is not required for _____.

    A. a gate operation   B. motor-vehicle detection

    C. the locomotive cab indications   D. the presence of a train detection

(4) When a train approaches the crossing, it will happen that _____.

    A. the gates are vertical

    B. the flashing warning lights on the signal gate assemblies are dark

    C. the warning bell is silent

    D. track-circuit relays are de-energized.

(5) The status of the loop detectors cannot _____.

   A. indicate whether a train is traveling over the crossing

   B. indicate whether a motor vehicle is stopped on the crossing

C. be passed to the non-vital portion of the processor, which directs the information to a data logger for recording

   D. indicate whether a motor vehicle is traveling over the crossing

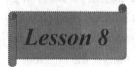 Centralized Traffic Control（调度集中）

Introduction

    Centralized Traffic Control, or CTC as it generally known, is an original development of General Railway Signal Company. It was first installed in 1927 on the New York Central Railroad between Stanley and Berwick, Ohio, with the CTC control machine located at Fostoria, Ohio.

    CTC is a signalling system used by railroads. The system consists of a centralized train dispatcher's office that controls railroad switches in the CTC territory and the signals that railroad engineers must obey in order to keep the traffic moving safely and smoothly across the railroad. In the dispatcher's office is a graphical depiction of the railroad on which the dispatcher can keep track of trains' locations across the territory that the dispatcher controls. Larger railroads may have multiple dispatcher's offices and even multiple dispatchers for each operating division.

    CTC was designed to enable the train dispatcher to control train movements directly, bypassing local operators and eliminating written train orders.[1] Instead, the train dispatcher could directly see the trains' locations and efficiently control the train's movements by displaying signals and controlling switches. It was also designed to enhance safety by detecting track occupancy and automatically preventing trains from entering signal blocks already occupied by other trains.

    What made CTC machines different from standard interlocking machines was that the vital interlocking hardware was located at the remote location and the CTC machine only displayed track state and sent commands to the remote locations. A command to display a signal would require the remote interlocking to set the flow of traffic and check for a clear route through the interlocking. If a command could not be carried out due to the interlocking logic, the display would not change on the CTC machine.

Control panel

    For a typical panel of a CTC control machine, above the panel is a track diagram which shows car capacities of the siding, lengths of intermediate tracks, and other information being helpful to operation. At the top of the panel are the names of the controlled points. Below these and above the track diagram are located the power-off lights, one for each controlled point or field location. These lights are normally dark. When steadily illuminated (red), a light indicates that the A-C power is off at that location.[2]

    The track diagram is laid out in geographic representation. Adjacent to it are signal symbols with identifying numbers and the number or name of the switch or crossover or other controlled facility. The track occupancy indicating lights for different sections of track circuits are located within the track line. White lights are generally provided for the OS track sections. These lights are normally dark and are illuminated during track occupancy or in the event of a broken rail or any other condition that causes the track relay to open its front contacts. An audible signal, bell or buzzer, may be provided to work with the OS lights or important approach lights. These are usually arranged to sound momentarily at the time the track-occupancy indication is firstly displayed.[3]

Below the track diagram are the switches, usually one for each controlled point. The switches controlling devices are two-position: on and off.

Next are the signal-clear indication lights, two for each signal lever. These indications are directional, that is, the light representing the signal which governs movements in one direction will be lit when the corresponding signal is clear in the field.

Next are signal levers, which are three-position rotary switches. Their normal position is in the center which calls for the corresponding group of signals to display their stop aspects.[4] To turn a lever to the right calls for a signal governing movement toward the right to clear; to turn a lever to the left calls for a signal governing movement toward the left. Where two or more signals govern in the same direction, selection of the one to clear is a field function, controlled by local signal selection circuits which are taken through switch-repeater relays, CTC controlled signals are usually arranged for stick operations, that is, they will remain at stop until again cleared by the operator. Non-stick operation may be provided if desired.

Below the signal levers are the switch levers, one for each switch or crossover, associated with the signals governed by the lever above. These levers are also rotary switches, normally two-position, being vertical position as normal. Turning 90 degrees to the right calls for the switch reverse. Engraved letters N and R show normal and reverse positions.

At the bottom of the panel are the start buttons, ordinarily used only if the CTC system coded. For example, when controls are to be sent out to reverse a switch and clear a signal for a train to enter the siding, the operator turns a signal lever and a switch lever to the right. Then he pushes the start button directly below these levers. The transmission of the controls to the field will not begin until the start button is pushed. The control message will ask for the switch to reverse and then for the lower unit on the signal to clear, indicating that a route is set up. The execution of these controls will, of course, be subject to the local interlocking circuits at the location, including detector locking, approach locking, track and block conditions, etc, as described in the section on relay interlocking.

At the time the switch lever is turned to the right, the switch correspondence light in the barrel of the lever is lighted, indicating to the operator that the switch in the field is not in correspondence with the position of the lever. This remains lighted until an indication message is received to the effect that the signal has cleared, the signal-clear indication light above end to the right of the signal lever is lighted.

New Words and Expressions

centralized traffic control　调度集中
bypass ['baipɑːs] *vt.*　绕过，避开，不顾
dispatcher [dis'pætʃə] *n.*　发报机，调度员

multiple ['mʌltipl] *adj.* 多样的，多重的
panel ['pænl] *n.* 面板，控制台
initiate [i'niʃieit] *v.* 引发，产生
siding ['saidiŋ] *n.* 股道
power-operated switch   电动道岔
interlocked signal   连锁信号机
controlled point   被控点
block section   闭塞区段
wayside facility   地面信号
inherently [in'hiərəntli] *adv.*   固有地，本来地
car [kɑː] *n.*   车列，车辆
capacity [kə'pæsiti] *n.*   流量
intermediate track   区间
field location   线路点
geographic representation   站场型表示
illuminate [i'ljuːmineit] *v.*   标志，标记，照明
audible signal   听觉信号，音响信号
buzzer ['bʌzə] *n.*   蜂鸣器
switch controlling device   道岔控制设备
signal-clear indication light   信号开放表示灯
rotary ['rəutəri] *adj.*   旋转的
engraved letter   铭牌
exertion [ig'zɜːʃən] *n.*   执行，实行
departure [di'pɑːtʃə] *n.*   退出
appropriate [ə'prəupriət] *adj.*   适当的
publication [,pʌbli'keiʃən] *n.*   出版物，刊物
a succession of   一个接一个的，一系列的
be informed of   知道
lay out   陈列，布局
in the event of   万一，即使
be subject to   须经，受……的支配
in preparation for   以备，为……作准备

Notes to the Text

1. CTC was designed to enable the train dispatcher to control train movements directly, bypassing local operators and eliminating written train orders.

   译文 调度集中可使调度员直接控制列车运行，而无需车站操作员，并且取消了手写列车命令。

   bypassing 和 eliminating 是现在分词作状语，也可以放在句子的前面。

2. These lights are normally dark. When steadily illuminated (red), a light indicates that the A-C power is off at that location.

译文　这些灯平时是熄灭的。当一个红灯亮时，表明对应车站的交流电源停了。

off 表示"不工作的，断开的"。

3. These are usually arranged to sound momentarily at the time the track-occupancy indication is firstly displayed.

译文　这些设备一般设计成轨道占用灯一亮就鸣叫。

These 是指上文中的 an audible signal, bell or buzzer.

4. Their normal position is in the center which calls for the corresponding group of signals to display their stop aspects.

译文　它们平时处于中间位置，要求相应的信号灯显示停车。

Exercises to the Text

Ⅰ. **Translate the following terms into Chinese.**
(1) be adapted to	(2) be applied to	(3) wayside facilities
(4) at a field location	(5) in preparation for	(6) in correspondence with
(7) clear a signal	(8) the signal-clear indication lights
(9) power-operated switches	(10) track occupancy
(11) in the event of	(12) a broken rail

Ⅱ. **Decide whether each of the following statements is true or false according to the text.**
(1) CTC was first installed on the New York Central Railroad. (　)
(2) All interlocking devices of a centralized traffic control system are controlled from a single console. (　)
(3) Above a typical panel of a CTC system, is a track diagram which can show some information being helpful to operation. (　)
(4) The signal lever has a two-position rotary switch. (　)
(5) The switch levers are also rotary switches, normally two-position, being vertical position as normal. (　)

Ⅲ. **Answer the following questions according to the text.**
(1) Where are the switch lever and the signal lever on the CTC control panel?
(2) What is a centralized traffic control system made up of?
(3) What does it mean when the signal lever is in the center?
(4) Which position of the switch lever is normal?
(5) Which light in the barrel of the lever is lighted when the switch lever is turned to the right?

Ⅳ. **Translate the following passage into Chinese.**
　　A centralized traffic control system is made up of a succession of interlocking, all controlled from a single console. Automatic block signals are usually provided on intervening track. Such a system may be adapted to any existing signal installation and may be applied to single or multiple track. The control console, located in an office within, adjacent to, or remote from the installation, provides means for initiating the desired controls and displaying the indication which keeps the operator informed train

movements and track conditions. Important switches and crossovers are power-operated to expedite the movement of trains into and out of sidings, junctions, etc.

Reading Material

The CTC Board

The CTC board, or dispatching machine, was not an interlocking machine, but a control console. It was 54" high and 16" deep, with or without a desk, and came in 2.5 ft and 5.0 ft sections, which were placed side by side as necessary. Inside the cabinet were the switch and indicator lamp bodies, relays, wire cables, power supplies, a bell, and so forth. The single-stroke bell announced the arrival of a train at an OS track section. It could be turned off for most sections so that it only announced the approach of a train to CTC territory. From top to bottom, the board showed a static track diagram with mileages and siding capacities, the illuminated track diagram showed the position of trains, a row of switch levers, a row of signal levers, toggle switches to turn on a light at each control point for calling a maintainer, and the code starting switches. As mentioned above, there were also stick or calling-on push buttons, code indicators, and code canceling buttons. Other controls, such as switches for the switch heaters used in winter, were also sometimes present. The board did not show the signal aspects as in the animation; these have been added to show you how the signals responded to the commands and changed in track occupancy.

The movement of trains was recorded on a strip chart where a pen for each OS track section (OS means "on sheet", from the traditional reports that telegraph operators made to the dispatcher to update his train sheet) made a mark when a train occupied it. An OS section was the piece of track containing the switch, or any other track circuit. The chart was 16.5" wide, and moved at 3" per hour. A 200-foot roll of paper would last a month. A pen could be provided for each of up to 40 OS sections. The dispatcher drew short lines between the dots to make a complete record. This was only a record, and was not very useful to the dispatcher in handling trains. The dispatcher signed the train sheet when going off duty.

The dispatcher also had a telephone, with a loudspeaker or, less conveniently, earphones, and could signal a train crew or signal maintainer to call him at a telephone box by displaying a light in its vicinity, usually on the relay box. This was very important, since there were no longer any operators along the line to handle messages. Now, of course, this has been replaced by continuous contact by means of radio.

To allow control of a complete operating division of 100 miles or more, with perhaps twenty control points, some way had to be found to economize on wires, since one could not use direct wire control. This was first done with the one-wire system, that managed each control point with only one wire. The machine in our example used the later two-wire system, a modern coded system, where each control point had a unique code, and commands could be sent to any of the control points, while any control point could report conditions to the dispatcher. This machine, obviously, was much more convenient to use than the old, and provided much more information. When switches and signals were in the vicinity of the CTC board (as in many small installations) they were controlled by direct wire, not coded signals. CTC was one of the earliest uses of pulse coding in electronics, which is now widespread.

Exercises to the Material

Choose the best answer according to the material.

(1) Which of the following is not true about the later two-wire system? _____.
A. It was a modern coded system
B. With the later two-wire system, each control point had a unique code, and commands could be sent to any of the control points, while any control point could report conditions to the dispatcher
C. It was much more convenient to use than the one-wire system, and provided much more information
D. All switches and signals were controlled by direct wire, not coded signals

(2) The word "economize" in last paragraph is closest in meaning to _____.
  A. saving   B. scanty   C. economy   D. retrench

(3) The dispatcher had all the following devices but _____.
  A. a loudspeaker   B. a radio   C. a pen   D. a computer

(4) The chart referred in second paragraph was used to _____.
  A. record the movement of trains
  B. record the work of the dispatcher
  C. help the dispatcher to control the train
  D. make a mark when a train was absent

(5) _____ were placed inside the cabinet of the CTC board.
  A. The switches and relays   B. Indicator lamp bodies
  C. Wire cables, power supplies, a bell   D. All of above

Lesson 9 Industrial Railroad Systems(工业铁路系统)

Introduction

The term "industrial railroad" covers a wide variety of installations. In general, it applies to the use of railroad equipment by an industry on its own property for special transportation and material handling purposes. Large-scale activities such as steel mills and open-pit mines may utilize miles of track, dozens of locomotives and hundreds of cars. Smaller installations may involve a few hundred feet of track, a single locomotive and only a few cars.[1] Locomotives and cars may be similar to equipment used by mainline railroads, or may be of special design related to the material transported and functions required.

Regardless of size of function, it is necessary that an industrial railroad operate safely and efficiently. Railroad signaling principles and apparatus can be applied to achieve these objectives. In some cases, these applications are similar to those for mainline operation. Thus switch machines, switch circuit controllers, color light signals, and crossing warning signals for in-plant roadways are used just as in ordinary railroad operation.[2] Similarly, car retarders with radar speed detectors are used to regulate the speed of cars rolling from industrial hump yards so that pushing can proceed at maximum rate while cars roll to empty-car tracks at speeds which hold coupling impacts to acceptable levels. In other cases, the requirements of industrial railroad may be quite different.

One of the systems developed by GRS is of particular importance to industrial railroads, that is radio remote control of locomotives. It permits locomotives to be started, accelerated, braked, stopped, reversed at any point within line of sight or distances up to 2 000 feet from man-carried portable control units.[3] Fixed transmitters are suitable when operations are concentrated in the vicinity of the control point and do not require the operator to do work around cars being switched. Portable transmitters are useful for operations over spread-out areas and when work is required on or about fixed and portable control equipment.

Since portable control has great flexibility of application, it is appropriate to focus attention on portable operation. With portable remote control, regardless of locomotive position in the train, an operator can at all times ride the leading end of the train where he can clearly see conditions ahead. He can alight to throw switches, couple and uncouple cars or to work anywhere along the train without the need for using hand signals being obscured or misread potentially. For heavy operations, such as loading and dumping, he can be off the train at a location which provides visibility so that he can accurately spot cars which are safely distant from any hazards.

New Words and Expressions

industrial railroad　工业铁路
property ['prɔpəti] n.　特性；性质
transportation [,trænspɔː'teiʃən] n.　运输
handling ['hændliŋ] n.　运送；调度；处理
steel mill　钢厂
open-pit min　露天矿
locomotive [,ləukə'məutiv] n.　机车，火车头
objective [əb'dʒektiv] n.　目的；目标
retarder [ri'tɑːdə] n.　减速器；缓行器
radar speed detector　雷达测速器
regulate ['regjuleit] v.　调整；调解
car rolling　钩车溜放场
hump yard　驼峰编组场
pushing ['puʃiŋ] n.　推送
coupling ['kʌpliŋ] n.　车钩
impact ['impækt] n.　碰撞；冲击
radio remote control　无线电遥控
accelerate [æk'seləreit] v.　加速
reverse [ri'vɜːs] vt.　颠倒，倒转
fixed [fikst] adj.　固定的
flexibility [,fleksi'biliti] n.　适应性；灵活性
ride [raid] v.　骑，乘，驾

alight [ə'laɪt] v. 落下；下车
couple car 挂钩车
hand signal 手信号
obscure [əb'skjuə] adj. 暗的，朦胧的，模糊的，晦涩的
misread [mɪs'riːd] v. 误认；误读
load [ləud] v. 装载
dump [dʌmp] v. 倾卸
spot [spɔt] vt. 认出，发现
in the vicinity of 在……附近；靠近……
be appropriate to 适合；合乎
focus attention on 把注意力集中在

Notes to the Text

1. Large-scale activities such as steel mills and open-pit mines may utilize miles of track, dozens of locomotives and hundreds of cars. Smaller installations may involve a few hundred feet of track, a single locomotive and only a few cars.

   译文 大规模的工业化铁路，比如钢厂和露天矿厂会使用若干英里的铁路、数十台机车和几百辆车厢；而较小规模的工业化铁路可能就只有几百英尺铁路、一辆机车和几个车厢。

   activities 和 installations 都是指上文中的 industrial railroad installations，即工业化铁路的装置或设备。

2. Thus switch machines, switch circuit controllers, color light signals, and crossing warning signals for in-plant roadways are used just as in ordinary railroad operation.

   译文 所以，道岔转辙机、道岔电路控制器、色灯信号机，以及用于内部车道的道口报警信号系统的使用与在普通铁路上的运用是一样的。

   as 表示"与……一样"。

3. It permits locomotives to be started, accelerated, braked, stopped, reversed at any point within line of sight or distances up to 2 000 feet from man-carried portable control units.

   译文 这套系统能从便携式控制单元发出命令允许机车在视觉距离直到 2 000 英尺范围内的任何地点启动、加速、减速、停车，甚至转向。

   it 指上文中 the systems developed by GRS。

Exercises to the Text

Ⅰ. **Translate the following terms into Chinese.**

(1) dozens of locomotives　　(2) hundreds of cars　　(3) in some cases

(4) regardless of size of function　(5) mainline operation　(6) in-plant roadways

(7) man-carried portable　　(8) in the vicinity of the control point

Ⅱ. **Decide whether each of the following statements is true or false according to the text.**

(1) The industrial railroad applies to the use of railroad equipment by an industry on its own property for special transportation and material handling purposes. (　)

(2) Large-scale industrial railroad may utilize a few hundred feet of track, a single locomotive and only a few cars. (　)

(3) Locomotives and cars of the industrial railroad can not be similar to the equipments used by mainline railroads. （　　）

(4) The safety of an industrial railroad is not as important as the mainline railroads. （　　）

(5) Portable control has great flexibility of application to the industrial railroad. （　　）

III. Answer the following questions according to the text.

(1) How many locomotives and cars are there in the large-scale industrial railroad?

(2) Are the switch machines in the industrial railroad just as in ordinary railroad operation?

(3) Who developed the radio remote control of locomotives that is particular importance to industrial railroads?

Reading Material

The GRS Radio Remote Control System

The GRS radio remote control system has capacity for control of up to 64 locomotives operating in the same area.

Command Transmission—Locomotive address and commands are transmitted via 100 ms pulses of frequency-modulated radio carrier. Pulses are repeated once a second at random intervals. Each carries complete address and command information. Between pulses the carrier is off.

Coding Principles—The carrier is modulated simultaneously by a number of tones which make up a code for the locomotive address and the functions command. Either of two tones may be transmitted in each of ten code channels. A pulse is valid only when each channel carries one (but not more than one) legitimate tone. Invalid pulses are rejected.

Encoder and Transmitter—In the sending unit, insertion of the address code selects the six address tones. The function switches and pushbuttons on the control unit act through a diode matrix to select the four tones for the command channels. The resulting 10 tones are applied to the modulator of the transmitter.

Receiver and Decoder—The frequency-modulated transmit pulses are received, the address and command tones extracted, and the tones amplified. The amplified tones are fed to address and command tone detectors. The address detectors are connected to the logic circuitry through the code plug in the transmitter.

As in all control system related to train operation, safety is a paramount consideration. With radio remote control, safety is assured by the closed circuit concepts, the locomotive must continue to receive a proper signal at periodic intervals to avoid an enforced stop.

Depending on the position of the direction control switch, the sending unit automatically transmits the forward, reverse, or neutral directional command as a keep-alive check pulse.

If either the sending unit or the receiving unit fails, periodic reception of the direction command ceases and the locomotive stops automatically. Automatic stop also occurs if the locomotive moves out of range of the sending unit, or if the safety posture switch opens, thus interrupting transmission.

An additional safety feature is achieved by transmission of commands on a priority basis. One and only one command is transmitted at a time. If more than one command switch or pushbutton should be operated simultaneously, only the more restrictive of the functions called for is transmitted.

Exercises to the Material

Choose the best answer according to the material.

(1) From the facts in the text we can safely say that _____.
A. the GRS radio remote control system can control over 64 locomotives operating in the same area
B. the GRS radio remote control system can control less 64 locomotives operating in the same area
C. the GRS radio remote control system can control only 64 locomotives operating in the same area
D. the GRS radio remote control system can control about 64 locomotives operating in the same area

(2) Between pulses of the locomotive address and commands the carrier is _____.
A. normal　　　　B. wrong　　　　C. present　　　　D. absent

(3) A pulse is valid only when each channel carries _____.
　A. more than one legitimate tone　　B. one legitimate tone
　C. one illegitimate tone　　　　　　D. more than one illegitimate tone

(4) The command channels are required to _____.
　A. select 10 tones　　　　　　B. select 6 tones
　C. select 4 tones　　　　　　　D. select 14 tones

(5) The safety is a _____ consideration with radio remote control.
　A. vital　　　　　　　　　　　B. exclusive
　C. efficient　　　　　　　　　D. considered

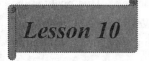 **Hump Classification Yard（驼峰编组场）**

Introduction

Now, GRS brings an advanced application of distributed microprocessor technology to the classification yard. In the new system, key functions once performed in a central minicomputer can now be distributed to dedicated microcomputer. The process control system of hump is built around a series of loosely coupled modules. Each module contains sufficient computing power to perform its individual function; appropriate modules contain interfaces to required field equipment.

Communication is handled through a simple interface which passes information from one module to another.[1]

The following are the leading features of the control system design.

Modular design

The backbone of the control system is a network of microprocessor modules that provide retarder and switch control. One module or set of modules is associated with each group, ensuring accurate and reliable control. This modularity allows quick repair and means that failure of a single group does not disable the yard.[2] The modules are interconnected via an appropriate communication interface.

The heart of the process control systems is the online processor, it automatically routes cars to their assigned tracks, regulates their speed to provide proper coupling, and supervises yard operation without a retarder operator.[3] Each yard has a standby alternate processor that automatically take over control if needed. This redundancy of key components minimizes any need for curtailing humping operations due to the failure of a vital part of the system.

The computer system is housed in the hump control tower, and all yard operations, with the exception of the pull down yard-master, are positioned in the same building. Once the new system went into service, the previous retarder operator positions were abolished, along with the buildings they were housed in.

Better information, better operation

Previously, the retarder operators used lists to indicate how to throw the car to the proper track via switches. The lists also showed the commodity of the car to indicate a reasonable coupling speed to the retarder operator.

Lists are still used to show how to route a car with the new process control system, but better information is used to calculate the best exit speed from the retarders.[4] Test sections measure the ability of the car, the effects of weather conditions, distance-to-couple, ability of the tracks, grades and direction of the tracks.

Two test sections are used to measure the ability of the cars. The test sections are located between the top retarder and the intermediate retarders because there is not enough space in the intermediate and group retarders, before the top factors are considered.

Instead of using operators to judge how full a track is, the process control system uses an automatic distance-to-couple sub-system to determine where the last car is located.[5] This enables the cars to couple at the desired speed of approximately four miles per hour. Weather has a significant impact on humping operations. To allow for this, a weather subsystem provides data about temperature, wind speed and direction, and wet or dry conditions. The process control system automatically compensates for the effects of weather.

Predicting the best exit speed is not enough, the retarders must be controlled so the actual exit speed closely matches the requested exit speed. Radar units at each retarder send speed measurements back to the system, which makes immediate changes as needed to control the cars to the requested exit speed. Speed control is so much more accurate with the new system that damage to the cars and their contents has been significantly reduced.

New Words and Expressions

hump classification yard　驼峰编组场
distributed microprocessor　分布式微处理器
key function　关键性功能
dedicated ['dedikeitid] *adj*.　专用的
process control　过程控制
loosely coupled module　积木式模块
backbone ['bækbəun] *n*.　主干；骨架
disable [dis'eibl] *v*.　使残废，使失去能力，丧失能力
communication interface　通信接口
assigned [ə'sain] *adj*.　指定的；分配的

supervise ['sju:pəvaiz] v. 监督
redundancy [ri'dʌndənsi] n. 冗余
curtail [kɜ:'teil] n. 缩短
control tower 控制塔
yardmaster ['jɑ:dmɑ:stə] n. 调车场主任
abolish [ə'bɔliʃ] v. 废除；废弃
commodity [kə'mɔditi] n. 物品；货物
exit speed 出口速度
sub-system ['sʌbsistim] n. 子系统
approximately [ə'prɔksimitli] adv. 近似地，大约
compensate ['kɔmpənseit] v. 补偿；校正
predict [pri'dikt] v. 预知，预言，预报
be distributed to 分配给
with the exception of 除……之外
go into service 投入运行
be based on 基于；根据
have a significant impact on 对……有显著影响

Notes to the Text

1. Communication is handled through a simple interface which passes information from one module to another.

   译文 通过一个简单的接口实现通信，使信息从一个模块传递到另一个模块。

   由 which 引导的从句修饰 a simple interface。

2. This modularity allows quick repair and means that failure of a single group does not disable the yard.

   译文 这种模块式结构可实现快速维修，意味着单个模块的故障不会导致驼峰不能工作。

3. The heart of the process control systems is the online processor, it automatically routes cars to their assigned tracks, regulates their speed to provide proper coupling, and supervises yard operation without a retarder operator.

   译文 过程控制系统的核心是在线处理器。它能自动地将车辆推送到指定的轨道，并自动调节速度以保证车辆正确勾挂，同时在没有减速器操作员的情况下监督驼峰场的工作情况。

4. Lists are still used to show how to route a car with the new process control system, but better information is used to calculate the best exit speed from the retarders.

   译文 新的过程控制系统仍然使用清单来表明如何按路线发送车辆，但使用更好的信息来精确计算减速器的最佳出口速度。

5. Instead of using operators to judge how full a track is, the process control system uses an automatic distance-to-couple sub-system to determine where the last car is located.

   译文 过程控制系统不再使用操作员去判断一个轨道的车辆是否饱和，而是用自动测量钩挂距离子系统来确定最后一个车皮在什么位置。

   instead of 引导介词状语。

Exercises to the Text

Ⅰ. **Translate the following terms into Chinese.**

(1) the classification yard (2) key function (3) the retarder operator
(4) an automatic distance-to-couple sub-system (5) the rollability of the cars
(6) wet or dry conditions (7) distributed microprocessor (8) be distributed to

Ⅱ. **Decide whether each of the following statements is true or false according to the text.**

(1) In the classification yard, key functions cannot be distributed to dedicated microcomputer with distributed microprocessor technology. ( )
(2) Modular design is one of the leading features of the process control system design. ( )
(3) Better information and better operation are the leading features of the process control system design too. ( )
(4) In the new process control system, lists are used to show how to route a car. ( )
(5) Weather has a significant impact on humping operations. ( )

Ⅲ. **Answer the following questions according to the text.**

(1) What is the backbone of the process control system?
(2) How to do with the weather that has a significant impact on humping operations?
(3) Where are the test sections located?

Reading Material

The Control System

This is a typical example of the control system, which uses distributed micro-process technology in yard classification operation. It includes five modules.

Operator communication, plus hump control (OPCOM+)

OPCOM+ is the central building block for the system. It provides communication switching between the electronic components of the system as well as communications between the system and the operators.

The hump control portion controls the message flow of the system. It receives messages from other modules, gives task to the appropriate module, and sends instructions. This module also keeps statistics and sends information for cuts currently in progress and calculates retarder exit speed. The exit speed takes into account the weight class of the cut, the measured rolling resistance and its projection to the destination track (length of curve, grade, etc.) and distance to couple. The exit speed determination also includes provision for modification of the rolling resistance, based on the weather (wind velocity, temperature, and moisture).

The operator communications portion provides communications between the system and the operators. Operators can enter commands and request information to be displayed on a CRT screen or printer.

There are two OPCOM+ modules, a prime and a backup. All keyboard inputs and MIS (Management Information System) inputs are received by the prime OPCOM+, and also sent to the backup OPCOM+. The backup OPCOM+ processes all messages received but suppresses all outputs. If the prime OPCOM+ should fail, the backup OPCOM+ is immediately ready to take over.

Automatic retarder control (MARC)

Using information from OPCOM+ and from the restarder equipment, MARC provides accurate and efficient control of the cut, MARC allows yard operation in automatic or semi-automatic mode.

Crest monitor (CMON)

CMON monitors all crest detection equipment, including wheel detectors, weight detectors, cut light detectors, bulkhead height detectors, loose flange detectors, dragging equipment detectors, and weight-in motion scales; it accommodates many variations in crest equipment and equipment placements.

Automatic switching control (MASC)

MASC operates and controls switches as the cuts approach. This offers a high degree of reliability in this critical function.

Automatic switching includes wheel detectors at switches, blocked track, stall detection and protection, corning prevention, and catch-up detection.

Distance-to-couple (MADTC)

MADTC surveys all throat tracks and maintains a "table of fullness" for each track. When requested, MADTC monitors a single cut's distance-to-couple at fixed intervals and forwards both the time and distance to the requester. MADTC determines if a cut is rolling forward or backward or if stopped. If a failure is detected in the automatic distance-to-couple sub-system, that track is automatically switched to a backup car count system.

MIS interface

The MIS process-control interface allows hump lists and other directives to be sent to the control system. As-humped records and other informative messages are sent to the MIS computer via this interface.

Exercises to the Material

Choose the best answer according to the material.

(1) From the facts in the text we cannot safely say that OPCOM+ provides communication switching between _____.

    A. the electronic components of the system   B. the train drivers and the operators

    C. the system and the operators   D. the control center of the system and the operators

(2) To calculate retarder exit speed, the following considerations must be took into account but _____.

A. the weight class of the cut and the measured rolling resistance

B. the mount of the rolling cars

C. its projection to the destination track (length of curve, grade, etc.) and distance to couple

D. provision for modification of the rolling

(3) From the text we cannot safely say that _____.

A. only the prime OPCOM+ receive all keyboard inputs and MIS inputs

B. the prime OPCOM+ and the backup OPCOM+ both receive all keyboard inputs and MIS inputs

C. the backup OPCOM+ processes all received messages but suppresses all outputs when the prime

OPCOM is normal

D. if the prime OPCOM+ should fail, the backup OPCOM+ is immediately ready to take over

(4) The word "critical" in paragraph 8 is closest in meaning to _____.

A. serious　　　　　B. different　　　　　C. pivotal　　　　　D. desperate

(5) Which of the following is not true about Distance-to-couple (MADTC)? _____.

A. MADTC determines if a cut is rolling forward or backward or stopped

B. MADTC surveys all throat tracks and maintains a "table of fullness" for each track

C. MADTC can detect a failure in automatic distance-to-couple sub-system

D. MADTC can monitor cuts' distance-to-couple at fixed intervals and forward both the time and distance to the requester

附录 A 专业英语中的常用语法知识

动词不定式

动词不定式是非谓语动词的一种，由不定式符号 to 加动词原形构成。之所以叫做"不定式"，因为它的形式不像谓语动词那样受到主语人称和数的限制。但是，动词不定式又具有动词的许多特点：它可以有自己的宾语、状语及宾语补足语。动词不定式和它的宾语、状语及宾语补足语构成不定式短语。除此之外，不定式还有时态和语态的变化。

例：Today we use computers to help us do most of our work.

译文：如今人们使用计算机帮助做大部分工作。

句中，动词不定式 to help 带有宾语 us 和宾语补足语 do most of our work。

动词不定式通常具有名词性、形容词性和副词性，因此可以充当句子的主语、表语、宾语、定语、状语和补足语。下面分别叙述动词不定式在句中的作用。

1. 做主语

动词不定式(短语)做主语，较多地用来表示一个特定的行为或事情，谓语动词需要用第三人称单数，且常用 it 做形式主语。

例：To know something about computer is important.

译文：懂得一些计算机的知识很重要。

句中，To know something about computer 是动词不定式短语，在句子中做主语。

不定式短语做主语时，为了句子的平衡，常常把它放在句尾，而用形式主语代替不定式放在句首。

例：It is necessary to learn Visual PASIC.

译文：学习 Visual PASIC 是很有必要的。

句中，It 是形式主语，而真正的主语是动词不定式 to learn Visual PASIC。

2. 做表语

不定式可放在系动词后面做表语。

例：To see is to believe.

译文：眼见为实。

句中，to believe 放在 is 后面做表语。

例：Our task today is to work out the design.

译文：我们今天的工作是把设计做出来。

3. 做宾语

不定式(短语)在某些及物动词后可做宾语。这类及物动词通常有 want, like, wish, hope, begin, decide, forget, ask, learn, help, expect, intend, promise, pledge 等。

例：This helps to save coal and reduce the cost of electricity.

译文：这有助于节约用煤以及降低发电成本。

例：They decided to do the experiment again.

译文：他们决定再次做这个实验。

当某些动词后面做宾语的不定式必须有自己的补语才能使意思完整时，要用 it 做形式宾语，而将真正的宾语(即不定式)后置。常用这种结构的动词有 think, find, make, consider, feel 等。

例：The use of semi-conductor devices with integrated circuits makes it possible to develop miniaturized equipment.

译文：半导体装置和集成电路一起使用使得发展微型设备成为可能。

句中，不定式短语 to develop miniaturized equipment 是形式上的宾语。

4. 做定语

动词不定式(短语)做定语时，通常放在它所修饰的名词(或代词)之后。

例：He never had the chance to learn how to use computers.

译文：他从来没有学习计算机的机会。

句中，to learn how to use computers 是动词不定式，在句中做定语，修饰和限定 the chance。

有时，动词不定式与它所修饰的名词是逻辑上的动宾关系。

例：We usually define energy as the ability to do work.

译文：我们通常将能量定义为做功的能力。

动词不定式做定语除修饰名词外，还可以修饰代词和数词。

例：There is something to do.

译文：还有一些事情要做。

5. 做状语

不定式做状语可以修饰句中的动词、形容词、副词或全句。主要表示目的、程度、结果、范围、原因等。

例：We are glad to hear that you have bought a computer.

译文：听说你买了一台计算机，我们十分高兴。(表示原因)

例：To meet our production needs, more and more electric power will be generated.

译文：为了满足生产的需要，将生产越来越多的电力。(表示目的)

例：Solar batteries have been used in satellites to produce electricity.

译文：人造卫星上已经用太阳能电池发电了。(表示结果)

应该注意，在 too...to 结构的 too 前面有 not，only，but，never 等含有否定意义的词时，后面的不定式就没有否定意义。

例：English is not too difficult to learn.

译文：英语并不难学。

6. 做宾语补足语

某些及物动词要求不定式做宾语补足语。宾语补足语是对宾语的补充说明。

例：A force may cause a body to move.

译文：力可以使物体移动。

句中，a body 是宾语，不定式 to move 是宾语补足语。

例：Conductors allow a large number of electrons to move freely.

译文：导体允许大量的电子自由运动。

当 make，let，have，see，hear，watch，notice，feel 等动词后面用不定式做宾语补足语时,不定式都不带 to。这一点特别重要。

例：I often hear people talk about this kind of printer.

译文：我经常听人们谈论这种打印机。

句中，talk about this kind of printer 是不带 to 的动词不定式短语，在句中做宾语 people 的补足语。

7. 做主语补足语

当主动语态的句子变成被动语态时，主动语态句子中的宾语补足语就在被动语态中变成主语补足语。若主动语态中的宾语补足语由动词不定式构成，则该句变为被动语态后它也相应地变为主语补足语。

例：He was asked to do the experiment at once.

译文：有人请他马上做实验。

但是，当 make，let，have，see，hear，watch，notice，feel 等动词的句子变为被动语态时，原来在主动语态时做宾语补足语的动词不定式这时也变为主语补足语，此时，动词不定式中的 to 不能省略。

例：He was made to finish repairing the printer.

译文：他被迫马上修好打印机。

分 词

分词是非谓语动词的一种。分词有现在分词和过去分词两种。规则动词的现在分词由动词原形加-ing 构成，过去分词由动词原形加-ed 构成；不规则动词的分词形式，其构成是不规则的。分词没有人称和数的变化，具有形容词和副词的作用；同时还保留着动词的特征，只是在句中不能独立做谓语。

现在分词所表示的动作具有主动的意义，而及物动词的过去分词表示的动作具有被动的意义。现在分词与过去分词在时间关系上，前者表示动作正在进行，后者表示的动作往往已经完成。现在分词表示的动作与谓语动词表示的动作相比，具有同时性，而过去分词则具有先时性。

分词在句子中具有形容词词性和副词词性，可以充当句子的定语、表语、状语和补足语。下面分别举例说明现在分词和过去分词在句子中的作用。

1. 现在分词

(1) 做定语

例：They insisted upon their device being tested under operating conditions.

译文：他们坚持他们的装置要在运转条件下检测。

例：An atom contains small particles carrying two kinds of electricity.

译文：原子含有带两种电荷的粒子。

(2) 做表语

例：The result of the experiment was encouraging.

译文：实验结果令人鼓舞。

(3) 做补足语

例：You'd better start the computer running.

译文：你还是把计算机启动起来好。

(4) 做状语

例：While making an experiment on an electric circuit, they learned of an important electricity law.

译文：他们在做电路实验时,学到了一条重要的电学定律。

2. 过去分词

(1) 做定语

例：The heat energy produced is equal to the electrical energy utilized.

译文：产生的热量与所用的电能相等。

例：The charged capacitor behaves as a secondary battery.

译文：充了电的电容就像一个蓄电池一样。

(2) 做表语

例：Some substances remain practically unchanged when heated.

译文：有几种物质受热时几乎没有变化。

(3) 做补足语

例：I don't know if we can get the computer repaired in time.

译文：我不知道我们能否按时修好计算机。

(4) 做状语

例：Given the voltage and current, we can determine the resistance.

译文：已知电压和电流，我们就可以求出电阻。

动 名 词

动名词是一种非谓语动词，由动词原形加词尾-ing构成，形式上和现在分词相同。由于动名词和现在分词的形成历史、意义和作用都不一样，通常把它们看做是两种不同的非谓语动词。它没有人称和数的变化。动名词具有动词词性和名词词性，因而又可以把它称为"动词化的名词"和"名词化的动词"。在句中充当主语、表语、定语和宾语等。

例：Excuse me for coming late.

译文：对不起，我来晚了。

句中，coming是动名词，late做coming的状语。

下面分别举例说明动名词在句子中的作用。

1. 做主语

动名词做主语表示一件事或一个行为，其谓语动词用第三人称单数。

例：Learning computer science is very important now.

译文：现在学习计算机很重要。

例：Changing resistance is a method for controlling the flow of the current.

译文：改变电阻是控制电流流动的一种方法。

动名词做主语时，也可用做形式主语，放在句首，而将真正的主语——动名词短语放在谓语之后。

例：It's no good using this kind of material.

译文：采用这类材料是毫无用处的。

2. 做宾语

动名词可以在一些及物动词和介词后做介词宾语。要求动名词做宾语的常用及物动词有finish, enjoy, avoid, stop, need, start, mean 等。

例：This printer needs repairing.

译文：这台打印机需要修理一下。

例：I remember having repaired this machine.

译文：我记得曾经修过这部机器。

英语中，suggest, finish, avoid, stop, admit, keep, require, postpone, practice, fancy, deny 等动词都用动名词做宾语，不能用不定式做宾语。但是在love, tike, hate, begin, start, continue, remember, forget, regret 等词后面可以用动名词做宾语，也可以用动词不定式做宾语。

例：Do you like watching / to watch TV?

译文：你喜欢看电视吗？

动名词做宾语时，如本身带有补足语，则常用it做形式宾语。而将真正的宾语——动名词放在补足语的后面。

例：I found it useless arguing with her.

译文：我发现与她辩论没有用。

下例是动名词做介词的宾语：

例：Thank you forgiving me so much help.

译文：谢谢你给我那么多帮助。

3. 做表语

动名词做表语为名词性表语。表示主语的内容，而不说明主语的性质。主语常为具有一定内涵的名词，这点与不定式做表语相似。动名词做表语与进行时的区别在于主语能否执行该词的行为。能执行，即为进行时；否则，即为动名词做表语(系表结构)。

例：The function of a capacitor is storing electricity.

译文：电容器的功能是存储电能。

例：Seeing is believing.

译文：眼见为实。

句中，动名词 seeing 做主语，believing 做表语。

4. 做定语

动名词做定语为名词性定语，说明名词的用途，与所修饰名词之间没有逻辑主谓关系，这点是与现在分词做定语相区别的关键：动名词做定语只能使用单词，不可用动名词短语；只能放在所修饰名词前面，不可后置。

例：Rubber is found to be a good insulating material.

译文：橡胶是一种良好的绝缘材料。

例：English is one of the working languages at international meetings.

译文：英语是国际会议上使用的工作语言之一。

5. 做宾语补足语

动名词在句中的作用相当于名词，故可做宾语补足语。动名词只能在少数动词后做宾语补足语，补充说明宾语的性质、行为或状态，与宾语具有逻辑主谓关系。

例：We call this process testing.

译文：人们称这个过程为检测。

句中，动名词 testing 做宾语 this process 的补足语。

被 动 语 态

语态是动词的一种形式，它表示主语和谓语的不同关系。语态有两种：主动语态和被动语态。主动语态表示句子的主语是谓语动作的发出者；被动语态表示主语是谓语动作的承受者。也就是说，主动语态句子中的宾语，在被动语态中做句子的主语。由于被动语态句子的主语是谓语动作的承受者，故只有及物动词才会有被动语态。

主动语态：He designed this building.

译文：他设计了这座大楼。

被动语态：This building was designed by him.

译文：这座大楼是他设计的。

在科技英语中，为了着重说明客观事物和过程，被动语态用得更为广泛。被动语态的构成如下：

主语+be+(及物动词)过去分词

1. 科技英语中主要时态的被动语态形式

(1) 一般现在时

一般现在时的被动语态构成如下：

主语+am (is, are) +及物动词的过去分词

例：I am asked to solve this problem by him.

译文：他请我解决这个问题。

例：The switches are used for the opening and closing of electrical circuits.

译文：开关是用来开启和关闭电路的。

(2) 一般过去时

一般过去时的被动语态构成如下：

主语+was (were) +及物动词的过去分词

例：That plotter was not bought in Beijing.

译文：那台绘图仪不是在北京买的。

例：The insulator was burned out by overheating.

译文：绝缘体因过热而被烧毁。

(3) 一般将来时

一般将来时的被动语态构成如下：

主语+will be+及物动词的过去分词

当主语是第一人称时，可用：

主语+shall be+及物动词的过去分词

例：I shall not be allowed to do it.

译文：不会让我做这件事的。

例：What tools will be needed for the job?

译文：工作中需要什么工具？

(4) 现在进行时

现在进行时的被动语态构成如下：

主语+is (are) being+及物动词的过去分词

例：Our printer is being repaired by John.

译文：约翰正在修理我们的打印机。

例：Electron tubes are found in various old products and are still being used in the circuit of some new products.

译文：在各种老产品里看到的电子管，在一些新产品的电路中也还在使用。

(5) 过去进行时

过去进行时的被动语态构成如下：

主语+was (were) being+及物动词的过去分词

例：The laboratory building was being built then.

译文：实验大楼当时正在建造。

例：The accident was being investigated.

译文：事故那时正在调查中。

(6) 现在完成时

现在完成时的被动语态构成如下：

主语+have (has) been+及物动词的过去分词

例：The letter has not been posted.

译文：信还没有寄出。

例：New techniques have been developed by the research department.

译文：研究部门发展了新技术。

(7) 过去完成时

过去完成时的被动语态构成如下：

主语+had been+及物动词的过去分词

例：When he came back, the problem had already been solved.

译文：他回来时，问题已经解决了。

例：Electricity had been discovered for more than one thousand years by the time it came into practical use.

译文：电在发现一千多年之后，才得到实际应用。

2. 常用被动语态的几种情况

(1) 当人们强调的是动作的承受者或给动作的承受者较多关注时，多用被动语态。这时由于动作的执行者处于次要地位，句子中 by 引导的短语可以省略。

例：The virus in the computer has been found out.

译文：计算机中的病毒已经找出来了。

(2) 当人们不知道或不想说出动作的执行者时，可使用被动语态。这时句子中不带由 by 引导的短语。

例：Electricity was discovered a very long time ago.

译文：电是很久以前发现的。

(3) 当动作的执行者是"物"而不是"人"时，常用被动语态。

例：This machine is controlled by a computer.

译文：这台机器由计算机控制。

(4) 当动作的执行者已为大家所熟知，而没有必要说出来时，也常常使用被动语态。

例：This factory was built twenty years ago.

译文：这座工厂是二十年前兴建的。

(5) 使用被动语态能更好地安排句子。

例：The professor came into the hall and was warmly applauded by the audience.

译文：教授走进大厅，大家热烈鼓掌。

定 语 从 句

定语从句又称关系从句，在句子中起定语作用，修饰一个名词或代词，有时也可修饰一个句子。被定语从句修饰的词叫先行词，定语从句通常跟在先行词的后面。

例：This is the software that I would like to buy.

译文：这就是我想买的那个软件。

that I would like to buy 是定语从句，the software 是先行词。

通常，定语从句都由关系代词 that, which, who, whom, whose 和关系副词 when, where, why, how 引导。关系代词和关系副词往往放在先行词和定语从句之间，起联系作用，同时还代替先行词在句中担任一定的语法成分，如主语、宾语、定语和状语等。

例：The man who will give us a lecture is a famous professor.

译文：将要给我们做讲演的人是位著名的教授。

该句中，who will give us a lecture 是由关系代词 who 引导的定语从句，修饰先行词 the mad，who 在从句中做主语。

定语从句根据其与先行词的密切程度可分为限定性定语从句和非限定性定语从句。

1. 限定性定语从句

限定性定语从句与先行词关系密切,是整个句子不可缺少的部分,没有它,句子的意思就不完整或不明确。这种定语从句与主句之间不用逗号隔开,译成汉语时,一般先译定语从句,再译先行词。

限定性定语从句如果修饰人,一般用关系代词 who,有时也用 that。若关系代词在句子中做主语,则 who 用得较多,且不可省略;若关系代词在句子中做宾语,就应当使用宾格 whom 或 that,但在大多数情况下都可省略。若表示所属,就应用 whose。

限定性定语从句如果修饰物,用 that 较多,也可用 which。它们可在句中做主语,也可做宾语。若做宾语,则大多可省略。

例:Those who agree with me please put up your hands.

译文:同意我的观点的人请举手。

who agree with me 是定语从句,修饰 those。who 既是引导词,又在句中做主语,who 不能省略。

例:PC tools are tools whose functions are very advanced.

译文:PC tools 是功能很先进的工具。

因为 functions 和 tools 之间是所属关系,故用所有格 whose。

例:The mouse is an instrument which operators often use.

译文:鼠标是操作员经常使用的一种工具。

which 引导的定语从句修饰 an instrument。因为 which 在从句中做 use 的宾语,故可省略。

下面各例也是限定性定语从句:

例:That is the reason why I am not in favor of the plan.

译文:这就是我不赞成该计划的原因。

例:Potential energy is the energy that a body has by virtue of its position.

译文:位能是指物体由于自身的位置而具有的能量。

例:I want to buy a car whose color is blue.

译文:我想买一辆蓝色的车。

2. 非限定性定语从句

非限定性定语从句与先行词的关系比较松散,从句只对先行词附加说明,如果缺少,不会影响句子的主要意思。从句与主句之间常用逗号隔开,译成汉语时,从句常单独译成一句。

非限定性定语从句在修饰人时用 who,whom 或 whose,修饰物时用 which,修饰地点和时间时用 where 和 when 引导。

例:We do experiments with a computer, which helps to do many things.

译文:我们利用计算机做实验,计算机可帮助做许多工作。

which 引导的非限定性定语从句是对先行词 a computer 的说明。

例:The meeting will be put off till next week, when we shall have made all the preparations.

译文:会议将推迟到下周,那时我们将做好一切准备。

例:They'll fly to America, where they plan to stay for 10 days.

译文:他们将飞往美国,计划在那逗留 10 天。

例:Mechanical energy is changed into electric energy, which in turn is changed into mechanical energy.

译文:机械能转变为电能,而电能又转变为机械能。

状 语 从 句

状语从句在句中起副词作用，故又称为副词从句。

状语从句可位于主句前，也可位于主句后；前置时，从句后常用逗号与主句隔开；后置时，从句前通常不使用逗号。状语从句一般由从属连词和起连词作用的词组来引导。

状语从句在句中做状语，修饰主句中的动词、形容词等。可表示时间、原因、目的、结果、条件、比较、方式、让步和地点等不同含义。

1. 时间状语从句

引导时间状语从句的连词或词组很多，但可根据所表示时间的长短以及与主句谓语动词行为发生的先后这两点去理解和区别。

这些连词或词组有：when (当……时候), as (当……时候，随着，一边……一边), while (在……期间), before (在……之前), after (在……之后), since (自从……以来), until (till) (直到……才), as soon as (一……就), no sooner...than (刚一……就……), once (一旦), every time (每次) 等。

例：It changes speed and direction when it moves.

译文：在运动时它改变速度和方向。

例：Check the circuit before you begin the experiment.

译文：检查好线路再开始做实验。

例：Electricity has found wide application since it was discovered.

译文：自从发现电以来，它就获得了广泛的应用。

例：No sooner had the push button been pressed than the motor began to run.

译文：按钮刚一压下，马达就开动了。

2. 原因状语从句

引导原因状语从句的连词和词组有 because (因为), as (由于), since (既然，由于), now that (既然), in that (因为) 等。其中前三个较常用，它们表示原因的正式程度依次为 because≥ since ≥as。

例：Electric energy is used most widely mainly because it can be easily produced, controlled, and transmitted.

译文：电能用得最广，主要是因为发电容易，而且控制和输送也方便。

3. 目的状语从句

目的状语从句由 in order that (为了，以便), so that (为了，以便), that (为了), lest (以免，以防), for fear that (以免，以防) 等引导。

例：He handled the instrument with care for fear (that) it should be damaged.

译文：他小心地弄那仪器，生怕把它弄坏了。

4. 结果状语从句

引导结果状语从句的连词有：so that (结果，以致), so...that (如此……以致), such...that (这样……以致) 等。注意 so 后接形容词或副词，而 such 后跟名词。

例：This problem is so difficult that it will take us a lot of time to work it out.

译文：这道题很难，我们要用很多时间才能解出。

5. 条件状语从句

条件状语从句用来表示前提和条件。通常由以下连词引导：

if (如果), unless (除非), provided / providing that (假如), as long as (只要), in case (如果), on condition that (条件是……), suppose / supposing (假如) 等。

例：A physical body will not tend to expand unless it is heated.

译文：除非受热，否则物体不会有膨胀的倾向。

6. 比较状语从句

比较状语从句经常是省略句，一般都是省略了重复部分；省略之后不影响句意，反而结构简练。部分比较状语从句还有倒装现象。

比较状语从句由下列连词引导：as...as (像……一样), than (比), not so (as)... as (不像……一样), the more...the more (愈……愈), as...so (正如……那样) 等。

例：Electron tubes are not so light in weight as semi-conductor devices.

译文：电子管的重量不如半导体器件那么轻。

例：He finished the work earlier than we had expected.

译文：他完成这项工作比我们预计的要早。

7. 方式状语从句

方式状语从句通常由下列连词引导：

as (如同，就像), as if (though) (好像，仿佛) 等。as 引导的方式状语从句常常是一个省略句。as if 引出的常是一个虚拟语气的句子，表示没有把握的推测，或是一种夸张的比喻。

例：The earth itself behaves as though it were an enormous magnet.

译文：地球本身的作用就像一个大磁铁一样。

8. 让步状语从句

让步状语从句表示在相反的(不利的)条件下，主句行为依然发生了。

引导让步状语从句的有：(al)though (虽然), even if (though) (即使), as (尽管), whatever (不管), however (无论怎样), no matter (how，what，where，when) (不管怎样、什么、哪里、何时), whether...or (不论……还是) 等。

例：It is important to detect such flows，even if they are very slight，before the part is installed.

译文：在安装部件之前，即使变形很轻微，也必须探测出来。

例：Much as computer languages differ，they have something in common.

译文：尽管计算机语言之间各不相同，但它们仍有某些共同点。

9. 地点状语从句

引导地点状语从句的词常用的有 where (在……地方，哪里), wherever (在任何地方), everywhere (每一……地方) 等。

例：She found her pen where she had left them.

译文：她的笔是她在原来放笔的地方找到的。

附录 B 轨道交通运输与信号专业英语术语

Ⅰ 轨道交通运输专业术语

1. 城市公共交通　　urban public transport
2. 公共交通方式　　public transport mode
3. 城市公共交通系统　　urban public transport system
4. 大运量客运系统　　mass transit system
5. 快速轨道交通　　rail rapid transit（RRT）
6. 地下铁道，地铁　　subway
7. 单轨运输系统　　monorail transit system
8. 新交通系统　　new transport system
9. 应急公共交通系统　　emergency public transport system
10. 公共交通信息系统　　public transport information system
11. 公共交通优先　　public transport priority
12. 公共汽车优先通行系统　　bus priority system
13. 城市公共交通企业　　urban public transport enterprise
14. 城市公共交通标志　　urban public transport sign
15. 公共交通工具　　public transport means
16. 公共交通线路　　public transport line
17. 公共交通线路设施　　public transport line facilities
18. 公共交通线路网　　public transport network
19. 公共交通车站　　public transport stop，public transport station
20. 公共交通停车场　　public transport parking place
21. 公共交通枢纽　　public transport junction
22. 城市公共交通规划　　urban public transport planning
23. 公共交通线路布局　　public transport network distribution
24. 公共交通场站布局　　public transport yard and station arrangement
25. 城市公共交通客流预测　　urban public transport passenger flow forecast
26. 城市公共交通客流调查　　urban public transport passenger flow investigation
27. 城市公共交通票价制　　urban public transport fare structure
28. 城市公共交通运行调度　　urban public transport scheduling
29. 客流　　passenger flow
30. 客流量　　passenger flow volume
31. 出行方式（出行采用的交通方式）　　trip mode
32. 出行时间（一次出行中，由起点到终点所花费的时间）　　travel time
33. 高峰时间（一天中，客流量最大的时段）　　peak time
34. 非高峰时间（客流高峰时间以外的时段）　　off-peak time

Ⅱ 轨道信号专业术语

1. 4 毫米锁闭　　check 4mm opening of a switch point
2. 矮型信号机　　dwarf signal
3. 安全电路　　vital circuit
4. 按钮　　push-in button
5. 按钮表示　　button indication
6. 半自动闭塞机　　semi-automatic block machine
7. 半自动闭塞联系电路　　liaison circuit with semi-automatic blocks
8. 半自动化驼峰系统　　semi-automatic hump yard system
9. 保护区段　　overlap protection block section
10. 备电源　　stand-by power source
11. 闭路式轨道电路　　close type track circuit
12. 闭塞分区　　block section
13. 标准分路灵敏度　　standard shunting sensitivity
14. 表示灯　　indication lamp
15. 表示电路　　indication circuit
16. 表示对象　　indicated object
17. 表示连接杆　　connecting rod for indication
18. 并联式轨道电路　　multiply connected track circuit
19. 并置信号点　　double signal location
20. 不对称脉冲轨道电路　　asymmetrical impulse track circuit
21. 不限时人工解锁　　manual non-time release
22. 操纵台　　operating console
23. 侧撞　　conering
24. 测长　　distance-to-coupling measurement
25. 测试环线　　test loop
26. 测速　　speed measurement
27. 测重　　weight sensing
28. 测阻　　rollability measurement
29. 车站控制　　station master control
30. 出站信号机　　starting signal
31. 磁路系统　　magnetic circuit
32. 错误办理　　wrong handling
33. 错误开放信号　　wrong clearing of a signal
34. 错误显示　　wrong indication
35. 单独操纵继电式电气集　　individual level type all-relay interlocking
36. 单轨条式轨道电路　　single rail track circuit
37. 单线臂板信号机　　single wire semaphore signal
38. 单线继电半自动闭塞　　single track all-relay semi-automatic block system

39. 导线导轮　　wire carrier
40. 到发线出岔电路　　protection circuit with switch lying in receiving
41. 道岔表示　　switch indication
42. 道岔表示电源　　power source for switch indication
43. 道岔表示器　　switch indicator
44. 道岔错误表示　　false indication of a switch
45. 道岔定位表示　　switch normal indication
46. 道岔动作电源　　power source for switch operation
47. 道岔反位表示　　switch reverse indication
48. 道岔封锁　　switch closed up
49. 道岔控制电路　　switch control circuit
50. 道岔控制电源　　power source for switch control
51. 道岔区段　　section with a switch or switches
52. 道岔人工解锁　　manual release of a locked switch
53. 道岔锁闭表示　　switch locked indication
54. 道岔中途转换　　switch thrown under moving cars
55. 道口信号机　　highway level crossing signal
56. 道口信号控制盘　　highway level crossing signal control panel
57. 敌对信号　　conflicting signal
58. 地面设备　　wayside equipment
59. 电动臂板信号机　　electric semaphore signal
60. 电空传送设备　　electropneumatic conveyer
61. 电码轨道电路　　coded track circuit
62. 电码轨道电路自动闭塞　　automatic block with coded track circuit
63. 电气锁闭　　electric locking
64. 调车表示器　　shunting indicator
65. 调车信号机　　shunting signal
66. 定点停车　　stopping a train at a target point
67. 定位接点　　normal contact
68. 定位锁闭　　normal locking
69. 额定值　　rated value
70. 扼流变压器　　impedance transformer
71. 二显示自动闭塞　　two-aspect automatic block
72. 发车表示器　　departure indicator
73. 发车表示器电路　　departure indicator circuit
74. 发车进路信号机　　route signal for departure
75. 发车线路表示器　　departure track indicator
76. 发车信号　　departure signal
77. 反位接点　　reverse contact
78. 反位锁闭　　reverse locking

79. 防护道岔　　protective turnout
80. 防护区段　　protected section
81. 非进路调车电路　　circuit to hold a route for shunting
82. 非联锁道岔　　non-interlocked switch
83. 非联锁区　　non-interlocking area
84. 分割区段　　cut section
85. 分路　　shunt
86. 分路道岔　　branching turnout
87. 分路灵敏度　　shunting sensitivity
88. 峰下减速器　　master retarder
89. 钢轨绝缘　　rail insulation
90. 钢轨绝缘不良　　bad rail insulation
91. 股道空闲　　track clear
92. 故障-安全　　fail-safe
93. 轨道变压器箱　　track transformer box
94. 轨道变阻器　　track rheostat
95. 轨道电抗器　　track reactor
96. 轨道电路电码化　　coding of continuous track circuit
97. 轨间电阻　　ballast resistance
98. 后退信号　　backing signal
99. 缓动继电器　　slow-acting relay
100. 缓放继电器　　slow-release relay
101. 缓放时间　　slow-release time
102. 缓吸继电器　　slow pick-up relay
103. 缓吸时间　　slow pick-up time
104. 机车接近通知　　approaching announcing in cab
105. 机车设备　　locomotive equipment
106. 机车信号测试区段　　cab signaling testing section
107. 机车信号作用点　　cab signaling inducter location
108. 机务段联系电路　　liaison circuit with a locodepot
109. 机械臂板信号机　　mechanically operated semaphore signal
110. 机械化驼峰设备　　mechanized hump yard equipment
111. 机械集中联锁　　mechanical interlocking
112. 机械锁闭　　mechanical locking
113. 基本进路　　basic route
114. 基本联锁电路　　fundamental interlocking circuit
115. 集中道岔　　centrally operated switch
116. 集中电源　　centrally connected power source
117. 集中供电　　centrally connected power supply
118. 继电器控制电源　　power source for relay control

119. 继电器灵敏度　　relay sensitivity
120. 继电器释放　　relay released
121. 继电器吸起　　relay energized
122. 继电式电气集中联锁　　all-relay interlocking
123. 加速推送信号　　humping fast signal
124. 检修不良　　not well inspected and repaired
125. 交流二元二位继电器　　AC two element two position relay
126. 交流计数电码轨道电路　　AC counting coded track circuit
127. 交流计数电码自动闭塞　　automatic block with AC counting code track circuit
128. 接车信号　　receiving signal
129. 接地报警　　grounding alarm
130. 接点闭合　　contact closed
131. 接点断开　　contact open
132. 接发车进路信号机　　route signal for receiving-departure
133. 接近区段　　approach section
134. 接近锁闭　　approach locking
135. 解除闭塞　　block cleared
136. 解锁电路　　release circuit
137. 解锁进路　　released route
138. 尽头信号机　　signal for stub-end track
139. 进路表　　route sheet
140. 进路表示器　　route indicator
141. 进路操纵作业　　semi-automatic operation by routes
142. 进路分段解锁　　sectional release of a locked route
143. 进路继电式电气集中连锁　　route type all-relay interlocking
144. 进路解锁　　route release
145. 进路人工解锁　　manual route release
146. 进路锁闭　　route locking
147. 进路锁闭表示　　route locking indication
148. 进路信号机　　route signal
149. 进路一次解锁　　route release at once
150. 进站信号机　　home signal
151. 开路式轨道电路　　open type track circuit
152. 控制点　　controlling point
153. 控制盘　　control panel
154. 快速转辙机　　quick-acting switch machine
155. 快吸继电器　　quick pick-up relay
156. 离去表示　　departure indication
157. 离去区段　　departure section
158. 励磁电路　　energizing circuit

159. 连锁表　　interlocking table
160. 连锁道岔　　interlocked switch
161. 连锁区　　interlocking area
162. 连锁图表　　interlocking chart and table
163. 连锁箱联锁　　interlocking by point detector
164. 列车运行控制系统　　train operation control system
165. 列车自动调速　　automatic train speed regulation
166. 列车自动限速　　automatic train speed restriction
167. 溜放进路自动控制　　automatic switching control of humping yard by routes
168. 溜放速度自动控制　　automatic rolling down speed control
169. 漏解锁　　missing release
170. 漏锁闭　　missing locking
171. 路签　　train staff
172. 脉冲继电器　　impulse relay
173. 脉冲式轨道电路　　pulse track circuit
174. 摩擦联结器　　frictional clutch
175. 排列进路　　route setting
176. 偏极继电器　　polar biased relay
177. 区段锁闭　　section locking
178. 区段遥控　　remote control for a section
179. 区段占用表示　　section occupancy indication
180. 区间封锁　　section closed up
181. 区间空闲　　section cleared
182. 区间联系电路　　liaison circuit with block signaling
183. 取消闭塞　　to cancel a block
184. 取消进路　　to cancel a route
185. 去禁溜线信号　　shunting signal to prohibitive humping line
186. 人工分路　　manual shunt
187. 人工解锁　　manual release
188. 闪光电源　　flashing power source
189. 失去联锁　　loss of interlocking
190. 施工妨碍　　construction interference
191. 事故照明　　emergency lighting
192. 释放时间　　drop away time
193. 释放值　　release value
194. 手柄　　handle
195. 受电端　　receiving end
196. 枢纽遥控　　remote control of a junction terminal
197. 双频感应器　　double frequency inductor
198. 双线继电半自动闭塞　　double track all-relay semi-automatic block system

199. 水分离器　water separator
200. 顺向重叠进路　route with overlapped section in the same direction
201. 四点检查　released by checking four sections
202. 四显示自动闭塞　four-aspect automatic block
203. 隧道通知设备　tunnel announciating device
204. 隧道遮断信号　tunnel obstruction signal
205. 锁闭杆　locking rod
206. 锁闭力　locking force
207. 条件电源屏　conditional power supply panel
208. 跳线　jumper
209. 停车信号　stop signal
210. 通过信号　through signal
211. 通过信号机　block signal
212. 推峰速度自动控制　automatic control for humping speed
213. 推送小车辆　propelling trolley
214. 推送信号　start humping signal
215. 脱轨表示器　derail indicator
216. 驼峰机车遥控　remote control of hump engines
217. 驼峰溜放控制系统　humping control system
218. 驼峰信号机　hump signal
219. 微机-继电式电气集中　microcomputer-relay interlocking
220. 微机联锁　microcomputer interlocking
221. 吸起时间　pick-up time
222. 吸起值　pick-up value
223. 线路区段　track section
224. 小站电气集中联锁　relay interlocking for small station
225. 信号复示器　signal repeater
226. 信号故障　signal fault

附录 C 科技英语写作

Skill Training (1)

Commonly-Used Opening Sentences and Closing Sentences of Letters 书信正文常用的开头语句和结尾语句

1. Commonly-Used Opening Sentences 常用的开头语句

(1) 表达"兹致函给您，通知您……"的句子

I beg to inform you that...

I am writing to you to ask about...

I am glad to tell you that...

(2) 表达"收到贵方*月*日来函，内容悉知"的句子

Thank you for your kind letter dated the 6th June.

Your kind letter of July 30 arrived this morning.

Your favor of the 5th inst. has come to hand and its contents have been noted.

注意：　①表示*月*日来函可有两种方法 a.用介词 of；b.用过去分词 dated。

　　　　②kind 在 letter 前常用，以示客气；favor 用在信函文字中就是指书信。

(3) 表达"迟复为歉"的句子

I must apologize for my delay in replying your recent letter.

I beg thousand pardons for not having written to you sooner.

2. Commonly-Used Closing Sentences 常用结束语句

在书信正文的末尾，常常表达盼回信、表祝愿和代问或嘱笔问候等意思，这种意思可以用句子表示，也可以用短语表示。用句子表示时，末尾用"."；用短语表示时，末尾用","。

(1) 表达盼回信的句子或短语

I hope to hear from you soon.

Hoping to hear from you soon,

Awaiting your early reply,

Your kind early reply will be appreciated.

(2) 表示祝愿的句子

With best regards,

Wish you the best of health and success.

Much love to you and your family,

(3) 表达转达、或嘱笔问候

Say hello to Joe.

Please remember me to your brother.

My mother joins me in love to you.

Skill Training (2)

Invitation　Card 请柬的写法

用于正式场合的英文请柬有固定的格式，注有 R.S.V.P.(请复柬)的，收柬人应及时回柬，告之自己应邀还是回绝。

例：
Mr. and Mrs. Li Dongwei
Vice president of ***University
request the pleasure of the company of
Mr. and Mrs. John Smith
Chancellor of *** Institute
at dinner
at 6: 00 pm on July 18
at Friendship Hotel
R.S.V.P.

从上柬可以看出，请柬是由一句话来表示。Mr. and Mrs. Li Dongwei 是主语，request 是谓语，the pleasure of the company of Mr. And Mrs. John Smith 是宾语。邀请者永远做主语，被邀请者永远在谓语之后。pleasure 做恩惠讲，在这里是"赏光"的意思,也可以用 honor 等词替换；company 是"作客"的意思，也可以用 reception 等词替换。

注意：主语和谓语的人称、数要一致。

下面看两个回柬。

1. 接受邀请的回柬

Mr. and Mrs. John Smith
Chancellor of *** Institute
accept with pleasure the kind invitation of
Mr. and Mrs.Li Dongwei
Vice president of ***University
for dinner
at 6: 00 pm on July 18
at Friendship Hotel

2. 婉言谢绝邀请的回柬

Mr. and Mrs. John Smith
Chancellor of *** Institute
regret that they are unable to accept
the kind invitation of
Mr. and Mrs. Li Dongwei
Vice president of ***University
for dinner
at 6: 00 pm on July 18
at Friendship Hotel

Skill Training (3)

Advertisement 广告的写法

广告是以付费的方式(公益广告除外)，通过一定媒介，向一定的人传达一定的信息。广告文案主要刊登在报纸杂志上或公共场所，用以介绍和推销商品，或宣传和促进某项事业。为此广告在写法上既重视宣传效果又重视节省费用。主要有两种写法。

1. 使用叙述文体

这种写法的文案构成包括：标题、正文、口号和随文四个部分。

Feel the Power of the World's First Turbo Copier

Introducing the new Toshiba 2230 Turbo, the first turbocharged copier in history. With it, you can produce 22 copies a minute. Or hit the turbo button and turn out 30 copies a minute. So now you have the power to work 40% more efficiently while using 33% less toner. And what is even more revolutionary we've managed to do is all without charging the price.

To be arranged for a free demonstration, just call 1-800-Go-TOSHIBA.

请体验一下世界首创涡轮式复印机的威力

隆重推出有史以来第一台新型 TOSHIBA 2230 涡轮式复印机。使用它，你一分钟可复印 22 份材料。如果按下涡轮键，一分钟则可复印 30 份。既可以提高效率 40%，又可以节省 33% 的色剂。更为革新的是我们并没有因此而提高价格。

如需安排演示，请电：1-800 转 TOSHIBA。

上文中 Feel the Power of the World's First Turbo Copier 是标题。由于它有一定的鼓动性，也可把它用做一句可以反复使用的广告口号。接下来是广告的正文。最后一句 To be arranged for a free demonstration, just call 1-800-Go-TOSHIBA. 是随文。用来告诉读者如何来响应这份广告。

2. 用缩略句或缩略词

SECRETARY/OFC. Position req. good command of English, organizational abilities, Sal. $ 980 mo. Resume to The Burdick Co. 238 Pitt St., Sydney, NSW2000.

招聘办公室秘书，职位要求：精通英语，有组织能力，月薪 $ 980，应聘请将履历表寄到新南威尔士州，悉尼市，郫街 238 号伯第克公司收。

此文不是由句子而是由名词或名词性短语罗列而成，虽然很短，但信息量却很大。其中使用了一些常用缩写词。如： ofc——office；req.——required(requirement)；sal.——salary；mo——month 等。

Skill Training (4)

Superscription 怎样写英文信封

英文信封和中文信封一样，包括收信人的姓名地址和发信人的姓名地址，再贴上邮票，就可以投到邮筒去了。

需要注意的是英文信封上收信人的姓名地址要放在信封的中间位置或略微往右、往下一些。第一行要写收信人的姓名，接下来写地址。英文地址的顺序要由最小单位，如房间号、门牌号到大单位，如城市、省、州和国家。如果需要写单位名称，要写在收信人的姓名之下，具体地址之上。发信人的姓名地址的写法同收信人的姓名地址的写法，只是位置要放在信封的左上角，或放在信封的背面上方。

注意：

(1) 收信人的姓名的前面通常加头衔，如：Mr., Mrs., Ms., Miss, Dr., 等等。而发信人的姓名前面往往不加头衔。

(2) 邮政编码永远放在省名或州名(包括直辖市)的后面。

(3) 城市名称与省名、州名之间使用逗号隔开。

请见下例：

LI HUA

STAMPS

MARKETING DEPT

*** CO
112 WEST UNIVERSITY RD
TIANJIN, 300000
CHINA

        MR JOHN SMITH
        WHOLESALES DEPT
        *** CO
        1356 GEORGE ST
        SYDNEY, 2000
        AUSTRALIA

如果拜托别人转收信件，可在受托人的姓名之前加上 C/O,（care of 的缩写）。而真正的收信人的姓名永远放在第一行。如上封信，如果收信人是 LI HONG 小姐，受托人是 JOHN SMITH，则信封应该这样写：

LI HUA

STAMPS
MARKETING DEPT
*** CO
112 WEST UNIVERSITY RD
TIANJIN, 300000
CHINA

        MISS LI HONG
        C/O MR JOHN SMITH
        WHOLESALES DEPT
        *** CO
        1356 GEORGE ST
        SYDNEY, 2000
        AUSTRALIA

如果拜托别人捎信，而不是寄信，则信封可以这样写：

Please forward
Mr. George Smith

Mr. George Smith
Kindness of Professor Zhang Ming

  第一种写法不特意交代出送信人，大致中文意思是"烦交(呈)乔治·史密斯先生"。第二种写法是特意交代出送信人的姓名，以表示出对送信人的尊重和强调。

Skill Training (5)

Personal Statement 自述的写法

  自述是一种记叙性短文。是对个人情况的表述。它和履历表一样，在现实生活中非常有用。

  请看下面实例。

My name is Gao Liang. I was born on July 28, 1978, in Shanghai. My father is a professor of English and my mother is a doctor in charge. I received a very good home education, both moral and intellectual, in my childhood.

When I was twelve years old, I entered Yaohua Middle School to complete my three-year junior and three-year senior middle school course. During the six years in the middle school, I was particularly interested in and fairly good at science subjects.

In 1996, I successfully passed the College Entrance Examination and was admitted into the Civil Engineering Department to major in bridge building in ** University where I stayed for four years during which I always got good marks in all major courses. I graduated from that university with the degree of BS in 2000.

After graduation I got a job as an assistant engineer in Tianjin Municipal Engineering Bureau. Since December 2001, I have become a lecturer in the Civil Engineering Department of ** University. I love my work and devote myself into it.

Since my young days, I have always been trying to cultivate a good character, paying attention to polite manners and noble ideas. Besides, I am of strong constitutions and temperate habits.

I have, of course, weakness and shortcomings. The conspicuous among them are impatience with difficulties and hesitation in making some decisions that I must make every effort to overcome.

Skill Training (6)

Letter Writing 书信的写法

先看下面一封求职信。

Dear Sir,

Having read your advertisement in today's newspaper for a secretary I wish to be considered as an applicant for the position, and beg to state my qualifications as follows:

I graduated from Foreign Language Department of *** University in 1999 with degree of Bachelor of Art. Since then I have been working in ABC Company as a secretary. ...

Feeling myself competent to meet your requirement, I beg to offer my services, should the position still be open. If I am successful in my application, I shall discharge my duties to the best of my ability.

Hoping you'll give my application your kind consideration,

Faithfully yours,

...

英文事务书信一般是开门见山，直截了当，使用简洁清楚的语言，但又注意客气、委婉。根据书信内容的不同，信的正文的开头语句和结尾语句不尽相同。但各种内容的书信都有自己的常用套语，熟练使用一些常用套语，就会逐渐运用自如书写信件了。

下面是一些最常用的书信开头语句和结尾语句。

1. 介绍信

(1) This is to introduce to you Mr.***

兹介绍***给您

(2) I have the honor(pleasure)to introduce to you Mr.***

我荣幸地(高兴地)向您介绍***

2. 证明信

(1) This is to certify that...

(2) It is hereby certified that...

(3) Let it be known that...

(4) It is my pleasure to give evidence that...

以上各句的基本含义是：兹证明……

3. 推荐信

(1) I have much pleasure in recommending Mr.*** to you.

我高兴地向你推荐***先生。

(2) I am confident that he will do his best wherever he may be placed and I cordially recommend him to you.

我向你担保，无论把他放在那里他都会努力工作，我诚心实意地把他推荐给你。

(3) I recommend Mr.*** and hope that he will be considered as one of the best applicants.

我推荐***先生，并希望你把他看做是最好的申请人之一。

4. 申请信（略，参见例信)

Skill Training (7)

The Structure of a Letter 信的结构

英文书信的结构主要包括：信头、信内地址、称呼、正文、结尾谦称和署名。另外，还有两个次要结构：再启和附件。

1. 信头

信头包括两部分内容：发信人的地址和写信的日期。以第四课给出的信封内容为例，信头应该是：

MARKETING DEPT

*** CO

112 WEST UNIVERSITY RD

TIANJIN，300000

CHINA

Sept. 28，2002

注意：日期的顺序，可以是日、月、年(英国习惯)，也可以是月、日、年(美国习惯)。

2. 信内地址

信内地址包括两部分内容：写信人的姓名和写信人的地址。以第四课给出的信封内容为例，信内地址应该是：

MR JOHN SMITH

WHOLESALES DEPT

*** CO

1356 GEORGE ST

SYDNEY，NSW 2000

AUSTRALIA

3. 称呼

通常，当知道收信人的姓名的时候，可以写：Dear Mr. John Smith,

通常，当不知道收信人的姓名的时候，可以写：Dear Sir or Madam,

称呼的后面可以用标点符号"，"或"："。

4. 正文(略)

5. 结尾谦称

结尾谦称与称呼相对应,反映出写信人与收信人之间的关系。

当写信人与收信人之间是平等的朋友或业务关系,最常使用的是:

Sincerely yours,

Truly yours,

Faithfully yours,

结尾谦称一般不用翻译出来,如果一定翻译的话,上述结尾谦称相当于"谨启"。如果收信人是写信人的长辈或上级,那么为了表达出写信人的谦恭,结尾谦称可用:

Respectfully yours,

Obediently yours,

译成汉语相当于"敬上"。结尾谦称的末尾要用","。

6. 署名

署名要亲笔签。当女士给不认识的人写信时,如果她认为有必要注明自己的头衔,以便对方在回信时知道如何称呼自己,她可以在自己的署名之前加上自己的头衔,如:Miss., Mrs., Ms. 等。

7. 再启

这个结构在事务信件中一般不用。在非正式信函中,当写信人写完信之后,又想添加一笔,可以在信后再单加上几句。而在事务信件中,如遇这种情况,应重新书写这封信。

8. 附件

附件在事务书信中倒还常见。如在一封信中附有一份履历表,附有一份学历证明的复印件,等等。附件用 Enclosure 来表示,缩写为:Enc.或为 Encl.。

如:

Encl. A copy of the certificate of graduation

下面是一封书信完整的结构:

        MARKETING DEPT

        *** CO

        112 WEST UNIVERSITY RD

        TIANJIN, 300000

        CHINA

        Sept. 28, 2002

MR JOHN SMITH

WHOLESALES DEPT

*** CO

1356 GEORGE ST

SYDNEY, NSW 2000

AUSTRALIA

Dear Mr. John Smith,

Body of the letter

Sincerely yours,
Li Hua
Encl.: A resume

Skill Training (8)

Notice 如何写通知和启事

通知是上级对下级、组织对个人发出通知、下达指示、提出要求的一种应用文体；启事是个人对公众，组织对公众发布信息的一种文体。但在英文表述上大体一样。

以下为一个放假通知和一个征婚启事。

Notice Giving a Holiday

30 April, 2002

Tomorrow being May Day, there will be no school. All teachers, staff members and students are expected to take part in the celebration to be held in the school. Classes will be resumed as usual on 7 May.

Bohai Vocational Technology School

放假通知

明天是"五一"节，不上课，希望全体教职员工和学生参加学校组织的庆祝活动。五月七日恢复上课。

渤海职业技术学校
2002 年 4 月 30 日

Seeking a Spouse

A male, aged 28, degree of BS, engineer, non-smoker, non-drinker, interested in sports and music, seeks a honest, quiet and warm female for long-term relationship. Calls are to be answered. Visits unnecessary.

Please contact: Ms. Wang Tel. 89123456.

征婚启事

某男，28 岁，理学学士学位，工程师，不嗜烟酒，爱好体育和音乐，征忠诚、恬静、热情女性为终身伴侣。电话联系，拒访。联系人：王女士，电话：89123456。

从以上两例可以看出，通知(启事)一般由四个结构组成：标题、正文、署名和发文日期。标题可简单写成 Notice 通知(启事)，也可加上定语，如：Meeting Notice 会议通知；还可以不用 Notice，直接点题，如：A Child Lost，寻人启事。

通知(启事)的正文写作特点是通知者和被通知者在正文中都以第三人称出现。发文单位的署名通常放在正文之下的右下角或标题之下。日期可放在署名之下的左下角或正文之上的右上角。

Skill Training (9)

Resume 履历表

简单的履历表包括两个部分，一是制表列项目，二是填写表格。列项目通常用名词来表示，填写项目通常用名词、名词性短语、介词短语、分词短语等来表示，一般不使用句子表示。例：

RESUME

NAME Wang Ping   [WB]SEX Female
DATE AND PLACE OF BIRTH   September 8, 1970 in Shanghai
NATIONALITY Han   PARTILIATIONS None

PRESENT OCCUPATION   Teacher of Tianjin Industrial Engineering University
OFFICE ADDRESS   288 Nanjing Rd Tianjin China 300000
TEL(OFC)   0862223300100   FAX   00862223300200
EDUCATION
September, 1988—July, 1992 majored in Bridge Building at the Civil Engineering Department of Tianjin University, BS
September, 1982—July, 1988 Yaohua Middle School
September, 1976—July, 1982 Xinhua Primary School
PROFESSIONAL EXPERIENCE

April, 1996—present Lecturer at Civil engineering Department of Tianjin Industrial Engineering University
July, 1992—April, 1996 Assistant engineer in Tianjin Municipal Engineering Bureau
HONOR, AWARD, PENALTY
Awarded the honorable title of "Three-Good Student" by Tianjin University in 1996
MEMBERSHIP OF PROFESSIONAL SOCIETIES
Member of Tianjin Mechanical Engineering Society

PUBLICATIONS
English for Highway Traffic published by Tianjin Science-technology Press in 1999

Skill Training (10)

Abstract 科技论文摘要的写法

一篇文章的摘要应能客观地反映该篇文章的主要内容的信息，具有独立性和自含性。它位于正文之前，通常不超过 200 个词。由于篇幅有限，必须十分简练，开门见山，直截了当，不使用多余的词或生僻的词，也避免使用冗长的句子。

科技论文摘要大致包括三个部分：

①说明论文的主题；②介绍主要内容；③提出结论或建议。

科技论文的摘要，在结构上和语言上相当程式化。以下介绍几种常用句型供参考。

1. 通常论文摘要的第一句应点题

常用的句型有：

(1) The author (writer) of the article reviews (presents, gives, points out, discusses, analyses, tries to describe, explores, holds, deals with, summarizes, examines, investigates, researches into...)...

作者回顾 (提出、指出、讨论、分析、描述、探讨、总结、检验、调查、研究……)……

(2) This article (paper, essay) approaches (holds, reports, reviews, touches upon, tells of, is about, concerns...)...

本文探讨 (认为、报告、回顾、论及、叙述、涉及……)……

2. 介绍内容的句子

常用的句型有：

(1) Examples of...demonstrate that...

……的例子表明……

(2) Data can be found in graphs and table.

数据显示在图表中。

(3) Statistics confirm that...

统计数字确认……

3. 关于结论和建议

常用的句型有：

(1) The author (writer) suggests (recommends, concludes, points out...) that...

作者建议（推荐、得出结论、指出……）……

(2) This article shows (suggests) that...

本文表明（建议）……

(3) The author's suggestion (conclusion) is that...

作者的建议（结论）是……

下面看两篇论文摘要。注意在英文摘要中，句子的主语通常使用第三人称，动词的时态以一般现在时为主。

(A)

Abstract: This article presents an account of contact problems in the classical theory of elasticity. It starts from fundamentals and aims to provide the reader with information on recent developments in this subject that he will need to widen his horizon of contact problems.

本文论述经典弹性理论中的接触问题。它从基本原理着手，给读者提供这门学科的最新信息，使读者扩大关于接触问题的知识面。

(B)

Abstract: This article tells of the importance of metals in daily life, particularly in machine building and engineering metals, of which the most widely used is iron. Therefore, production of iron has much to do with the development of a nation.

本文论述金属在日常生活中，特别是在机械制造和工程建设中的重要作用。用于工业的金属称为工程金属，其中，铁的用途最为广泛。因此，铁的生产对一个国家的发展关系重大。

Skill Training (11)

Key Words 关键词

关键词是反映文章主题概念的词或词组。一般每篇文章可选3～8个。中文文章的关键词应尽量从《汉语主题表》中选用。未被词表收录的新学科、新技术中的重要术语也可作为关键词标注。多个关键词之间用分号隔开。注意，英文的关键词是由名词和相当于名词的词组、短语构成的，如名词、名词词组、动名词、动名词短语等。

附录 D 单 词 表

I 轨道交通运输部分单词表

A

a touch of 一点，少许
lag [læg] n. 落后
abandoned [ə'bændənd] adj. 被抛弃的，自甘堕落的，没有约束的，放荡的
accelerate [æk'seləreit] v. 加速，促进
access ['ækses] n. 通路，入门
accessory n. 附件
accident ['æksidənt] n. 意外事件，事故
accommodate [ə'kɔmədeit] v. 接纳，使适应
accommodation [ə,kɔmə'deiʃən] n. 住处，预定铺位
accompany [ə'kʌmpəni] vt. 陪伴，伴奏
accounting [ə'kauntiŋ] n. 会计学，清算账目
accurate ['ækjurit] adj. 正确的，精确的
achievement [ə'tʃi:vmənt] n. 成就，功绩
actuality [,æktju'æliti] n. 实在，现状
adapt to v. 适合
adhesion [əd'hi:ʒən] n. 黏着，附着，支持，信奉
adjust [ə'dʒʌst] vt. 调整，调节
admit [əd'mit] v. 容许，承认，接纳
adopt [ə'dɔpt] vt. 采用，收养
adorn [ə'dɔ:n] v. 装饰
advanced [əd'vɑ:nst] adj. 高级的，年老的，先进的
Advanced Cab 高级软卧包厢
advantage [əd'vɑ:ntidʒ] n. 优势，有利条件，利益
advocate ['ædvəkit] vt. 提倡，鼓吹
n. 提倡，鼓吹
affect [ə'fekt] v. 影响
affiliate to 附属于，合并成为其中的一部分
agency ['eidʒənsi] n. 代理行，代理权
aggregate ['æɡriɡət] n. 集合物，填料，集料
agreement [ə'ɡri:mənt] n. 协定，协议
aisle [ail] n. 坐席之间的纵行通道
albeit [ɔ:l'bi:it] conj. 尽管，虽然
alignment [ə'lainmənt] n. 结盟

alleviate [ə'li:vieit] v. 减轻，缓和
allocation [,æləu'keiʃən] n. 分配，分配物
alongside [ə,lɔŋ'said] prep. 横靠
adv. 在旁，横靠
alphabetic [,ælfə'betik] adj. 照字母次序的，字母的
altiplano [,ælti'plɑ:nəu] n. 高原
altitude ['æltitju:d] n. （指海拔）高度
amount [ə'maunt] n. 数量
Amtrak "美铁"，全国铁路客运公司
amusement [ə'mju:zmənt] n. 娱乐，消遣
analyst ['ænəlist] n. 分析者
ancillary [æn'siləri] adj. 从属的，辅助的
appearance [ə'piərəns] v. 出现，外观，外貌
application [,æpli'keiʃən] n. 应用，运用，施用
approach [ə'prəutʃ] n. 方法，途径
appropriate [ə'prəupriət] adj. 适当的
approved [ə'pru:vd] adj. 经核准的，认可的
arguably ['ɑ:ɡjuəbli] adv. 可论证地
argue ['ɑ:ɡju:] vi. 争论，辩论
array [ə'rei] v. 配置，排列
arrival [ə'raivəl] n. 到达，抵达
artistic [ɑ:'tistik] adj. 艺术的，有美感的
artwork ['ɑ:tw3:k] n. 插图，艺术作品
as follow 依下列各项
as of 到……时为止，从……时起
as well as 也，又
aside from 除……以外
assessment [ə'sesmənt] n. 估价
associate [ə'səuʃieit] vt. 使发生联系，使联合
attack [ə'tæk] v. 攻击
authorization [,ɔ:θərai'zeiʃən] n. 授权，认可
automatic [,ɔ:tə'mætik] adj. 自动的，无意识的，机械的
automobile ['ɔ:təməubi:l] n. 汽车
availability [ə,veilə'biliti] n. 可用性，有效性，实用性

available [ə'veiləbl] *adj.* 可用到的，可利用的，有用的
aviation [,eivi'eiʃən] *n.* 航空
avoid [ə'vɔid] *vt.* 避免，消除
award [ə'wɔ:d] *v.* 授予，判给
axle load 轴载重，轴负重

B

backbone ['bækbəun] *n.* 脊柱，主脊
background ['bækgraund] *n.* 背景
baggage ['bægidʒ] *n.* 行李
baggage car 行包车厢
ballast ['bæləst] *n.* 压舱物，沙囊
balloon [bə'lu:n] *n.* 气球
ban [bæn] *n.* 禁令
vt. 禁止，取缔（书刊等）
baseplate ['beispleit] *n.* 基础板，基板
be attached to 附属于
be capable of 能够
be comparable to 可比较的，比得上的
be inferior to 次于，低于
bearing ['bɛəriŋ] *n.* 轴承
behind [bi'haind] *adj.* 落后的
belt [belt] *n.* 环行线路，地带，区
bilateral [bai'lætərəl] *adj.* 有两面的，双边的
block [blɔk] *n.* 区间，闭塞
vt. 妨碍，阻塞
boast [bəust] *v.* 自豪
bodily ['bɔdili] *adj.* 整个地，完全地
bolster ['bəulstə] *n.* 承枕，支承架
bond [bɔnd] *n.* 债券
Boston ['bɔstən] 波士顿
brake [breik] *n.* 制动器，刹车，闸
break down 倒塌，垮掉，分解
break up 分解，分裂
breakthrough ['breik'θru:] *n.* 突破
bunk [bʌŋk] *n.* （轮船，火车等）铺位
by means of 依靠

C

cabin ['kæbin] *n.* 小屋，船舱
calculate ['kælkjuleit] *v.* 计算，考虑

capacity [kə'pæsiti] *n.* 能力，容量
capital ['kæpitəl] *n.* 资本
cargo ['kɑ:gəu] *n.* 船货，（车、船、飞机等运输的）货物
carrier ['kæriə] *n.* 运送者
carry out 完成，实现，执行
cart [kɑ:t] *n.* 大车，小车
cast iron 铸铁
catastrophic [,kætə'strɔfik] *adj.* 悲惨的，灾难的
causeway ['kɔ:zwei] *n.* 堤道，（穿越湿地的）堤道
centerpiece [sentəpi:s] *n.* 中心装饰品，（餐桌中央的）摆饰
challenge ['tʃælindʒ] *v.* 挑战
characteristic [kæriktə'ristik] *adj.* 特有的，典型的
charge [tʃɑ:dʒ] *n.* 费用
check [tʃek] *v.* 托运，寄存，检查
check in 签到
Chicago [ʃi'kɑ:gəu] 芝加哥
chipping ['tʃipiŋ] *n.* 碎屑，破片
cite [sait] *vt.* 引用，引证，举（例）
civil engineering 土木工程
classification yard 铁路编组场
classify ['klæsifai] *v.* 分类
climb up 爬上
clip [klip] *vt.* 夹住
clog [klɔg] *v.* 障碍，妨碍，填满
coach [kəutʃ] *n.* 四轮大马车，长途汽车
coarse [kɔ:s] *adj.* 粗糙的，粗鄙的
code [kəud] *n.* 代码，代号，编码
cog [kɔg] *v.* 吻合，欺骗
collide [kə'laid] *v.* 碰撞
colliery ['kɔljəri] *n.* 煤矿（包括建筑物和设备等在内）
collision [kə'liʒən] *n.* 碰撞，冲突
colonization [,kɔlənai'zeiʃən] *n.* 殖民化，殖民地化
combination [,kɔmbi'neiʃ(ə)n] *n.* 结合，联合，合并
combined transportation 联合运输
comfortable ['kʌmfətəbl] *adj.* 舒适的
commercial [kə'mɜ:ʃəl] *adj.* 商业的，贸易的

communicate [kə'mju:nikeit] v. 沟通，通信，传达
commuter traffic 通勤交通
commuter train 通勤列车
compact ['kɔmpækt] adj. 紧凑的，紧密的，简洁的 n. 契约，合同
company ['kʌmpəni] n. 公司
compartment [kəm'pɑ:tmənt] n. 间隔间，车厢
compatibility [kəm,pæti'biliti] n. 兼容性
compatible [kəm'pætib(ə)l] adj. 兼容的
compete [kəm'pi:t] vi. 比赛，竞争
competition [kɔmpə'tiʃ(ə)n] n. 竞争，竞赛
competitive [kəm'petitiv] adj. 竞争的
completion [kəm'pli:ʃ(ə)n] n. 完成
complexity [kəm'pleksiti] n. 复杂性
component [kəm'pəunənt] n. 成分
comprehensive [kɔmpri'hensiv] adj. 全面的，广泛的
concourse ['kɔŋkɔ:s] n. 车站大厅，场所，中央广场，宽阔的大街
concrete slab 混凝土板
conduct ['kɔndʌkt] v. 引导，传导
configuration [kən,figju'reiʃən] n. 构造，结构，配置，外形
confine to 限制
congestion [kən'dʒestʃ(ə)n] n. 充满，拥挤
connection [kə'nekʃən] n. 连接
connotation [,kɔnəu'teiʃən] n. 内涵，含蓄，意义
consignee [,kɔnsai'ni:] n. 收货人
consignment [kən'sainmənt] n. 托运的货物，托运，委托
consignor [kən'sainə(r)] n. 发货人
consist of 由……构成
console [kən'səul] vt. 安慰，藉慰
consortium [kən'sɔ:tiəm; (US) kən'sɔ:rʃiəm] n. 合伙，社团，财团
constraint [kən'streint] n. 约束，强制，局促
construction [kən'strʌkʃən] n. 建筑，施工，建筑物
consumption [kən'sʌmpʃ(ə)n] n. 消费，消费量
containerize [kən'teinəraiz] vt. 用集装箱装
continuation [kən,tinju'eiʃən] n. 继续，续集，延长，延长物，扩建物
continuous [kən'tinjuəs] adj. 连续的，持续的
continuous welded rail 无缝钢轨
contractor [kən'træktə] n. 订约人，承包人
convenient [kən'vi:njənt] adj. 便利的，方便的
conventional [kən'venʃən(ə)l] adj. 常规的，习俗的，传统的，惯例的
converge vi. （线条、运动的物体等）会于一点，向一点会合，（趋于）相似或相同
convert…to 把……转换
corridor ['kɔridɔ:] n. 走廊，通道（corridor train: 从头到尾有走廊的列车）
cost effectiveness 成本效率
couchette [ku:'ʃet] n. 坐卧两用车厢
couple ['kʌpl] v. 连合，连接
coupler ['kʌplə] n. 联结者，配合者
cradle ['kreidl] n. 托架，支架
crest [krest] n. 鸟冠，盔上的装饰（如羽毛），顶部，顶峰，浪头
critic ['kritik] n. 批评家，评论家
crosstie ['krɔstai] n. 枕木
crucial ['kru:ʃiəl, 'kru:ʃəl] adj. 至关紧要的
current ['kʌrənt] adj. 当前的，通用的，现在的，最近的 n. 电流
curvature ['kɜ:vətʃə] n. 弯曲，曲率
curve [kɜ:v] n. 曲线，弯曲 vt. 弯，使弯曲 vi. 成曲形
cushion…against 把……加以衬垫以防

D

date back 回溯至
deadly ['dedli] adj. 致命的，极度的，必定的
decade ['dekeid] n. 十年，十
decelerate [di:'seləreit] v. 减速
declaration [,deklə'reiʃən] n. 宣布，宣言，声明
decline [di'klain] vt., vi. 降，下垂
decrease [di'kri:s] vi., vt. 减少
dedicated ['dedikeitid] adj. 专注的，献身的

define [di'fain] vt. 定义，详细说明
definition [,defi'niʃən] n. 定义，规定
defrost [di(:)'frɔst] v. 解冻
deliberately [di'libəritli] adv. 故意地
delivery [di'livəri] n. 运送，交付
demonstration [,deməns'treiʃən] n. 演示，论证，显示，证明
denote [di'nəut] vt. 指示，表示
dense [dens] adj. 密集的，浓厚的
departure [di'pɑ:tʃə(r)] n. 出站
departure station 旅客出发站
depict [di'pikt] v. 描绘，描画，描写
depot ['depəu; 'di:-] n. 火车站，仓库
descend [di'send] v. 下来，下降，遗传（指财产，气质，权利），突击，出其不意的拜访
describe [dis'kraib] vt. 描写，记述，形容，形容
designate ['dezigneit] vt. 指明，指出，任命，指派
detail ['di:teil, di'teil] n. 细节，详情
Detroit [di'trɔit] 底特律
diamagnetic [,daiəmæg'netik] adj. 抗磁的，反磁性的
diesel ['di:zəl] n. 柴油机
diminish [di'miniʃ] v. （使）减少，（使）变小
direction [di'rekʃən, dai'rekʃən] n. 方向，指导，趋势
disadvantage [,disəd'vɑ:ntidʒ] n. 不利，劣势
discharge [dis'tʃɑ:dʒ] v. 卸货
discreetly adv. 谨慎地
disorder [dis'ɔ:də] n. 杂乱，混乱，无秩序状态
dispatch [dis'pætʃ] vt. 分派，派遣 n. 派遣，急件
dispense [dis'pens] vt. 分发，分配
dispute [dis'pju:t] v. 争论，争执
distinct [dis'tiŋkt] adj. 清楚的，明显的，独特的
distinction [dis'tiŋkʃən] n. 区别，差别，级别
distort [dis'tɔ:t] vt. 扭曲，歪曲（真理、事实等）
ditch [ditʃ] n. 沟，沟渠，壕沟
divide [di'vaid] v. 划分，分开，隔开
dome [dəum] n. 圆屋顶

double track 复线
doubt [daut] n. 怀疑，不信
down train 下行车
downtown ['dauntaun] n. 商业区，闹市区
drainage ['dreinidʒ] n. 排水，排泄，排水装置
due to 由于，应归于

E

economic and social returns 经济和社会收益
economical [,i:kə'nɔmikəl] adj. 节约的，经济的
ecosystem [i:kə'sistəm] n. 生态系统
efficiency [i'fiʃənsi] n. 效率，功效
efficient [i'fiʃənt] adj. 有效率的，生效的
electric [i'lektrik] adj. 电的，导电的，电动的，电气
electrify [i'lektrifai] v. 电气化
electrocute [ilektrəkju:t] v. 使……触电身亡
element ['elimənt] n. 元素，成分
elevated ['eliveitid] adj. 提高的
eliminate [i'limineit] vt. 排除，消除，除去
embankment [im'bæŋkmənt] n. （铁路的）路堤
embed [im'bed] vt. 使插入，使嵌入，嵌入
embellish [im'beliʃ] v. 装饰，美化
emergency [i'mɜ:dʒnsi] n. 紧急情况，突然事件，非常时刻，紧急事件
emphasis ['emfəsis] n. 强调，重点
employ [im'plɔi] vt. 雇用，使用
enclose [in'kləuz] vt. 装入，环绕
encode [in'kəud] v. 编码
endless ['endlis] adj. 无止境的，无穷的
endure [in'djuə] v. 耐久，忍耐
engine ['endʒin] n. 发动机，机车，火车头
engineer [,endʒi'niə] n. 工程师
enquiry [in'kwaiəri] v. 调查，询问
ensure [in'ʃuə] vt. 保证，担保
enterprise ['entəpraiz] n. 企业
entirely [in'taiəli] adv. 完全地，全然地，一概地
epidemic [,epi'demik] adj. 流行的，传染的，流行性 n. 时疫，疫疾流行
equipment [i'kwipmənt] n. 装备，装置，铁路车辆
error ['erə] n. 误差，过失，错误
essential [i'senʃ(ə)l] adj. 本质的，实质的，基本的，

　　　　　　　　　精华的
essentially [i'senʃəli] adv. 本质上，本来
evacuate [i'vækjueit] v. 疏散，撤出，撤离
eventual [i'ventjuəl] adj. 最终发生的，最终，有可能的
eventually [i'ventjuəli] adv. 最后，终于
exert [ig'zɜ:t] vt. 施加，努力，发挥，竭尽全力
expansion [iks'pænʃən] n. 膨胀，扩大，张开
expansion joint 伸缩接头，膨胀节
experimental [ik,speri'mentl] adj. 实验的
exploitation [,eksplɔi'teiʃən] n. 开发，开采，剥削，自私的利用，宣传，广告
extended [ik'stendid] adj. 扩展的，延伸的
extensive [iks'tensiv] adj. 广大的，广阔的，广泛的
extremely [iks'tri:mli] adv. 极端地，非常地
extrinsic [eks'trinsik] adj. 外在的

　　　　　　　　　F
facade [fə'sɑ:d] n. 正面，外观
facilitate [fə'siliteit] vt. 使容易，使便利
facility [fə'siliti] 设备，工具
falling gradient 下坡道
fasten ['fɑ:sn] vt. 扎牢，扣住，闩住，拴紧，使固定 vi. 扣紧，抓住
feedback ['fi:dbæk] n. 反馈
financially 财政上，金融上
finding ['faindiŋ] n. 发现，发现物，决定，[律]裁决
fitting ['fitiŋ] n. 装配，装置
fix [fiks] vt. 安装，使固定，装置
fixed [fikst] adj. 固定的，确定的
flange [flændʒ] n. （机）法兰　（铁路）轨底
flank [flæŋk] v. 位于……的侧面
flash butt welding 闪光对接焊
flat-shunted yard 平面调车场
flaw [flɔ:] n. 缺点，缺陷
flexible ['fleksəbl] adj. 柔韧性，易曲的，灵活的，柔软的，能变形的，可融通的
flywheel ['flaiwi:l] n. 调速轮
focus on 集中
footprint ['futprint] n. 足迹，脚印
formality [fɔ:'mæliti] n. 拘谨，礼节，仪式，正式手续，拘泥形式
formerly ['fɔ:məli] adv. 从前，以前，原来
foster ['fɔstə] vt. 养育，抚育，培养，鼓励，抱（希望）
fragment ['frægmənt] n. 碎片
frail [freil] adj. 脆弱的，薄弱的
Frank Sprague　（人名）弗兰克·斯普拉格
free Trade Zone　自由贸易区
freight [freit] n. 货物，货运　vt. 货运
frequency ['fri:kwənsi] n. 频率，周次，发生次数
friction ['frikʃən] n. 摩擦力，摩擦
funding ['fʌndiŋ] n. 资金

　　　　　　　　　G
gain ground　发展，普及，壮大
gap [gæp] n. 缺口，裂口，间隙，缝隙
gear to　使适合
general fast train　普通旅客快车，普快
generate ['dʒenə,reit] v. 产生，引起，造成
geographic [,dʒiə'græfik] adj. 地理学的，地理的
geography [dʒi'ɔgrəfi, 'dʒiɔg-] n. 地理，地形
geometry [dʒi'ɔmitri] n. 几何学，图形
George Stephenson　（人名）乔治·史蒂芬森
give access to　接见，准许出入
give prominence to　突出
go ahead　继续下去，进展，前进
go without　没有……也行
goods [gudz] n. 货物
government ['gʌvənmənt] n. 政府
grade crossing　平面交叉
gradient ['greidiənt] n. 梯度，倾斜度，坡度
gravity yard　重力调车场
grid [grid] n. 格栅
Guangzhou Arts College　广州美术学院
guarantee [gærən'ti:] n., v. 保证，担保
guide [gaid] n., v. 指导，支配，管理，操纵

　　　　　　　　　H
halfway ['hɑ:f'wei] adj. 中途的，部分的，不彻底的 adv. 半路地，在中途，在半途

halt [hɔ:lt] vt. 使停止，使立定
handle ['hændl] v. 处理
hard seat 硬座
hard sleeper 硬卧
hard-nut 棘手的，难以解决的
hardware ['hɑ:dwɛə] n. 硬件，部件
harsh [hɑ:ʃ] adj. 严厉的，苛刻的
haul [hɔ:l] v. 托运，托
haulage ['hɔ:lidʒ] n. 托运，牵引力，公路（铁路）运费，公路（铁路）货运业
headway ['hedwei] n. 列车班距；发车间距；车间距；运转空间；班距
heavy-duty adj. 重型的，耐受力强的
herdsmen n. 牧人，牧主
high-density n. 高密度
high-grade adj. 高级的
highway ['haiwei] n. 公路
hinge [hindʒ] n. （门、盖等的）铰链，枢纽，关键
vt. 装铰链
vi. 装以铰链，依……而转移
hold back 抑制，控制，隐瞒，滞留
homemaking market 家政市场
horse-drawn adj. 马拉的（车）
hostel ['hɔstəl] n. 宿舍，招待所
house [hauz] v. 给……房子住，收藏，覆盖
hump yard 驼峰调车场
Huntingdon Beaumont （地名）亨廷顿·博蒙特
hydraulic [hai'drɔ:lik] adj. 水力的，水压的

I

identifier [ai'dentifaiə] n. 检验人，标识符
immense [i'mens] adj. 巨大的
immobilization [i,məubilai'zeiʃən] n. 无机动性，固定不动
impact ['impækt] n. 冲击，影响，冲突
improve [im'pru:v] v. 改善，改进
in charge of 负责
in competition with 与……竞争
in effect 实际上，事实上
in excess of 超过
in line with 一致，成一直线

in place 在适当的位置，适当
in response to 响应，适应
in reverse 反过来
in surplus 过剩
in the case of 在……的情况
in the event of 如果……发生
in the long term 从长远观点来看，长期
in the stage of 在……时期
inaugurate [i'nɔ:gjureit] v. 开始，为……举行就职典礼
incline [in'klain] n. 倾斜，斜坡，斜面
include [in'klu:d] vt. 包含，包括
incorporate [in'kɔ:pəreit] v. 包含
independent [indi'pendənt] adj. 独立自主的，不受约束的
indicate ['indikeit] vt. 指出，显示，象征，预示
induce [in'dju:s] v. 引诱，引起，感应
infrastructure ['infrəstrʌktʃə(r)] n. 基础，行政机构
ingenious [in'dʒi:njəs] adj. 有独创性的，巧妙的
inhabitant [in'hæbitənt] n. 居民，居住者
inherit [in'herit] vt. 继承，遗传而得
initial [i'niʃəl] adj. 最初的，开头的
inland ['inlənd] n. 内地
innovative ['inəuveitiv] adj. 创新的，革新的
inspection [in'spekʃən] n. 检查，视察
install [in'stɔ:l] vt. 安装，安置
instance ['instəns] n. 实例，情况，场合
vt. 举……为例，获得例证
institute ['institju:t] n. 学院，协会
insurance [in'ʃuərəns] 保险
integrate ['intigreit] v. 使结合成为整体，（使）融入
integration [,inti'greiʃən] n. 综合
intellectual [,inti'lektjuəl] adj. 智力的，有智力的
intense [in'tens] adj. 强烈的，紧张的
interaction [,intər'ækʃən] n. 相互作用
interchange [intə'tʃeindʒ] v. 互换，交替变化
intercity [,intə'siti] adj. 城市间的
InterCity Express 城市特快
interfere with 妨碍，干涉，干扰

interim ['ɪntərɪm] adj. 中间的，临时的，间歇的
interior [ɪnˈtɪərɪə] n. 内部
interlock [ˌɪntəˈlɔk] v. 连锁，使……连锁
intersection [ˌɪntə(ː)ˈsekʃən] n. [数]交集，十字路口，交叉点，交，交点
interstate [ˌɪntə(ː)ˈsteɪt] adj. 州际的
interval [ˈɪntəvəl] n. 间隔
intolerance [ɪnˈtɔlərəns] n. 不容忍
intrinsic [ɪnˈtrɪnsɪk] adj. 内在的
investigate [ɪnˈvestɪgeɪt] v. 调查，研究
investigation [ɪnˌvestɪˈgeɪʃən] n. 调查，研究
investment [ɪnˈvestmənt] n. 投资
ironworks [ˈaɪənwɜːks] n. 炼铁厂
isolate [ˈaɪsəleɪt] vt. 使隔离，使孤立
issue [ˈɪʃuː, ˈɪsjuː] v. 发行，发表

J

James Watt （人名）詹姆斯·瓦特
Jessop （人名）杰瑟普
jet [dʒet] v. 喷出，喷射
joint bar 钢轨连接板
joint venture 合资企业
jointly adv. 共同地，连带地
jumbo [ˈdʒʌmbəu] adj. 巨大的

L

lag screw 方头螺钉
landmark [ˈlændmɑːk] n. 界标，里程碑
landscape [ˈlændskeɪp] n. 前景，地形
latest [ˈleɪtɪst] adj. 最新的
launch [lɔːntʃ, lɑːntʃ] v. 发动，发起，开办，开始
lavishness n. 浪费，过度
lay down 敷设，规定，制定（计划，规划，原则等），放下，交出，献出（生命）
lead to 导致，通向
lease out 租赁
ledge [ledʒ] n. 壁架
levitate [ˈlevɪteɪt] v. 升空，将……悬置
levitation [ˌlevɪˈteɪʃən] n. 轻轻浮起，升在空中
link [lɪŋk] v. n. 连接，联合
loan [ləun] n. 贷款，借款

locomotive [ˌləukəˈməutɪv] n. 机车，火车头
longitudinal [ˌlɔndʒɪˈtjuːdɪnl] adj. 经度的，纵向的
Los Angeles 洛杉矶
luggage [ˈlʌgɪdʒ] n. 行李

M

macroeconomic adj. 宏观经济学的
magnetic [mægˈnetɪk] adj. 磁的，有磁性的
maintenance [ˈmeɪntɪnəns] n. 维修
major [ˈmeɪdʒə(r)] adj. 主要的，大部分的
make out 填写，进展，说明，理解，了解，辨认
make use of 使用，利用
manipulation [məˌnɪpjuˈleɪʃən] v. 操作，操纵
manually [ˈmænjuəli] adv. 手工的，用手
manufacturing [ˌmænjuˈfæktʃərɪŋ] adj. 生产的，制造的
n. 制造业
marshalling yard 铁路货运编组站
mass transit 公共交通
measure [ˈmeʒə] n. 尺寸，方法，测量
mechanical [mɪˈkænɪkl] adj. 机械的，机械制的，呆板的
mechanize [ˈmekənaɪz] v. 机械化
mention [ˈmenʃən] vt. 提起，说及
merchandise [ˈmɜːtʃəndaɪz] n. 商品
merge [mɜːdʒ] v. 合并，使合并
metro [ˈmetrəu] n. 地下铁道
metropolitan [metrəˈpɔlɪt(ə)n] adj. 首都的，大城市的，主要城市的
Mexico City 墨西哥
mezzanine [ˈmezəniːn] n. 底层
micro-regulation 微观调控
mine [maɪn] n. 矿藏
miscellaneous [ˌmɪsəˈleɪnɪəs] adj. 杂的，各种各样的
mitigation [ˌmɪtɪˈgeɪʃən] n. 缓解，减轻，平静
mixture [ˈmɪkstʃə] n. 混合，混合物
monopolistic [məˌnɔpəˈlɪstɪk] adj. 垄断的
monopolize [məˈnɔpəlaɪz] vt. 独占，垄断
monorail [ˈmɔnəureɪl] n. 单轨，单轨铁路

moot [mu:t] adj. 未决议的，无实际意义的
motive power 动力
move [mu:v] v. 移动，离开
multiple ['mʌltipl] adj. 多样的，多重的
Multiple Unit 动车组
multipurpose ['mʌltipɜ:pəs] adj. 多种用途的
municipal [mju(:)'nisipəl] adj. 市政的
mural ['mjuərəl] n. 壁画
mute [mju:t] adj. 缄默的

N
namely ['neimli] adv. 即，也就是
nature ['neitʃə] n. 本性，天性
negotiation [ni,gəuʃi'eiʃən] n. 谈判
Newcastle （地名）纽卡斯尔
nomenclature [nəu'menklətʃə] n. 名称，命名
nominally ['nɔminəli] adv. 标称的，名义上的
normal time 正常时间
noticeably adv. 引人注目地，显著地
notion ['nəuʃən] n. 概念，观念，想法，主张
nuclear ['nju:kliə(r)] n. 核武器

O
obstacle ['ɔbstək(ə)l] n. 栅栏
occupy ['ɔkjupai] vt. 占用，占领，占据
offer ['ɔfə] vt. 提供，使出现
on the contrary 相反
open up 开发，开始
operate ['ɔpəreit] v. 操作，运转
opportunity [ɔpə'tju:niti; (US) -tu:n] n. 机会，时机
optimize ['ɔptimaiz] vt. 使最优化
option ['ɔpʃən] n. 选项，选择权
orbital ['ɔ:bitl] adj. 轨道的
order ['ɔ:də] vt. 定购，定制
orient ['ɔ:riənt] vt. 使朝东，使适应，确定方向
outfit ['autfit] n. 配备，装备
outset ['autset] n. 开端，开始
outsource v. 外部采办
overcome [,əuvə'kʌm] vt. 战胜，克服，征服
overlap [,əuvə'læp] v. （与……）交叠 和……重叠
overnight [,əuvə'nait] adj. 通宵的，晚上的，前夜的

P
painstaking ['peinsteikiŋ] adj. 艰苦的，下工夫的
pallet ['pælit] n. 托盘
parallel ['pærəlel] adj. 平行的，类似的
parlor ['pɑ:lə] n. 客厅，会客室
partition [pɑ:'tiʃən] n. 隔板，间壁
passageway ['pæsidʒwei] n. 走廊，过道
passenger ['pæsindʒə] n. 乘客，旅客
passenger station 客运站
passenger volume 客运量，客流量
passive ['pæsiv] adj. 被动的，消极的
patrol [pə'trəul] n., v. 巡逻，巡查
pattern ['pæt(ə)n] n. 模式，式样
pavilion [pə'viljən] n. 亭子
peak [pi:k] 顶点，最高峰
periphery n. 外围，边缘
perishable ['periʃəbl] n. 易腐品
permafrost ['pɜ:məfrɔ(:)st] n. 永久冻结带
permanent ['pɜ:mənənt] adj. 永久的，持久的
permissive [pə'misiv] adj. 许可的
peruvian [pə'ru:vjən] adj. 秘鲁的，秘鲁人的
pervasive adj. 无处不在的，遍布的，充斥各处的
phase [feiz] n. 阶段
phosphate ['fɔsfeit] n. 磷酸盐，磷肥
physical ['fizikəl] adj. 物质的，自然的，物理的
piggyback ['pigibæk] n. 在平车上的背负式（运输）
plague [pleig] vt. 折磨，使苦恼，使受灾
plateau ['plætəu, plæ'təu] n. 高原
plateway 板式铁路
plaza ['plɑ:zə] n. 广场
pocket n. 袋，口袋
point out 指出
policy ['pɔlisi] n. 政策，方针
polish ['pəuliʃ] v. 擦亮，磨光
populous ['pɔpjuləs] adj. 人口多的，人中稠密的
portal ['pɔ:təl] n. 入口，大门
postal ['pəustəl] adj. 邮政的
potentially [pə'tenʃəli] adv. 潜在地
pour [pɔ:, pɔə] v. 倒

practical ['præktikəl] adj. 实践的，应用的，实用的
preceding train 先行列车
precise [pri'sais] adj. 精确的，准确的
prefer [pri'fɜː] vt. 提到，涉及，提交，谈及
present [pri'zent] vt. 呈现，提出
preservation [ˌprezə(ː)'veiʃən] n. 保存，保管，储藏，维持
preside [pri'zaid] v. 主持
primarily ['praimərili, prai'meərili] adv. 首先，主要地，根本上
primary ['praiməri] adj. 主要的，初级的，原来的，根源的
principal ['prinsip(ə)l] adj. 主要的，首要的
prior to 在前，居先
privatization n. 私有化
procession [prə'seʃən] n. 行列，一排
procure [prə'kjuə] v. 获得
productive [prə'dʌktiv] adj. 生产的，多产的
profit ['prɔfit] n. 利润，得益
project ['prɔdʒekt] n. 设计，方案，工程
prologue ['prəulɔg] n. 序言，开端
promise ['prɔmis] v. 允诺，答应
propel [prə'pel] v. 推进，推动
property ['prɔpəti] n. 财产，所有权，性质，特性
propose [prə'pəuz] vt. 建议，向……提议
propulsion [prə'pʌlʃən] n. 推进，推进力，推进器
prototype ['prəutətaip] n. 原型，模范

Q

qualify as 取得……资格
queue [kjuː] n. 队列，长队

R

radical ['rædikəl] adj. 彻底，根本的
railroad car 火车车厢，机动车辆
railway bureau 铁路局
rake [reik] v. 搜索，掠过，用耙子耙，（使）倾斜
ramp [ræmp] n. 斜坡，坡道，敲诈
rank as 排列
rapid ['ræpid] adj. 迅速的，飞快的
rational ['ræʃənl] adj. 合理的，理性的

reach the conclusion 得出结论
realign [ˌriə'lain] v. 重新排列，再结盟
receptacle [ri'septəkl] n. 容（贮）器
record ['rekɔːd] n. 最高纪录
reduction [ri'dʌkʃən] n. 减少，缩影
reflect [ri'flekt] v. 反射，反映，表现，反省，细想
reform [ri'fɔːm] v. 改革，改造
regulation [regju'leiʃən] n. 规则，规章，调节，校准
reinforce [ˌriːin'fɔːs] vt. 加强，增援，补充
relatively ['relətivli] adv. 相关地
relieve [ri'liːv] vt. 减少，解除
remain [ri'mein] vi. 保持
remnant ['remnənt] n. 残余，残迹
renewal [ri'njuː(ː)əl] n. 更新，复兴
represent [ˌriːpri'zent] vt. 呈现，提出，介绍，引见
repulsive [ri'pʌlsiv] adj. 排斥的
require [ri'kwaiə] vt. 需要，要求，命令
rescue ['reskjuː] vt. 援救，营救
n. 援救，营救
reservation [ˌrezə'veiʃən] n. 保留，预订
reshuffle [riː'ʃʌfl] v. 改组
residential [rezi'denʃ(ə)l] adj. 住宅的
resilience [ri'ziliəns] n. 弹回，有弹力，恢复力，顺应力
resistance [ri'zistəns] n. 抵抗，抵制
respective [ris'pektiv] adj. 分别的，各自的
result in 导致
resume [ri'zjuːm] vt. 再继续，重新开始，重新占用，再用，恢复
retarder [ri'tɑːdə] n. 阻滞剂，缓凝剂，减速器
revenue ['revənjuː] n. 收入，税收
revive [ri'vaiv] v. （使）苏醒，复兴
revolution [ˌrevə'luːʃən] n. 革命，旋转
Richard Trevithick （人名）理查·特尔维域克
Richmond （城市名）里士满
ridership ['raidəʃip] n. [总称]<主美>公共交通工具乘客（人数）
roster ['rəustə] n. 值勤人员表
roughly adv. 粗略地，大体上，大致上
round [raund] n. 一轮

round-trip ticket 往返票，双程票
rubber-tired 橡胶式的，胶轮式的
run over 在……上压过
rust [rʌst] v. 生锈

S

Saint Louis 圣路易
scenery ['si:nəri] n. 风景，景色
schedule ['ʃedju:l; 'skedʒjul] v. 确定时间
scheme [ski:m] n. 计划，安排，配置
sculpture ['skʌlptʃə] v. 雕刻
search for 搜寻
secondary ['sekəndəri] adj. 次要的，二级的，中级的，第二的
second-line 次线
section ['sekʃən] n. 部分，断片，部件，节，项，区，地域，截面
sector ['sektə] n. 部分，部门
secure [si'kjuə] v. 固定，紧固
segmentation [ˌsegmən'teiʃən] n. 分割，分节现象
seismological [ˌsaizmə'lɔdʒikəl] adj. 地震学上的
semaphore signal 臂板信号
senior ['si:njə] adj. 年长的，资格较老的，资深的
separate ['sepəreit] adj. 分开的，分离的，个别的，单独的
v. 分开，隔离，分散，分别
separation [sepə'reiʃən] n. 分离，分开
set back 使退步
severely [si'viəli] adv. 严格地，激烈地
share [ʃɛə] vt. 分享，共有，分配
shed [ʃed] n. 棚，小屋
shelter ['ʃeltə] n. 躲避，掩避
Sherlock Holmes 夏洛克·福尔摩斯
Shinkansen ['ʃi:n'kɑ:nsen] 新干线（日本的高速客运列车）
shipment ['ʃipmənt] n. 运送，发送，运送的货物
shortage ['ʃɔ:tidʒ] n. 不足，不足之额
showcase ['ʃəukeis] v. 使……展现
showpiece ['ʃəupi:s] n. 展览品，供展览的样品
showy ['ʃəui] adj. 浮华的，（过分）艳丽的，炫耀的，卖弄的
shrink [ʃriŋk] v. 收缩，（使）皱缩，缩短
shunt [ʃʌnt] v. 逃避
shunter ['ʃʌntə(r)] n. 扳道员，能干的组织者
shunting capacity 调车容量
shunting engine 调车机车
siding ['saidiŋ] n. 铁路的侧线，旁轨
signal ['signl] n. 信号的
simultaneously [ˌsiməl'teiniəsli] adv. 同时地
single ['siŋgl] adj. 单一的，专一的，个别的
skate [skeit, skit] n. 冰鞋，溜冰
slab n. 平板，厚板，厚片，混凝土路面，背板
slate [sleit] n. 石板，石片
sleeper ['sli:pə] n. 轨枕，枕木
slope [sləup] n. 斜坡，斜面
socio-economic adj. 社会经济的
soft seat 软座
soft sleeper 软卧
solid ['sɔlid] adj. 可靠的，结实的
sorting office 邮件分拣处
source [sɔ:s] n. 来源，出处
Soviet Union 苏联
space out 留间隔，把……拉开距离
span [spæn] n. 跨度
specialist ['speʃəlist] n. 专家
specialty ['speʃəlti] n. 专业
specification [spesifi'keiʃ(ə)n] n. 规格，规范
specify ['spesifai] vt. 指定，详细说明，列入清单
spike [spaik] n. 长钉，钉鞋，道钉
split [split] v. 分裂，分离
spot [spɔt] v. 认出，发现
spring up 突然出现，长出，跳出
stabilize ['steibilaiz] v. 稳定
stable ['steibl] adj. 稳定的
stably ['steibli] adv. 稳定地，坚固地，坚定地
stack [stæk] v. 堆叠
stairway ['stɛəwei] n. 楼梯
standard ['stændəd] n. 标准，规格，本位
adj. 标准的，权威，第一流的

state-owned *adj.* 国有的
statistic [stəˈtistik] *n.* 统计，统计学
steadily [ˈstedili] *adv.* 稳定地，有规则地
steam engine 蒸汽机车
steam-powered 蒸汽动力的
steelworks [ˈstiːlwɜːks] *n.* 炼钢厂
steep [stiːp] *adj.* 陡峭的，险峻的，急剧升降的
steer [stiə] *v.* 指导，驾驶
step into 进入
stimulate [ˈstimjuleit] *v.* 刺激，激励
Stockton and Darlington Railway 史托顿及达灵顿铁路
straddle [ˈstrædl] *v.* 跨骑
strain [strein] *v. n.* （使）紧张
stranded [ˈstrændid] *adj.* 束手无策的，进退两难的
strategic [strəˈtiːdʒik] *adj.* 战略上的，战略的
strategically [strəˈtiːdʒikəli] *adv.* 战略的，战略上用的，对全局有重要意义的
strategy [ˈstrætidʒi] *n.* 策略，战略
streetcar [ˈstriːtkɑː] *n.* 路面电车
street-crossing 十字路口
strenuous [ˈstrenjuəs] *adj.* 奋发的，使劲的，紧张的
stretch [stretʃ] *v.* 伸展，伸长
strive to 努力
subscription [sʌbˈskripʃən] *v.* 认捐
substantial [səbˈstænʃəl] *adj.* 坚固的，实质的，真实的，充实的
sufficient [səˈfiʃənt] *adj.* 充分的，足够的
sum up 总结，概括
superconducting [ˌsjuːpəkənˈdʌktiŋ] *adj.* 超导的
supervision [ˌsjuːpəˈviʒən] *n.* 监督
supplemental [ˌsʌpliˈmentl] *adj.* 补足的，追加的
surge [sɜːdʒ] *n.* 巨涌，汹涌，澎湃
vi. 汹涌，澎湃，振荡，滑脱，放松
vt. 使汹涌奔腾
surpass [sɜːˈpɑːs] *vt.* 超越，胜过
surplus [ˈsɜːpləs] *n.* 过剩，盈余
Surrey Iron Railway 萨里铁铁路
survive [səˈvaiv] *v.* 幸免于，幸存，生还

susceptible [səˈseptəb(ə)l] *adj.* 易受感动的，敏感的
suspend [səsˈpend] *v.* 悬，悬浮
swift [swift] *adj.* 迅速的，敏捷的
switch [switʃ] *n.* 道岔
synergy [ˈsinədʒi] *n.* 协同作用，增效

T

tackle [ˈtækl] *v.* 对付，处理，解决
tailor [ˈteilə] *vt.* 适合，适应
take into account 重视，考虑
take into consideration 考虑
target [ˈtɑːgit] *n.* 目标，对象
tariff [ˈtærif] *n.* 关税率，关税，收费表
telecommunication [telikəmjuːniˈkeiʃ(ə)n] *n.* 电信
telegraph [ˈteligrɑːf] *v.* 发电报，打电报说
terminus [ˈtɜːminəs] *n.* 终点，终点站，目标
TGV (Train à Grande Vitesse) 巴黎、里昂间高速火车
thanks to 由于；凭借
the Andes *n.* 安第斯山脉（南美洲）
the central government 中央政府
The European Union 欧盟
the Expo 2010 site 2010年世界博览会场馆
the following train 后行列车
the one way ticket 单程票
thereon [ðeərˈɔn] *adv.* 在其上，在那上面，……之后立即
thermite [ˈθɜːmait] *n.* 铝热剂，灼热剂
throughout [θruː(ː)ˈaut] *prep.* 一直，自始至终
thrust [θrʌst] *n.* 插进，力推
tie [tai] *n.* 带，联系
tile [tail] *n.* 瓦片，瓷砖
timetable [ˈtaimteib(ə)l] *n.* 时间表
toll-road 收费道路
Toronto [təˈrɔntəu] 多伦多
tough [tʌf] *adj.* 坚硬的
township [ˈtaunʃip] *n.* 镇区
track [træk] *n.* 轨道
track layout 轨道配置
track wear 轨道磨损

traction ['trækʃən] n. 拖，牵引，牵引动力
traffic flows   运输流量
trail [treil] v.   跟踪，托着
trailing unit   挂车组
train schedule   列车明细表
transaction [træn'zækʃən] n.   交易，办理
transfer [træns'fɜ:] vt.   转移，调转，调任
transit ['trænsit] n.   运输，转运，通过
transmit [,trænz'mit] v.   传送，传达，传导
transparent [træns'pærənt, trɑ:-] adj.   透明的，显而易见的
transport [træns'pɔ:t] n.   传送，运输
traverse ['trævɜ:s] v.   横过
tray [trei] n.   托盘，托架
trend [trend] n.   倾向，趋势
trunk line n.   干线
tube ['tju:b] n.   管，管子
tundra ['tʌndrə] n.   冻原，苔原，冻土带
tunnel ['tʌnl] n.   隧道，地道
turboprop ['tɜ:bəuprɔp] n.   涡轮螺旋桨发动机
turmoil ['tɜ:mɔil] n.   动乱
turnaround ['tɜ:nəraund] n.   回车场
turnkey ['tɜ:nki:] adj.   一切齐全即可使用的
extend Time   加班时间
Tyne   泰恩河

U

ultra ['ʌltrə] adj.   前缀，表示"过，超"
uncouple ['ʌn'kʌpl] vt.   解开，分开
underneath [,ʌndə'ni:θ] adv.   在下面，向下面
underpass ['ʌndəpɑ:s] n.   地道，地下过道
underside ['ʌndəsaid] n.   下面，底面
unique [ju'ni:k] adj.   唯一的，独特的
unlade [ʌn'leid] vt.   卸下，卸货
unreliable [ʌnri'laiəbl] adj.   不可靠的
unstable [ʌn'steibl] adj. 不稳定的，不牢固的
unworkable [ʌn'wɜ:kəbl] adj. 难运转的，不能实行的

up train   上行车
updated [ʌp'deitid] adj.   最新的

upgrade ['ʌpgreid] vt.   使升级，提升，改良品种
upper ['ʌpə] adj.   上面的，上部的
urgent ['ɜ:dʒənt] adj.   紧急的，急迫的
usage ['ju:zidʒ] n.   使用，用法
utility [ju:'tiliti] n.   公用事业，效用

V

vacation [və'keiʃən] n.   假期，休假
Valencia [və'lenʃiə]   巴伦西亚
Vancouver [væn'ku:və]   温哥华
vary ['vɛəri] vt.   改变，变更，修改
vehicle ['vi:ikl] n.   交通工具，车辆
velocity [vi'lɔsiti] n.   速度
ventilate ['ventileit] v.   通风，排气
ventilation [venti'leiʃən] n.   通风，公开讨论
via ['vaiə] prep.   经，通过，经由
view [vju:] v.   观察，观看
Virginia   （地名）弗吉尼亚
vision ['viʒən] n.   景象，先见之明
volume ['vɔlju:m; (US) -jəm] n.   体积，量，大量
overhead [əuvə'hed] adj.   在上头的，高架的

W

wagonway n.   马车铁路
Washington D.C.   华盛顿
welfare ['welfɛə] n.   福利，安宁，幸福
width [widθ] n.   宽度
with the advent of   随着……到来
with the developing of   随着……的发展
withdraw [wið'drɔ:] v.   收回，撤退
workshop ['wɜ:kʃɔp] n.   车间
workstation ['wɜ:ksteiʃ(ə)n] n.   工作站，智能终端
worldwide ['wɜ:ldwaid, -'waid] adj.   全世界的
wrap [ræp] vt.   包装，卷，缠绕

Z

Zhongshan Memorial Hall   中山纪念堂
zigzag ['zigzæg] n.   蜿蜒曲折，盘旋弯曲

Ⅱ 轨道信号部分单词表

A

left-hand switch　左开道岔
right-hand switch　右开道岔
a series of　一系列；一连串
a succession of　一个接一个的，一系列的
AC counting code track circuit　交流计数电码轨道电路
abolish [ə'bɔliʃ] v.　废除；废弃
accelerate [æk'seləreit] v.　加速
according to　按照；根据
act as　充当；起……作用
actuate ['æktʃueit] v.　动作
adjoining [ə'dʒɔiniŋ] adj.　邻接的
adjust [ə'dʒʌst] v.　调节；调整
advantage [əd'vɑ:ntidʒ] n.　优点
advisable [əd'vaizəbl] adj.　可行的；合理的
affect [ə'fekt] v.　影响；对……起作用
alight [ə'lait] v.　落下；下车
align [ə'lain] vt.　使结队，使成一行
all-relay interlocking　继电式电气集中联锁
alternately adv.　交替地
aluminum [ə'lju:minəm] n.　铝
apparatus [ˌæpə'reitəs] n.　装置；设备
appliance [ə'plaiəns] n.　设备；装置
approach [ə'prəutʃ] vt.　接近；逼近
appropriate [ə'prəupriət] adj.　适当的
approximately [əprɔksi'mətli] adv.　近似地，大约
armature ['ɑ:mətjuə] n.　衔铁
arrangement [ə'reindʒmənt] n.　布局，安排
as well as　以及；像……一样
assign [ə'sain] vt.　分配，指派
association [əˌsəusi'eiʃən] n.　协会；学会
assume [ə'sju:m] v.　假定
asymmetrical high voltage impulse track circuit　不对称脉冲轨道电路
attract [ə'trækt] vt.　吸引
attribute [ə'tribju:t] n.　属性；特性
audible signal　听觉信号，音响信号
audio-frequency n.　声（音）频
automatic block signaling　自动闭塞信号
automatic gate　自动栏木
availability [əˌveilə'biləti] n.　可用性；现有
available [ə'veiləbl] adj.　备有的；通用的

B

backbone ['bækbəun] n.　主干；骨架
ballast resistance　轨间电阻
barrier ['bæriə] n.　栅栏
be appropriate to　适合；合乎
be associated with　与……有关联
be base on　基于；根据
be combination with　配合；和……共同结合
be dependent on　依靠，依赖
be different from　与……不同；不同于
be distributed to　分配给
be divided into　划分成
be fundamental to　对……很重要
be immune to　不受影响
be informed of　知道
be similar to…　与……相似；类似
be subject to　须经，受……的支配
be sufficient to　足够（做）……
be used to　过去习惯于
bell [bel] n.　电铃
block section　闭塞区段
both directions　双向
braking distance　制动距离
broken-rail detection　断轨检测
buzzer ['bʌzə] n.　蜂鸣器
bypass ['baipɑ:s] vt.　绕过，避开，不顾

C

cab signal　机车信号
call for　要求；需要
capacity [kə'pæsiti] n.　通过能力，流量
car [kɑ:] n.　车列，车辆
car rolling　钩车溜放场
categorize ['kætigəraiz] v.　把……归类；把……列作
centralized traffic control　调度集中

characteristic [ˌkærɪktəˈrɪstɪk] adj. 特有的，表示特性的，典型的
charge [tʃɑːdʒ] v. 使充电
classification yard 编组场
clear a crossing signal 开放道口信号
code transmitter 电码发送器
coil [kɔɪl] n. 线圈；绕组
commercial power n. 市电
commodity [kəˈmɔdɪti] n. 物品；货物
communication interface 通信接口
compensate [ˈkɔmpənseɪt] v. 补偿；校正
comprise [kəmˈpraɪz] v. 包含，包括，由……组成
concurrent [kənˈkʌrənt] adj. 并发的，协作的，一致的
condition [kənˈdɪʃən] n. 条件
conflicting route 敌对进路
consecutive [kənˈsekjutɪv] adj. 连续的；依次相连的
consist of 由……组成
contact [ˈkɔntækt] n. 接点
contribute [kənˈtrɪbjuːt] v. 促使；有助于
control tower 控制塔
controlled point 被控点
conversion [kənˈvɜːʃən] n. 转换；转化
couple car 挂钩车
coupling [ˈkʌplɪŋ] n. 车钩
crossing at grade 平交道口
crossing gate 道口栏木
curtail [kɜːˈteɪl] v. 缩短
cut section n. 分割区段

D

decoding transformer 译码器
dedicated [ˈdedɪkeɪtɪd] adj. 专用的
define…as… 把……定义为……
definition [ˌdefɪˈnɪʃən] n. 定义
density [ˈdensɪti] n. 密度
departure [dɪˈpɑːtʃə] n. 离开，离去
derail [dɪˈreɪl] vt., vi. 出轨
derive from 由……起源

descend [dɪˈsend] v. 落下
desirable [dɪˈzaɪərəbl] adj. 所希望的；想要的
diameter [daɪˈæmɪtə] n. 直径
differ from 不同于；与……有区别
disable [dɪsˈeɪbl] v. 使残废，使失去能力，丧失能力
dispatcher [dɪsˈpætʃə] n. 发报机，调度员
display [dɪˈspleɪ] n. 陈列，展览，显示
v. 显示
distance-to-couple adj. 钩挂距离
distributed microprocessor 分布式微处理器
diverge [daɪˈvɜːdʒ] vi. 分开；偏离；分歧
divide into 分成；分为
dump [dʌmp] v. 倾卸

E

efficiency [ɪˈfɪʃənsɪ] n. 性能
electric motor 电机
electric operation switch 电动道岔
electric switch machine 电动转辙机
electrified railroad n. 电气化铁路
elimination [ɪˌlɪmɪˈneɪʃən] n. 消除
engine [ˈendʒɪn] n. 机车
engineman [ˈendʒɪnmæn] n. 司机
engraved letter 铭牌
essentially [ɪˈsenʃəlɪ] adv. 实质上；基本上
excessive [ɪkˈsesɪv] adj. 过大；过量
execute [ˈeksɪkjuːt] vt. 处决，执行，实现
exert [ɪgˈzɜːt] v. 施加
exertion [ɪgˈzɜːʃən] n. 执行，实行
exit speed 出口速度

F

factor [ˈfæktə] n. 因素
far apart 离得很远；间距很大
field location 线路点
fixed [fɪkst] adj. 固定的
flange [flændʒ] n. （机械等的）凸缘，（火车的）轮缘
flashing light signal 闪光信号机
flexibility [ˌfleksəˈbɪlɪtɪ] n. 适应性；灵活性
focus attention on 把注意力集中在

FSO track circuit　移频重叠轨道电路
furthermore [ˌfɜːðəˈmɔː(r)] adv.　此外

G

geographic representation　站场型表示
go into service　投入运行
govern [ˈgʌvən] v.　控制；调解；管理
grade [greid] n.　坡度
grade crossing　平交道口
guard rail（check rail）　护轨

H

hand signal　手信号
handling [ˈhændliŋ] adj.　操作的
n.　运送；调度；处理
have a significant impact on　对……有显著影响
headway [ˈhedwei] n.　（前后两车）车间时距；时间间隔
HF track circuit　高频轨道电路
highway crossing warning　道口预警
hinge [hindʒ] vt., vi.　用铰链连接（某物），给（某物）装上铰链
horizontal [ˌhɔriˈzɔntl] adj.　地平线的，水平的
hump classification yard　驼峰编组场
hump yard n.　驼峰编组场
hydraulic [haiˈdrɔːlik] adj.　液力的，液压的

I

illuminate [iˈljuːmineit] v.　标志，标记
illustrate [ˈiləstreit] v.　举例说明
illustration [ˌiləsˈtreiʃən] n.　插图，说明，图解
impact [ˈimpækt] n.　碰撞；冲击
impedance [imˈpiːdəns] n.　阻抗
impedance bond　阻抗联结器
in accordance with　按照；根据
in addition　另外还有；此外
in correspondence with　和……相一致
in preparation for　以备，为……作准备
in relation to　与……有关
in response to　响应
in series with　与……串联
in terms of　就……而言，从……方面说来，根据

in the event of　万一，即使
in the presence of　在……的情况下
in the vicinity of　在……附近；靠近……
in as much as　因为；由于
individual [ˌindiˈvidjuəl] adj.　各个的；特殊的
induction affect n.　感应效应
industrial railroad　工业铁路
inherently [inˈhiərəntli] adv.　固有，本来
initiate [iˈniʃieit] v.　引发，产生
insulated joint failure　绝缘节破损；绝缘不良
insulated section　绝缘区段
interconnect [ˌintəkəˈnekt] v.　互联；相互联系
interlocked signal　联锁信号机
interlocked switch　联锁道岔
interrupt [ˌintəˈrʌpt] v.　间断
intersection [ˌintəˈsekʃən] n.　交叉点
interval [ˈintəvəl] n.　间距
introduction [ˌintrəˈdʌkʃən] n.　介绍，序言，导言

J

joint [dʒɔint] n.　道岔连接部分
junction point　枢纽

K

key function　关键性功能

L

lag [læg] v.　滞后；迟延
lamp lighting circuit　电灯电路
lateral [ˈlætərəl] adj.　侧面的，从旁边的，至侧面的
lay out　陈列，布局
leakage [ˈliːkidʒ] n.　漏，泄漏，渗漏
linkage [ˈliŋkidʒ] n.　结合；联系；联动装置
load [ləud] n.　负荷，重担，装载量，工作量，负载，加载
v.　装载
locality [ləuˈkæliti] n.　地点；位置
locomotive [ˌləukəˈməutiv] n.　机车，火车头
loosely coupled module　积木式模块

M

magnetic circuit　磁路系统
magnetization [ˌmægnitaiˈzeiʃən;-tiˈz-] n.　磁化

make compensation for　补偿
manually ['mænjuəli] adv.　用手地，人工地
mast [mɑ:st] n.　桅杆；支座
mechanical [mi'kænikl] adj.　机械的
medium ['mi:diəm] adj.　中等的；中级的
microwave ['maikrəuweiv] n.　微波
misread [mis'ri:d] v.　误认；误读
modify ['mɔdifai] v.　修改；改进
motor generator set　发电机组
mount [maunt] v.　安装
multiple ['mʌltipl] adj.　多样的，多重的
multiple proceed aspects　多显示

N

negative post　负极
no longer　不再；已不
normal ['nɔ:məl] adj.　正常的，正规的，标准的

O

objective [əb'dʒektiv] n.　目的；目标
obscure [əb'skjuə] adj.　暗的，朦胧的，模糊的，晦涩的
vt.　使暗，使不明显
of course　当然；自然
open-pit min　露天矿
opposing signal　反向信号
out of　由……制成
outline ['əutlain] n.　摘要

P

panel ['pænl] n.　面，板，控制台
passage ['pæsidʒ] n.　通过，经过
peak [pi:k] n.　峰值
permissible [pə'misəbl] adj.　容许的；许可的
personnel [,pɜ:sə'nel] n.　（全体）人员；职员
pertinent ['pɜ:tinənt] adj.　相应的；有关的
pickup value　吸起值
plurality [pluə'ræliti] n.　多元化，多重性，众多
pneumatic [nju(:)'mætik] adj.　充气的，由压缩空气操作[推动]的，风动的
point blade　尖轨
polar-frequency code track circuit　极频轨道电路
polar-impulse track circuit　极性脉冲轨道电路

positive post　正极
power-operated switch　电动道岔
predict [pri'dikt] v.　预知，预言，预报
preliminary [pri'liminəri] adj.　预备的，初步的
primary ['praiməri] adj.　初级的
principle ['prinsəpl] n.　法则，原则，原理
process control　过程控制
property ['prɔpəti] n.　特性；性质
propulsion current n.　牵引电流
protect…against…　保护……以防（免遭）……
provided with　拥有
publication [,pʌbli'keiʃən] n.　出版物，刊物
pushing ['puʃiŋ] n.　推送

R

radar speed detector　雷达测速器
radii ['reidiai] n.　半径
radio remote control　无线电遥控
rail bonding　钢轨引接线
railroad switch　铁路道岔
rated input n.　额定输入
reactor [ri(:)'æktə] n.　反应堆，电抗器
redundancy [ri'dʌndənsi] n.　冗余
refer to as　称为
regardless of　不管；与……无关
regulate ['regjuleit] v.　调整；调解
relay ['ri:lei] n.　继电器
release [ri'li:s] v.　解锁
release value　释放值
remain [ri'mein] v.　保持
remote control system　遥控
repeater [ri'pi:tə] n.　复示器
represent [,repri'zent] v.　代表；表示
resistance [ri'zistəns] n.　电阻
resistor [ri'zistə] n.　电阻器
restricted [ri'striktid] adj.　限制的，严格的
retain [ri'tein] v.　保留
retarder [ri'tɑ:də] n.　减速器；缓行器
reverse [ri'vɜ:s] n.　相反，背面，反面，倒退
adj.　相反的，倒转的
vt.　颠倒，倒转

ride [raɪd] n. 骑，乘
rob of 使……失去
rotary ['rəutəri] adj. 旋转的
route [ruːt] n. 进路

S

safeguard ['seifɡɑːd] n. 安全装置，安全措施 v. 防护
satisfactorily [ˌsætɪsˈfæktərɪlɪ] adv. 满意地
secondary ['sekəndəri] adj. 次级
serve as 用作；供作……之用
set forth 规定；宣布
set up 建立
shunting sensitivity 分路灵敏度
siding ['saidiŋ] n. 股道
sign [sain] n. 标志
signal-clear indication light 信号开放表示灯
single-rail track circuit 单轨条轨道电路
so long as 只要
spot [spɔt] vt. 认出，发现
standby ['stændbai] n. 备用的
station stop 车站定点停车
steel mill 钢厂
stock rails 基本轨
storage cell 蓄电池
substantially [səbˈstænʃ(ə)li] adv. 实质上；本质上
subsystem ['sʌbˌsistim] n. 子系统
succeed [səkˈsiːd] v. 接续；接着……发生
supervise ['sjuːpəvaiz] v. 监督
switch [switʃ] n. 道岔
switch controlling device 道岔控制设备

T

tap [tæp] vt. 开发，利用
taper ['teipə] vt., vi. （使）一端逐渐变细

terminology [ˌtɜːmɪˈnɒlədʒi] n. 术语
territory ['teritəri] n. 区域；区段
tie [tai] n. 轨枕
track transformer n. 轨道送电变压器
trailing ['treiliŋ] adj. 拖尾的，曳尾的，被拖动的
trailing direction 背向
train operation 行车；列车运行
transformer [trænsˈfɔːmə(r), trɑː-] n. 变压器
transportation [ˌtrænspɔːˈteiʃən] n. 运输
two-element track relay 二元轨道继电器
typically ['tipikəli] adv. 一般

U

underground cable 地下电缆
upper portion 上方
utilize [ˈjuːtɪlaɪz] v. 利用

V

vary with 随……而变化
vertical ['vɜːtikəl] adj. 垂直的，直立的，顶点的
via ['vaiə] prep. （经）由；借助于
video monitor 视频监视器
voltage ['vəultidʒ] n. 电压

W

warning device 预警设备
warning sign 预告标
watt [wɔt] n. 瓦特
wayside facility 地面信号
wheel and axle 轮轴
whether…or 或者……或者
with provision for 考虑到
with the exception of 除……之外

Y

yardmaster [ˈjɑːdˌmɑːstə(r);-ˌmæs-] n. 调车场主任